Team Players

ALSO BY MARK MURPHY

*Hiring for Attitude: A Revolutionary Approach to Recruiting
and Selecting People with Both Tremendous Skills and Superb Attitude*

*Hundred Percenters: Challenge Your Employees to Give It
Their All, and They'll Give You Even More*

Team Players

THE FIVE CRITICAL ROLES YOU NEED TO BUILD A WINNING TEAM

Mark Murphy

BASIC

VENTURE
NEW YORK

Basic Venture
Hachette Book Group
1290 Avenue of the Americas, New York, NY 10104
www.basic-venture.com

Printed in the United States of America

First Edition: October 2025

Published by Basic Venture, an imprint of Hachette Book Group, Inc. The Basic Venture name and logo is a registered trademark of the Hachette Book Group.

The Hachette Speakers Bureau provides a wide range of authors for speaking events. To find out more, go to hachettespeakersbureau.com or email HachetteSpeakers@hbgusa.com.

Basic Venture books may be purchased in bulk for business, educational, or promotional use. For more information, please contact your local bookseller or the Hachette Book Group Special Markets Department at special.markets@hbgusa.com.

The publisher is not responsible for websites (or their content) that are not owned by the publisher.

Print book interior design by Sheryl Kober.

Library of Congress Control Number: 2025932368

ISBNs: 9781541705975 (hardcover), 9781541706026 (ebook)

LSC-C

Printing 1, 2025

To Andrea, Isabella, and Andrew

Contents

INTRODUCTION

W HAT ARE THE QUALITIES OF A GREAT TEAM? YOU'VE PROBABLY been taught that team success requires building trust, fostering psychological safety, and cultivating a unified mindset. Seems logical. You might have learned that consensus is important and hierarchies are bad. Okay. You've undoubtedly been given that old chestnut, "There's no I in team." A classic. Team building 101. It's conventional wisdom, and yet it completely misses the paradox of teams: While companies often focus on merging everyone into a single homogeneous entity, truly great teams embrace the distinct, diverse roles and talents of their team members.

On the best teams, "team players" aren't cookie-cutter replicas, molded to fit arbitrary standards of agreeableness and conscientiousness. Greatness in groups comes from leveraging everyone's unique talents so that each member adds something important and valuable.

Hard-nosed decision-makers, tireless doers, meticulous planners, diplomatic peacekeepers, and bold visionaries don't always fit the cliché definition of "team player," but make no mistake, their diverse talents and personalities are vital for team success.

Here's the irony: You already know that exceptional groups succeed by harnessing distinct and diverse roles. Think about your favorite rock band. Do the band members play identical instruments or share carbon-copy personalities? Of course not. Each instrument and personality contributes something unique to the group.

Take the Beatles, for example. They had the visionary John Lennon, with a penchant for social commentary and challenging norms; the melodious Paul McCartney, who brought an unparalleled sense of melody and pop sensibility; the avant-garde George Harrison, who infused spirituality and diverse musical influences; and the affable and grounded Ringo Starr, whose unassuming demeanor formed a steady foundation.

Need more? Okay, how about your favorite sports team? If you're a basketball fan, does every player on the court have the same skills or demeanor? Hardly. When the Denver Nuggets won the 2023 NBA title, their victory was driven by one of the all-time great duos in Finals history: Nikola Jokić and Jamal Murray. Metaphorically, Jokić is the Nuggets' head; just before the Finals started, a teammate noted that Jokić knew the game better than anyone he's played with or worked with in his basketball career. Murray, by contrast, is the team's heart; he's been described as "fire in human form," and his fierce enthusiasm is palpable. Jokić and Murray are wildly different talents and personalities, and that's an essential part of their magic. As ESPN's Ramona Shelburne described this dynamic duo, "The personalities have to be different enough to fill all the types of needs a championship team has."[1]

This truth about teams and team players has been staring us in the face all along, evident in every concert we've attended and every game we've watched. We all have favorite players and musicians, and it's their distinctiveness, not their homogeneity, that appeals.

Yet somehow, when we step into the corporate world, we often forget these fundamental truths about what makes teams truly effective. We fall into the trap of trying to create uniformity where diversity is needed, of focusing on team building before we've even selected and assembled the right mix of talents.

THE FIVE CRITICAL ROLES

In the office, we don't have guitarists and singers, or point guards and centers; instead, we have **Directors**, **Achievers**, **Stabilizers**, **Harmonizers**, and **Trailblazers**. The best teams contain members who fill these five vital roles, and the absence of even one role can lead to a team's downfall.

Every high-performing group in an organization will have someone who takes the lead on making decisions (the Director), somebody who produces work and achieves results (the Achiever), another who keeps the group on track and on schedule (the Stabilizer), another who keeps the relationships healthy (the Harmonizer), and someone who challenges the group with ideas outside the norm (the Trailblazer).

No amount of team building, communication skills, trust, psychological safety, or shared vision can overcome having the wrong mix of people in the room. Similarly, if you select the right team members—people who can fulfill each of the five roles necessary to make a team function properly—most of the problems that plague teams today simply go away.

In these pages, we'll explore how understanding and embracing these roles can transform the way we build and lead teams. Whether you're a team leader, a team member, or someone who's ever been frustrated by ineffective teamwork, this team-building method will change the way you think about collaboration and collective success.

EACH ROLE CONTRIBUTES SOMETHING UNIQUE

The capacity crowd at Harvard University's Sanders Theatre was transfixed as Wynton Marsalis spoke. Yes, spoke. While the nine-time Grammy winner and the first jazz artist to win a Pulitzer Prize is deservedly known for his otherworldly range, tone, and improvisation on the trumpet, his words are every bit as captivating. In an event billed as "lecture and performance," Marsalis, alongside his world-class band, illuminated American music for a rapt audience.

He had loftier goals than delivering a team-training workshop, yet as he enlightened the audience on the nuances of swing, he divulged a profound insight about the structure of teams: "The rhythm section's job is to turn time into 'the' time, and that time is called swing. In a four-beat measure, the bass presides over one and three. James Chirillo on the guitar is gonna show us that, though he plays on all four beats, he presides over two and four. So we got our one, two, three, four going. Here comes the piano, free to cover all, none, or some of the beats at will. The drummer is in charge of the shuffle that is the foundation of swing. And the bass guitar is responsible for making sure that the drummer doesn't rush or drag.... And when it's balanced, it feels so good; you just have to join in."[2]

What Marsalis so eloquently described is a beautiful metaphor for thinking about the different roles on a team. One member of his team keeps the first and third beats in check while a colleague takes the helm for the second and fourth. Yet another ensures a steady pace without rushing or dragging, paving the way for a teammate to add a dash of spice, weaving in and out of all four beats.

Like a great jazz band, you've got to empower and nurture the different voices and talents in your group, show off their distinct sounds, and highlight the uniqueness they bring. Erasing individuals' distinctiveness to create cookie-cutter team members only weakens the group. It's the distinctive and complementary sounds and functions of the different instruments that make beautiful music. You don't want your trumpet to sound or function like the bass guitar; each instrument provides something special that the others can't replicate.

DISCOVERING THE FIVE ROLES

Like many discoveries, the five team roles emerged unexpectedly from a completely different line of research. In one of my previous books, *Hiring for Attitude*, I explored why some new hires succeed while others fail. The research behind that book shocked quite a few people.

With my team at Leadership IQ, the training and research company I founded two decades ago, we tracked twenty thousand new hires and discovered that 46 percent failed within their first eighteen months. Even more stunning was that 89 percent of those failures were due to attitudinal issues rather than a lack of technical skills.

But hiring for attitude isn't as simple as hiring people with great attitudes, because different companies need radically different attitudes to succeed. For every Southwest Airlines that wants fun-loving personalities, there's a Four Seasons seeking quiet sophistication. Google and Apple are both successful companies but require very different attitudes to thrive.

That message resonated with a lot of leaders, and I saw thousands of companies figure out their unique cultures and improve their hiring. But I also discovered that some organizations were taking things a step too far.

I was coaching a cutting-edge technology company whose culture prized innovation above all else. Their hiring profile sought out creative, flexible thinkers who could ideate the next breakthrough product. And it worked—they were hiring some remarkably innovative people.

But while talking with one of their senior engineering leaders, he confided something that initially struck me as heretical to their culture. "I know this'll sound strange," he said, leaning forward and lowering his voice, "but my team actually needs some non-innovative people. We've got plenty of brilliant minds dreaming up the next big thing, but we're drowning in ideas and falling behind on execution. I desperately need some rigid taskmasters who can drive our project schedules, and I need people who aren't looking to revolutionize everything but who'll put their heads down and just get work done."

I couldn't get that conversation out of my head. Here was a company that had masterfully defined their cultural attitude, yet one of their best leaders was telling me that too much of a good thing was actually hurting his team's performance. As we dug deeper, we found similar sentiments across other departments. The innovation-obsessed culture was creating teams stacked with idea generators but lacking the people who could transform those ideas into reality.

This insight sparked a new direction in my research: I began studying not just the attitudes that made companies successful but also the different roles that made teams successful. My team and I analyzed thousands of high-performing teams and discovered something remarkable: The best teams weren't homogeneous groups of people sharing the same attitudes—they were diverse groups where different people played distinctly different roles.

Some people were natural Directors, making the tough calls that kept projects from stalling. Others were Achievers, the doers who could be counted on to produce high-quality work. The Stabilizers kept everything organized and on track. The Harmonizers maintained relationships and resolved conflicts. And yes, the Trailblazers brought that innovative thinking—but their creativity was valuable because other roles could translate their ideas into reality.

I've been studying, coaching, and training leaders for more than two decades, and yet, this was a complete paradigm shift in how I thought about building great teams. The fatal flaw in some organizations' hiring and team-building approaches was that they were trying to shoehorn everyone into a suffocatingly narrow archetype of success—like trying to build a championship basketball team with five centers or a world-class jazz band with only drummers. They were creating teams full of Trailblazers with no Stabilizers, or teams loaded with Directors but missing Harmonizers.

This discovery explained so many of the team dysfunctions I'd witnessed over the years. It explained why "dream teams" of top performers often failed—they were usually collections of people trying to play the same role. It explained why traditional team-building exercises focusing on trust and communication sometimes fell flat—they weren't addressing the fundamental imbalance in team roles.

Perhaps most importantly, it revealed that every person has the potential to be a vital team player—they just need to find their proper role. Not everyone needs to be an innovator, an organizer, or a peacekeeper, but every team needs all of those roles to truly excel.

The five roles framework finally allowed us to see the full picture of team effectiveness. It wasn't just about having the right culture or the right attitudes—it was about having the right mix of roles that complement and balance each other. That's the paradox of teams: The best ones don't try to make everyone the same; they succeed by embracing and leveraging their differences.

WHERE WE'RE GOING NEXT

In the chapters that follow, I'll introduce the five roles you need to have on your team and show what happens when even one of them is missing. We'll explore the nuances and real-life examples of Directors, Stabilizers, Trailblazers, Harmonizers, and Achievers.

After understanding these roles, we'll look at curating your team, identifying role gaps, and building the right balance of strengths for a cohesive and effective group.

I'll show you how to think like all five roles, broadening your perspective to improve collaboration and decision-making, and we'll uncover the power of adaptive hierarchies, where the right person leads at the right time for the best outcomes.

You'll learn strategies for making better decisions by encouraging diverse perspectives and reducing conformity bias, and we'll explore the science of great meetings, turning them into productive, goal-driven events. Finally, I'll guide you through selecting new team members, focusing on attitude and role fit to build a team that truly elevates its performance.

Together, these chapters will equip you with the tools to assemble, lead, and thrive with a team that leverages the unique strengths of its members. Let's get started!

CHAPTER 1

THE FIVE TEAM ROLES

W E KNOW THAT THERE ARE A BUNCH OF DIFFERENT ROLES THAT need filling on a team. But what are they? Here's a simple way to think about it. Picture the teams you're a part of. What's really happening in your team meetings? What sort of work gets done? What discussions are taking place?

At some point, hopefully, someone pushes the group to make some decisions. And though it might not be a daily occurrence, there are likely times when a bit of peacekeeping is necessary, as a bit of tension or even conflict in meetings is nearly inevitable.

Of course, keeping everyone accountable to deadlines and agendas is a must, so there's likely a person who keeps the group focused on deadlines and timelines. And every group needs someone willing to stop talking and start doing—the person who rolls up their sleeves and writes the big report. There may even be someone urging the team to think more creatively.

Over the past few decades, my team and I have studied thousands of teams, from executive teams and boards to task forces and project teams. And in any high-functioning group, five roles nearly always emerge:

- The Director assumes a leadership role within the team, guiding its direction and making important, difficult, and even unpopular decisions.

- The Achiever immerses themselves in the details of accomplishing tasks and getting things done, with a keen eye for delivering error-free work.
- The Stabilizer keeps the team on track with meticulous planning, processes and procedures, clear timelines, and organization.
- The Harmonizer brings collaboration and camaraderie, builds relationships, and resolves conflict.
- The Trailblazer brings innovation, creativity, and out-of-the-box thinking, along with the courage to challenge conventional wisdom.

Another way to picture the five roles on a team is as vital parts of a body. Think of the Director as the brain. It's the control center of the body, responsible for making decisions, processing information, and guiding actions. Just as the brain oversees the body's functions, the Director guides the team's direction, making important and sometimes difficult decisions.

The Achiever is like the hands, instrumental in performing tasks, skilled in detail work, and capable of manipulating tools and materials to achieve desired outcomes. The Achiever immerses themselves in the details of work, focusing on executing tasks effectively and efficiently.

The Stabilizer is akin to the spine, providing structure and support, keeping the body upright and stable. The spine is essential for maintaining balance and bearing the weight of the body. In a similar way, the Stabilizer provides the team with structure and support through planning, organization, and maintaining clear timelines, ensuring the team remains focused and on track.

The Harmonizer is the heart, central to sustaining life and pumping blood to nourish and maintain the body's functions. The heart is also a common metaphor for emotions, relationships, and empathy. The Harmonizer, like the heart, nurtures team relationships, fosters collaboration, and resolves conflicts, ensuring the emotional and social well-being of the team.

Think of the Trailblazer as the eyes. Eyes provide vision and perspective, allowing us to see beyond our immediate surroundings and, in a figurative sense, imagine possibilities. Likewise, the Trailblazer provides innovation, creativity, and a vision for the future, challenging conventional wisdom and exploring uncharted territories.

THE FIVE TEAM ROLES RESEARCH

The five roles aren't formal jobs, like vice president or engineer, and the role that you play on one team might be radically different than the role you fill on another. Have you ever found yourself on a disorganized team where chaos reigned supreme? Even if you're not a natural organizer, you might have felt frustrated enough to jump into the Stabilizer role. Have you ever been trapped in a meeting room where the air was thick with acrimony and discord seemed to be the only constant? You may not consider yourself a master of emotional intelligence, but for that hour, you may have been compelled to don the mantle of Harmonizer.

In one form or another, teams need all of the five roles fulfilled. In fact, my research team found that people describe their most effective teams as containing a blend of all the roles. We asked 1,200 professionals to analyze the most effective team they've ever been on. Among their tasks, they sorted every member of their team into one of the five roles. And we discovered that a whopping *97 percent* of those great teams filled every role.

If you're concerned about locating the right person for a specific role or face limitations in modifying your team composition, don't worry. As we'll explore in later chapters, people can often quite easily switch roles. You just have to curate the right balance.

If balance is the characteristic that defines the best teams, imbalance defines the worst. The first line of Leo Tolstoy's novel *Anna Karenina* holds true: "Happy families are all alike; every unhappy family is unhappy in its own way." That's precisely what we found when we asked those 1,200 professionals to analyze the worst teams they've ever been on. Sometimes those terrible teams were overloaded with Directors, while others had none. There were groups loaded with Stabilizers and no Trailblazers, but we also saw the reverse.

The configurations of ineffective teams were seemingly endless, but one commonality did emerge: Regardless of the exact mix, the worst teams had serious imbalances among the five roles (or were missing roles entirely). In fact, in contrast to the best teams, only 21 percent of the worst teams managed to fill every role. Moreover, even when all roles were filled, their allocation was markedly disproportionate.

We saw teams stacked with Directors, where each member believes they know the best path forward. Under this configuration, meetings quickly turn into power struggles, with everyone talking over each other and trying to assert their vision. Without Harmonizers, conflicts escalate, creating tension and hostility. And the absence of Stabilizers means there's not a structured process for decision-making or execution.

There were teams filled with Achievers, highly focused on getting tasks done and delivering perfect results. However, because everyone is buried in their own work, there's minimal collaboration or discussion. Meetings are purely status updates, lacking strategic thinking or innovative problem-solving. The team churns out a high volume of work, but it's often duplicative or misaligned because no one is challenging objectives or thinking ahead.

What if you had a team full of creative Trailblazers and enthusiastic Achievers? They'd generate a constant flow of new ideas and launch multiple initiatives simultaneously. However, without anyone to keep track of deadlines, prioritize projects, or ensure follow-through, projects would be half-baked or abandoned midway. The team would constantly start new things without ever finishing or implementing them properly.

On more than a few occasions, teams with an abundance of Harmonizers and little else appeared. In this scenario, meetings are pleasant and filled with empathy, but the team rarely tackles difficult decisions or confronts poor performance. The group avoids conflict to the point where underperformers are never addressed and tough decisions are postponed endlessly.

We saw a team full of Stabilizers who were exceptionally skilled at planning, organizing, and following processes. However, without Directors to set a clear direction or Trailblazers to bring fresh ideas, the team became overly bureaucratic and rigid, sticking to outdated procedures and failing to adapt to new challenges.

YOU CAN'T JUST THROW A BUNCH OF I'S INTO A ROOM

In 2011, Vince Young was no ordinary backup quarterback. With other-worldly athleticism and high-wattage charisma, he commanded everyone's attention. He entered the NFL in 2006 after a college career for the ages, winning the National Championship and finishing second in Heisman Trophy voting. Once in the NFL, with the Tennessee Titans, he won Offensive Rookie of the Year, became the first rookie quarterback to rush for more than five hundred yards, and shortly thereafter was selected to be the Madden NFL 08 cover athlete.

Although his passing inaccuracy and number of thrown interceptions would cost him his starting job with the Titans, his college and early NFL success, combined with his magnetism and marketability, meant he was still a star. He landed as the Philadelphia Eagles' backup quarterback in 2011, his introductory press conference had the buzz and media attention of a big-time signing. And Young was just the latest in a bevy of star players signing with the Eagles, joining the likes of Nnamdi Asomugha, Dominique Rodgers-Cromartie, and Jason Babin.

When Young was asked about those recent big-name acquisitions, he said, "Aww, Dream Team, heh, heh, heh, heh. From Nnamdi to Cromartie, to Jason to myself, you know they are going to do some more things. It's just beautiful to see where we're trying to go."[1]

Those two words, "dream team," would hang over the Eagles like the sword of Damocles all season. The Eagles had signed a cadre of stars, it's true, but their on-field performance was anything but dreamy. After losing three of their first four games that season, starting quarterback Michael Vick tried to bury the dream team moniker, telling reporters, "I think the 'Dream Team'—that word is dead now. Can't talk 'Dream Team' anymore. Maybe it put pressure on some players, maybe it didn't, but I think just the fact that it was lingering around and people were talking about it creates a sense of pressure."[2]

Sports history is littered with examples of putative dream teams that fell miles short of their on-paper potential. From the 2004 US men's Olympic basketball team to the 2004 New York Yankees, from the 1998 Brazil World Cup squad to the 2010–2011 Miami Heat, there are too many examples to list them all. But why do dream teams often fall so far short of their potential? A study of star Wall Street analysts offers us a clue.

A group of Harvard researchers analyzed what happens when you have a bunch of star equity analysts at Wall Street investment banks.[3] If you've ever sat in an airport bar, you've probably watched at least a few minutes of CNBC. When analysts come on to discuss a hot new stock or the one you need to sell immediately, those folks are typically sell-side equity analysts. They scrutinize the financials and operations of companies and industries to make informed predictions and investment recommendations. Their performance is ranked by groups like Institutional Investor, and the stars are lavishly rewarded with millions of dollars, influence, and media coverage.

You'd imagine that every Wall Street investment bank would want offices filled with those star analysts. But the researchers discovered a phenomenon eerily similar to the one faced by the Philadelphia Eagles. The study discovered that performance peaked if around 65 percent of the group were star analysts; any more stars than that and performance actually waned.

The performance drop-off was even worse if those analysts had similar areas of expertise. In cases where the analysts covered similar areas, performance fell off if more than 45 percent of the analysts were stars. It seems that you can only have so many stars on a team before they cancel each other out and performance erodes. And when those stars all play the same role or cover the same territory, you'll run into trouble even faster.

TRUST IS GOOD, BUT IT'S NOT ENOUGH

Nineteenth-century doctors treated patients based on the leading medical belief that "bad air" caused disease. Patients were encouraged to avoid foul-smelling areas, which indeed had some positive effects. Less stench meant fewer immediate discomforts and, to some extent, fewer diseases. However, germ theory would eventually prove that this approach to disease prevention was merely superficial.

When Louis Pasteur and Robert Koch discovered that microorganisms—bacteria and viruses—were the real culprits behind diseases, it transformed medicine. Suddenly, it wasn't just about avoiding bad smells; it was about targeting the actual causes of illness. This shift led to groundbreaking practices: sterilizing surgical instruments, developing vaccines, and using antibiotics. Medicine became proactive, not just reactive.

Before Robert Koch's discovery of Mycobacterium tuberculosis in 1882, the most widely accepted treatment for tuberculosis (TB) was a lengthy stay in a sanatorium—a specialized medical facility where patients were isolated in mountain or seaside locations thought to offer healing climates. In sanatoria they rested, followed strict hygiene protocols, and received fresh air and light exercise, believing this could counteract the effects of "bad air."[4]

Now, most of us could benefit from a lot more rest, fresh air, and exercise; those sound like delightful recommendations. However, even with those remedies, tuberculosis remained a major killer.

Koch's identification of the tubercle bacillus as the true cause of tuberculosis led to major changes. Medical understanding shifted from vague environmental or hereditary theories to a targeted approach: isolating infected individuals to control transmission, advancing hygiene practices, and, eventually, developing the BCG vaccine and antibiotics like strepto-mycin. These treatments allowed for direct targeting of the bacteria, making it possible to cure TB and saving millions of lives worldwide. Unlike the passive measures of sanatoria, the discovery enabled proactive, scientifically grounded interventions that transformed TB from a rampant epidemic to a treatable disease.

Traditional team-building practices like trust, psychological safety, and cohesion are akin to avoiding bad smells or getting more rest, fresh air, and exercise. They certainly aren't harmful and can absolutely be beneficial. However, they don't address the deeper truth: The thing that can really make or break a team is the role that each person plays and how well those roles complement each other.

TEAMS FAIL WHEN THEY'RE MISSING ROLES

Team success requires a specific mix of roles; it's a balanced ecosystem that brings together differing talents and perspectives. When critical roles are absent, however, the results can be disastrous: innovation is stifled, conflicts simmer unaddressed, and priorities can swing wildly without a steadying hand. Teams lacking this balance often fail, not because of individual incompetence, but because key perspectives are missing or drowned out.

When You're Missing a Trailblazer

In the early 1980s, the semiconductor industry was abuzz with the quest for blue LEDs. While red and green LEDs had been available since the 1960s, blue remained elusive. Some readers might not think this an earth-shattering scientific pursuit, but there's a good chance that the room you're sitting in right now is lit by LED lights. Light-emitting diodes (LEDs) currently account for around half of all light sources, and that's expected to grow to around 90 percent by 2030.[5] And the real kicker is that you can't get white LED light without blue LED light.

Scientists in the 1980s considered two materials as possible candidates for creating blue LEDs: zinc selenide and gallium nitride. Most scientific teams focused on zinc selenide for blue LEDs due to its lower dislocation density, dismissing gallium nitride as impractical.

Across the globe, major semiconductor companies posed this question to their research teams: "We're here to ensure we're on the right path to blue LEDs. Zinc selenide or gallium nitride?"

In team after team, the responses were eerily similar:

"Zinc selenide is the obvious choice. It's well-studied, and the scientific community clearly favors it."

"The dislocation density in zinc selenide is much lower than in gallium nitride. Everyone knows good LEDs need low dislocation density."

"Switching to gallium nitride would be too risky. We could miss deadlines, and the whole project could fail."

Even when a lone voice would suggest potential in gallium nitride, they quickly backtracked, unwilling to go against the consensus. This scene played out repeatedly across the industry. Teams were so focused on the safe path that they overlooked the potential of gallium nitride.

At that time, it was more challenging to produce defect-free crystals with gallium nitride. Zinc selenide was more familiar, and scientists had techniques to grow it with fewer defects. However, it couldn't withstand the high power needed for bright, stable blue light. Gallium nitride's stability and ability to emit intense blue light made it the right choice long-term, but without a Trailblazer to pursue and refine the technology, most teams didn't realize that its challenges could be overcome with the right innovations.

Meanwhile, at a small two-hundred-person chemical company in Japan, there was a Trailblazer hard at work. A scientist named Dr. Shuji Nakamura eschewed the safe path in favor of gallium nitride. The people above and around him tried to force him back in line; "When people learned I worked with gallium nitride," he shared with me, "they told me I was crazy and a foolish scientist."[6]

You can probably guess what happened next. Dr. Nakamura won the Nobel Prize in 2014 for discovering blue LEDs using gallium nitride.

How did the fleet of well-funded teams at major semiconductor companies fail to recognize this crucial breakthrough? It's not like they didn't know about gallium nitride's existence. Dr. Nakamura talked with the big semiconductor companies' teams, and what he heard was, "We have meetings where we talk about which material to use, and out of ten scientists, nine scientists say we have to use zinc selenide, while only the one foolish guy says we should try gallium nitride." Some teams embrace and recruit Trailblazers, whereas others call them "foolish" (or eschew them entirely).

When You're Missing a Director or an Achiever

In 1991, a series of well-intentioned but financially imprudent decisions led to a catastrophic financial collapse of California's Richmond Unified School District. For only the second time in the state's history, a school district filed for bankruptcy protection.

The school board's members were educated, community-oriented individuals who convened regularly, and their discussions were filled with aspirations to revolutionize education in their district. Ambitious and charismatic Superintendent Walter L. Marks spearheaded numerous initiatives to enrich the curriculum and establish magnet schools. His vision was grand—to transform the educational landscape through innovative programs and enhanced resources.

The board sat in rapt attention as Marks passionately outlined his vision. They were captivated by the promise of educational reform, their eyes reflecting a shared dream of uplifting their schools. Like most school board members, they wanted everything for their district. They envisioned a community in harmony; parents, teachers, and students aligned in achieving a world-class educational experience.

So it wasn't too surprising that, as Marks detailed his plans for staff expansion and the purchase of new equipment, no one smacked the table and loudly exclaimed, "Absolutely not. I don't care if everyone gets mad at me;

we can't afford this." There wasn't a single voice that said, "As someone who loves nitty-gritty detail, I've read every line of this budget. Even though district revenues grew by 49 percent in the past few years, our expenditures grew 76 percent. And our annual deficit is now $18.1 million."

The atmosphere of the meetings was optimistic and collegial, but behind the scenes, the district's expenses spiraled out of control. Staff numbers grew by 25 percent, salaries increased without sustainable funding, and equipment purchases were made recklessly. The district's revenues, though increasing, could not keep pace with its skyrocketing expenditures.

The grand jury investigating the district's collapse attributed the blame to "a large dose of wishful thinking" and an inability to withstand pressure from school employees' unions and community groups. "The primary motive of members in seeking election," it added, "was to influence educational, not financial, policies and practices." They noted that the board didn't challenge the superintendent on his plans for curriculum enrichment and magnet schools, nor did they question his erroneous claim that everything could be funded with federal and state grants.[7]

In short, the school board was missing a Director—someone who, unbothered by criticism, could make unpopular decisions. They also clearly lacked an Achiever—someone whose love of detail would have propelled them to scour every line of the budget reports.

When You're Missing a Stabilizer or a Harmonizer

In the late 1950s, the city of Sydney, Australia, embarked on what was to become one of the most iconic architectural undertakings of the twentieth century—the Sydney Opera House. The design, created by the Danish architect Jørn Utzon, was a beacon of innovation, destined to challenge conventional architectural norms. Utzon, a Trailblazer in every sense, introduced bold forms inspired by natural shapes and sails, a radical departure from the prevalent architectural styles of the time. My work has brought me around the world, and I can't recall ever being as mesmerized by the artistry of a building as I was on Bennelong Point in front of the opera house.

However, beneath the surface of this architectural marvel lay a turbulent saga of mismanagement and oversight failures that almost derailed the entire project. The project commenced in 1959 with a four-year timeline and a budget of AUD$7 million. Ultimately it took fourteen years to complete and cost AUD$102 million. For those doing the math, that's a cost overrun of about 1,400 percent.[8]

At the heart of the myriad problems was the lack of a strong Stabilizer, someone who loves maintaining timelines, project scopes, and budgets. While a Stabilizer was technically part of the team in the form of the project engineer, his voice and influence were significantly minimized.

The innovative roof structure, for example, which resembled sails and was Utzon's signature element, presented unforeseen engineering challenges. The roofs were initially designed as parabolic shells but had to be reconfigured into the complex geometry of spherical sections to be feasible, a solution that came after significant trial and error, delays, and cost overruns.

At one point, the team realized that the design would require heavier supports than the ones already built. The solution was dynamiting the existing supports during rush hour traffic to hide the noise (and avoid scrutiny of the project's bungles). Unfortunately, a chunk of concrete was blown so far into the harbor that it landed on a ferry passing by.

Utzon's role as a Trailblazer, while visionary, contributed to tensions with contractors and the engineering team. His insistence on aesthetic perfection and last-minute changes without thorough consultation exacerbated the project's logistical and financial woes. While the problems began amid the absence of a strong Stabilizer, the lack of a Harmonizer worsened the situation, especially when a new Minister for Public Works took office. The new official, ostensibly in an effort to control ballooning costs, withheld payments and angrily demanded more project oversight. Utzon received some warnings to respond diplomatically and tread lightly, but they were too little and too late. Following a heated meeting with the new minister, and without a Harmonizer to mediate or smooth ruffled feathers,

Utzon resigned from the project. His departure marked a significant turning point, leading to further complications and changes in design direction under subsequent architects.

Eventually the Sydney Opera House was completed (in 1973), but the project's mismanagement is a testament to the dangers of teams missing key roles. Beyond the years and money wasted, however, there was also a personal cost. Utzon never got to visit the iconic architectural masterpiece he designed. Near the end of Utzon's life, he was visited by British architect John Pardey. When Pardey suspected the older man's pain at never having seen the opera house, Pardey offered to help Utzon make the trip. But Utzon's wife took Pardey aside to let him know it wasn't possible. "It would kill him," she said.[9]

TEAMS NEED ALL FIVE ROLES

Why did those teams fail? The semiconductor teams failed because they were missing a Trailblazer like Shuji Nakamura, someone who, unfazed by risk, had both the insight and courage to challenge conventional wisdom. The school board failed because they lacked a Director, someone who could make difficult and even unpopular decisions. They also lacked an Achiever, the person who immerses themselves in the details with a keen eye for error. The Sydney Opera House's failure was initially the result of a marginalized Stabilizer, someone who keeps the team on track with meticulous planning, clear timelines, and organization. The lack of a Harmonizer also contributed significantly to the project's woes and resulted in heavy personal costs.

Teams need to fill the five roles. They also need to appreciate the importance of each role. Roger Waters and David Gilmour, the two most famous members of Pink Floyd, have been feuding for years. Gilmour joined the band in 1968, and notwithstanding their millions of record sales and legendary tours, conflict eventually led to Waters quitting the band in 1985. I'll spare you the gory details of the various lawsuits, the attempt to dissolve the band, and all the other madness that's taken place. Much to everyone's surprise, the group did reunite for a benefit concert in 2005. But as a testament to the lingering problems between Waters and Gilmour, they turned down a $150 million offer for the reunited group to perform a US tour.

Now, here's the reason why I'm mentioning this story. In a 2018 interview, Pink Floyd's drummer, Nick Mason, offered his take on the source of the trouble between Roger Waters and David Gilmour: "I think the problem is Roger doesn't really respect David. He feels that writing is everything and that guitar playing and the singing are something that, I won't say anyone can do, but that everything should be judged on the writing rather than the playing. I think it rankles with Roger that he made a sort of error in a way that he left the band assuming that without him, it would fold."[10]

Whether it's writing or singing, scientific discoveries or engineering, Directors, Achievers, Stabilizers, Harmonizers, or Trailblazers—every single role on the team is vital. And people who don't recognize that are doomed to a miserable team experience.

TEAM BUILDING DOESN'T FIX THOSE PROBLEMS

Some people love team building. But—and this is hard for some people to hear—many people do not love team building (at least as it's typically conducted).

Ask a group about their experiences with corporate team-building activities, and you're likely to hear a chorus of groans. From trust falls to ropes courses and personality tests to scavenger hunts, team-building exercises are often met with eye rolls and quiet dread. A quick online search reveals countless articles, social media posts, and memes mocking the futility and awkwardness of forced team bonding. Even as companies continue to invest time and money in these activities, many employees view them as a waste of time at best and a source of genuine discomfort at worst.

Team-building activities frequently fall short because they fail to recognize and leverage the diverse roles and talents of individual team members. Instead of allowing people to contribute in ways that align with their natural strengths and preferences, generic team-building exercises often force everyone into the same mold.

Think about what it takes to be a successful participant in a team-building exercise offsite. Being extroverted certainly helps, as does a high level of sociability. A sense of humor is practically a requirement, and it doesn't hurt to be comfortable with looking a bit awkward. The people who love classic team-building exercises are energized by group interactions, enjoy engaging with others, and are comfortable voicing their opinions.

Now, here's the problem. Some of your most valuable team members won't meet any of those criteria. A one-size-fits-all approach ignores the fact that effective teams need a variety of complementary skills and personalities. When people aren't positioned to play roles that suit them, they're inevitably going to feel inauthentic and disengaged.

There's another issue that bugs a fair number of professionals. Traditional team building often emphasizes superficial bonding activities over meaningful collaboration aligned with work goals. Forced socialization and artificial challenges rarely translate to improved teamwork in real job contexts. Instead, they can create discomfort and resentment, especially for those whose strengths don't align with the chosen activities. Effective teams allow each member to find their niche and make unique contributions. By failing to account for individual differences and forcing people into roles that don't fit them, most team-building exercises miss the opportunity to harness the full potential of diverse talents and perspectives.

Team building has a place; I've conducted more team-building exercises than I can count. The key to successful team building, however, is first, to make it relevant to the real world. Second, team building needs to enable, empower, and embrace the diversity of roles, talents, and personalities that exist on your team.

Here's an irony of embracing the diversity of roles on your team: Empowering differences gives you a way to make every single person engaged and productive. There's a lid for every pot. Whether someone is introverted, extroverted, solitary, social, innovative, impatient, task-focused, unstructured, the adult in the room, the free spirit, or whatever else, the five roles offer every unique individual a way to make an important and meaningful contribution to the team.

Before my freshman year of high school, I tried out for the summer basketball league. I was younger, but honestly, I was also shorter, fatter, slower, and weaker than the other guys on my team. Our captain was a junior in high school who could've passed for a thirty-year-old adult. He had more body hair at seventeen than I do at fifty-three. My recollection is a bit fuzzy, but I'm pretty sure he already had a receding hairline. He was a man among boys.

I heard a few grumbles from some of the other guys when I showed up for the first practice. It might be worse in my head than it was in reality, but I remember hearing, "How is this doughy little freshman going to help the team?" As we walked onto the court for a scrimmage, the captain sidled up to me and asked, "Can you do anything decent?" "Shoot threes," was all I could muster.

A few minutes into the first scrimmage, I was wide open (nobody guards the guy they think is useless). The captain saw, passed me the ball, and, by some miracle, I sank a three-pointer. The scenario repeated a minute later, and, again, I hit my shot. "Murph just toasted you!" the captain shouted to the guy who was supposed to guard me.

I wasn't the team's MVP. I wasn't the coolest guy. I was trying to sprout a single chest hair while my teammates were dating cheerleaders. But the captain found a way I could be useful. I felt wanted and valuable. I wasn't a worthless freshman; I had a role.

If I had been forced into a trust fall or made to build a tower out of toothpicks and newspapers, I would never have found my place on that team. I didn't have the "cool kid" status, physical confidence, or interpersonal dominance to be anything more than a bystander in a social bonding ritual. (If our team building had involved an academic challenge, I would've been fine, but that's a pretty unusual team-building exercise.) Absent the artificial exercises, however, the captain found a useful place for me in situ, out on the basketball court.

IT'S ABOUT COMPARATIVE ADVANTAGE

Building a great team requires finding everyone's comparative advantage. Now, I need to explain that concept because 99 percent of people misunderstand it. When most people hear the phrase "comparative advantage," they think it means competitive advantage. But it's a totally different idea.

Competitive advantage is when a person (or company) can outperform their rivals. If you can run faster than everyone in your home country, you've got a competitive advantage (and you're probably going to the Olympics). If you can make project plans better than anyone else in your company, you've got a competitive advantage.

By contrast, a comparative advantage is the idea that someone should focus on what they are relatively best at, even if they aren't the best at it overall. It's not about being the best; it's about being better at one thing compared to other things you can do.

My comparative advantage in basketball was shooting threes. I did that better than any of the other things I tried to do in basketball. However, I did not have a competitive advantage because the captain of the team was better than me at every single aspect of the game. He shot threes better, rebounded better, and drove to the basket better. But, of all the things that could be done on a basketball court, I shot threes better than I did anything else. That was my comparative advantage.

Now that you understand the concept, here's a big aha: Every single person on your team has a comparative advantage. You might not have a team where everyone has a competitive advantage, but literally every person on your team has something they do better than all the other things they could possibly do. And creating a great team is about finding everyone's comparative advantage.

Imagine a Director of a project team who is exceptionally skilled not only at leading and making strategic decisions but also better than anyone else at the tasks typically handled by other team roles. Maybe this Director is more efficient than the Achiever at completing tasks, more organized than the Stabilizer, more empathetic and skilled in conflict resolution than the Harmonizer, and more innovative than the Trailblazer.

Despite the Director's capability to excel in multiple areas (their competitive advantage), their comparative advantage is making strategic decisions; that's the thing they're best at. And that's where their time and effort should be focused.

"But wait," some will say, "they're better at everything, so they should just fill all the roles!" Okay, let's think this through. It might seem logical for a highly skilled Director, who excels in all areas, to take on all the roles within a team, but the opportunity cost makes this counterproductive. Even if the Director is better than everyone else at various tasks, their comparative advantage lies in strategic decision-making and leadership—where their unique skills and insights have the greatest impact. The opportunity cost of the Director handling roles that others could manage is the lost value of their time and effort that could have been spent on high-level decisions and guiding the team's overall strategy.

And, let's be realistic: Attempting to fill all the roles risks spreading the Director too thin, leading to burnout and a decline in effectiveness. This approach also underutilizes other team members, who may become disengaged and demotivated if they don't have a way to contribute meaningfully. Relying on one person for everything stifles diverse perspectives and creates a bottleneck, resulting in role fatigue and delays.

Finally, I'm going to be brutally honest here: Your investors and stakeholders will lose their minds if they learn that one person is doing everything and unable to delegate or offload responsibilities. Whether your stakeholders are Wall Street or your boss, venture capitalists or the executive team, it's career suicide to essentially say, "I don't know how to pick good people for my team and harness their abilities."

Building great teams isn't about having one superstar who can do it all; it's about leveraging the unique comparative advantages of each team member. When every person is given the opportunity to focus on what they do relatively best—whether that's being a Director, Trailblazer, Harmonizer, Stabilizer, or Achiever—the entire team becomes stronger.

This approach not only maximizes the team's productivity but also fosters a sense of ownership, engagement, and collaboration. Your job isn't to dominate all the roles but to identify, cultivate, and strategically position the right people in the right roles.

NAKED MOLE RATS GET IT

Books on teams rarely recognize and embrace different roles, but the animal kingdom is no stranger to the idea. Naked mole rats aren't generally considered the sexiest of mammals, but in the subterranean catacombs of East Africa, every naked mole rat has a well-defined role.[11]

There's the indomitable queen, the only female in the colony that can reproduce. While her primary role is reproduction, she also plays a part in guiding the colony and maintaining order. The breeding male is a highly selective role, filled by one to three male mole rats. As the relationships between the queen and breeding males may last for years, other females are temporarily sterile, and the nonbreeding males take on other roles.

Physical size has a hand in determining those other roles. Smaller workers expand the empire and forage for food, excavating new spaces and bringing sustenance to the colony. The larger workers are tasked with protection roles and stand ready to defend against attacks. There's even a disperser role: These male mole rats are morphologically, physiologically, and behaviorally distinct from the other colony members. Equipped with generous fat reserves for long journeys, they look to leave the burrow when they see a chance for escape. Their primary job is to mate with individuals from foreign colonies.

Naked mole rats aren't the most glamorous creatures, yet somehow they've figured out that in order to survive, the colony needs to embrace and leverage distinct roles.

CHAPTER REFLECTION GUIDE

- Think about the most effective team you've ever been a part of. Which of the five roles (Director, Achiever, Stabilizer, Harmonizer, Trailblazer) were present? Was any role missing? How did the presence or absence of certain roles impact the team's success?
- Think about a team you are currently a part of. Which of the five roles (Director, Achiever, Stabilizer, Harmonizer, Trailblazer) do you see most clearly represented? Are there any roles missing? How does this balance—or imbalance—affect the team's dynamics and outcomes?
- The chapter discusses comparative advantage versus competitive advantage. What is your comparative advantage on your current team? What role allows you to contribute most effectively, even if you're not the "best" at everything?
- Reflect on how well your team values and leverages the unique strengths of its members. Are there opportunities to better appreciate or support teammates who play different roles from your own?

Visit **www.leadershipiq.com/teamplayers** to find more resources, such as exercises, assessments, and additional tools.

CHAPTER 2

THE DIRECTOR

I N 1997, AFTER A TWELVE-YEAR INTERREGNUM, IMMERSED IN
other ventures like NeXT and Pixar, Steve Jobs returned to Apple.
And the company to which he returned was in trouble. On $7 billion in
revenue, the company would end that year losing more than $1 billion.
And when rival Michael Dell was asked what he'd do if he was running Apple, he replied, "I'd shut it down and give the money back to the
shareholders."[1]

Among Apple's many problems was its sprawling and confusing product lineup that epitomized the company's lack of focus. Overlapping product lines, convoluted naming schemes, and a diluted brand identity left
consumers bewildered and the company floundering.

It was into this bureaucratic mess that Jobs stepped with his unique
brand of decisiveness. During a product review shortly after rejoining, Jobs
discovered that Apple was selling a rebranded version of Hewlett-Packard's
DeskJet printer under the label StyleWriter. More importantly, he also discovered that Hewlett-Packard made its money through a "razor and blade"
business model, selling the hardware near breakeven and making a profit
through the blades (or ink cartridges). In fact, Wall Street analysts at the
time estimated that companies like Hewlett-Packard earned 60 percent
margins on inkjet cartridges. At that time, a milliliter of Hewlett-Packard's

ink was more expensive than a milliliter of Dom Perignon champagne. And consumers were buying it in droves.[2]

Thunderstruck by these discoveries, Jobs made a decision. His preeminent biographer Walter Isaacson uncovered what happened: "'I don't understand,' Jobs said at the product review meeting. 'You're going to ship a million and not make money on these? This is nuts.' He left the room and called the head of HP. Let's tear up our arrangement, Jobs proposed, and we will get out of the printer business and just let you do it. Then he came back to the boardroom and announced the decision."[3]

There was ample justification to exit the printer business; months of further study likely wouldn't have added much clarity, and with the company in dire straits, someone needed to make a decision. Making decisions is arguably the most important function performed by a team's Director. Decision-making could mean saying "No," "Yes," or "Hold your horses, we're about to walk off a cliff." However, decision-making is emphatically not about procrastinating until the choice is so glaringly obvious that it shields the decider from all possible criticism.

WHO IS THE DIRECTOR?

Whenever I walk into a team meeting room, whether it's an executive team, board of directors, project team, or what have you, the Director is typically easy to spot. Maybe it's the tap-tap-tap of their pen impatiently hitting the conference table; it could be the tension in their shoulders as they lean forward primed for action; or if they're leaning back, it might be the hint of a furrow in their brow that says, "If we could get this done ten minutes ago, that would be great."

Directors are decisive; they're not looking for hours, let alone weeks, of deliberation. They want decisions made, and they want them made yesterday. In simplest terms, Directors make decisions, especially the kinds of decisions that stymy or vex others.

Psychologically, the Director role typically attracts individuals with strong, assertive personalities—people who naturally gravitate toward leadership positions. They thrive on making decisions, taking charge, and steering the course for others.

They have a higher-than-average drive for power and influence, and they enjoy having the ability to affect outcomes and guide others. Directors are typically quick and decisive in their decision-making, relying more on facts and logic than emotions. They're often goal-oriented and focused, with a talent for seeing the big picture and developing strategies to achieve objectives.

Unless they're purposefully restraining their natural impulses, you'll rarely see a Director sitting off to the side in a meeting. In the center of the action is where they'll be, and that's because Directors make decisions. Owing to the power required to enact and enforce decisions, most of the Directors on the teams I train and study are in leadership or at least highly influential roles. More often than not, when I'm working with an executive team, the CEO is the de facto Director. (There are exceptions, of course, and we'll explore those in Chapter 9.)

When a team calls me in because "we can't make a decision," it's often because that team is missing a Director. One of the biggest tells that a team is lacking a Director occurs when you ask the group, "What should we decide?" When there's not a Director in the group, the most common responses I hear sound like, "Let's get some more options," "Let's take a few days to think about it," "Let's not rush into anything," or "Let's get so-and-so to study it and give us some additional options."

If you've ever felt agitated, frustrated, or even enraged by a group's inability to decide, you understand one of the biggest benefits of having a Director on your team. They make decisions swiftly and with confidence, and in doing so, they keep the group moving forward and avoid stagnation.

Jobs's swift decision to exit the printer business exemplifies another crucial aspect of the Director role: the willingness to act decisively without getting bogged down in endless studies and reviews (known as analysis paralysis). When presented with information about the unprofitability of the StyleWriter printer, Jobs didn't hesitate. He immediately recognized the strategic implications, made a decision on the spot, and took action by calling HP's head to terminate the arrangement.

To be sure, there are decisions that require in-depth study, but impetuousness is a far less common source of team failure than analysis paralysis. "Death by discussion" threatens most teams at one time or another, and having a sufficiently empowered Director on your team offers a counterweight.

A POTENTIAL DILEMMA

Now, when taken to an extreme, the Director's assertiveness and confidence can come across as domineering, even autocratic. Not everyone wants to be on the hot seat for making the tough decisions, but neither do they want to feel utterly sidelined or that their contributions are worthless.

I remember walking into a boardroom for a strategy session with a large retail company. Before anyone said a word, I had spotted the Director. She had a stack of notes in front of her, a pen gripped tightly in her hand, and the muscles in her face tensed with an intensity that told me, "Let's get this show on the road."

I started to worry when her assistant told me how many presentations were scheduled to offer various solutions to a supply chain problem. I understand that supply chains can be complicated, and I'm a pretty patient guy, but even I was experiencing some dread at the prospect of listening to six different proposals.

Even more than my own dread, I was worried that this was going to push the Director over the edge. And sure enough, as her team laid out option after option, I'm pretty sure I saw steam coming out of her ears. Finally, she'd had enough: "We've been debating this for too long. It's time to move. We're going with Option Three. I want an implementation plan on my desk by Friday." The room fell deathly silent, a miasma of both relief and hurt feelings filling the room.

After the meeting, she pulled me aside. "I know I came on strong in there," she said, a hint of doubt creeping into her voice. "But we can't afford to keep spinning our wheels. Did I make the right call?"

This is the Director's dilemma. On the one hand, teams need to make decisions quickly and confidently; on the other, there's the risk of steamrolling the people who've worked hard to develop detailed analyses and recommendations.

There is, however, a way to think about this that I find usually helps Directors. The Director's role is to ensure that the team isn't mired in indecision, empty rhetoric, analysis paralysis, death by discussion, or some other form of "decisional procrastination" (that's the technical term for being unable or unwilling to make a decision).

The platonic ideal of the Director assesses and analyzes the situation while avoiding unnecessarily lengthy deliberations. In statistics, there's a concept called the elbow point: it's the point of diminishing returns for adding more variables, clusters, or components to a model. When you're looking at a graph, and the curve bends like an elbow, that's typically the point where adding additional variables isn't worth the cost.

I've taught this concept to thousands of Directors, and it resonates with nearly all of them. They know when the options they're seeing start to blend together, when each additional alternative simply wasn't worth the time and effort it took to create it. Directors understand the elbow point.

Directors aren't usually statisticians, but they do have an intuitive sense of when additional analysis offers diminishing returns. It's as though they can see a few weeks or months into the future and know that additional deliberation won't change anything. These traits also enable Directors to make tough, sometimes unpopular decisions and to stand firm in the face of opposition or criticism.

Upon Jobs's return to Apple, he wanted to reprice executives' stock options to stop them from abandoning the company (given Apple stock's ghastly performance, their options were essentially worthless). When the board wanted to conduct a two-month study on the matter, Jobs made clear the cost of their resistance to quick decisions, telling them: "Guys, if you don't want to do this, I'm not coming back on Monday. Because I've got thousands of key decisions to make that are far more difficult than this, and if you can't throw your support behind this kind of decision, I will fail. So if you can't do this, I'm out of here." The board acquiesced and the next day, Apple's chairman told Jobs, "We're going to approve this, but some of the board members don't like it. We feel like you've put a gun to our head."[4]

A decade ago, I conducted a study called "Why CEOs Get Fired." My team and I interviewed board members who had recently fired their CEO with the goal of discovering the undisclosed reasons behind the CEO dismissals. Among the most pervasive causes was this gem: too much talk, not enough action. It turned out that speechifying and endless meetings without taking action were bigger causes of CEO terminations than unprofitability. Once the board got the sense that the CEO was paralyzed by indecision, they lost confidence, and the writing was on the wall.

It's worth noting that Directors do more than make tough decisions or break voting ties; they excel in setting clear goals, strategizing effectively, and ensuring the team is aligned with a shared vision. Yet when someone is decisive, that trait is typically highly correlated with being able to corral the team into a common goal and vision.

Effective decision-making provides clarity; so too does setting a clear direction and vision. Both skills require distinguishing between signal and noise and then choosing and articulating the signal. Directors prefer clarity over chronic ambiguity, and it's that characteristic that drives their decision-making and strategic talents.

It also doesn't hurt that Directors tend to be assertive and confident, because that fuels their capacity for making difficult choices that would intimidate others. Directors often see themselves as experts or authority figures, and they're not afraid to voice their opinions or provide criticism when necessary. Not everyone wants the spotlight shining on them; Directors don't necessarily need the spotlight, but they certainly don't mind it.

MAKING DECISIONS WHEN OTHERS WON'T (OR CAN'T)

Nestled on the serene shores of Lake Geneva, Évian was a glittering jewel of the French Riviera in 1938. Its Belle Époque architecture and healing mineral springs drew Europe's elite to bask in its rarefied air. Such was the location for the Évian Conference, a gathering of delegates from thirty-two countries, there ostensibly to solve the plight of Jewish refugees fleeing Nazi persecution. Despite more than a week of heartfelt speeches and lofty rhetoric, nearly all participating nations refused to meaningfully increase their refugee quotas (the Dominican Republic being a notable exception).

Conference attendee and future Israeli minister Golda Meir would later write, "Sitting in that wonderful hall listening to the representatives of thirty-two countries standing up one after another and explaining how terribly glad they would be to receive a larger number of refugees and how terribly sorry they were that they unfortunately could not—it was a shattering experience."[5]

It's against that historic backdrop of willful impotence and irresolution that German Chancellor Angela Merkel faced the Syrian refugee crisis in 2015. As waves of refugees sought sanctuary in Europe, Hungary responded not with open arms but by constructing barriers of razor wire; Austria and Bulgaria also announced their fencing intentions.[6] As anti-immigration and nativist sentiment surged, so too did the humanitarian crisis.

You might remember the heart-rending image of Alan Kurdi, a three-year-old Syrian boy whose drowned body washed ashore on a Turkish beach, his sodden red shirt and blue shorts a stark reminder of the desperate journeys families were taking across the Mediterranean Sea to escape the violence in Syria.[7] Or perhaps you recall when Austrian officials discovered an abandoned truck containing the decomposing bodies of seventy-one refugees who had likely suffocated in the sweltering heat, their desperate bid for a new life ending in a metal tomb.[8]

Amidst these horrors, inaction, and vitriol, Merkel declared, "Germany will not turn away refugees," asserting, "I don't want to get into a competition in Europe of who can treat these people the worst."[9]

Over the next year, Germany would take in more than a million refugees, far more than any other European country. And the backlash was swift and intense. The far-right Alternative for Germany Party surged in popularity. Anti-immigrant protests abounded. One paper wrote, "She has exacerbated a problem that will be with us for years, perhaps decades." Even former US Secretary of the Treasury Hank Paulson noted, "Of course, she did the right thing. But I was afraid it would be her political undoing."

But Merkel didn't waver. She acknowledged the difficulties while insisting Germany could and must rise to the challenge. "Wir schaffen das" ("We can handle this" or "We'll manage this") was the phrase that Merkel repeated when challenged about the increase in refugees.

Even when that phrase was mocked, memed, twisted, and weaponized, she remained largely resolute. Although her legacy is still being written, this example is but one of many examples of why *Forbes* named her the most powerful woman in the world fourteen years in a row.

For all of the worries about this decision causing her political demise, the data would suggest her decisiveness did, in fact, positively change minds. In 2018, 82 percent of Germans said they supported taking in refugees fleeing violence and war (for comparison, the US was at 66 percent, the UK at 74 percent, and Hungary at 32 percent).[10] And she left office in 2021 with a 71 percent approval rating, easily erasing the slight ratings downturn she experienced during the height of the refugee crisis.[11]

Merkel's handling of the Syrian refugee crisis exemplifies another vital aspect of the Director role: the willingness to break through indecision and empty rhetoric and withstand the repercussions of an unpopular decision. In a situation where many European leaders were paralyzed by inaction or resorting to populist measures, Merkel took a bold stance by declaring,

"Germany will not turn away refugees." This decision cut through the collective indecision that had characterized much of Europe's response to the crisis.

Merkel's persistence in the face of intense backlash demonstrates the Director's capacity to stand firm behind difficult decisions. Despite protests, political challenges, and criticism from various quarters, she maintained her position with her "Wir schaffen das" (We can handle this) mantra. This steadfastness in the face of adversity is a hallmark of effective Directors, who must often make and stick to decisions that may be unpopular in the short term but align with their long-term vision.

INDECISION AS SABOTAGE

When a team can't make a decision, and the team lacks a Director willing to curtail fruitless debate and force a resolution, the result is so painful that it's tantamount to a form of team sabotage.

In 1944, the United States Office of Strategic Services, now the CIA, published a document called the "Simple Sabotage Field Manual." The guide was for use by agents to recruit potential foreign saboteurs (US sympathizers) and to give those folks the means to inflict sabotage and help the Allies win the war.[12]

The guide covers a wide range of sabotage, including electric power, railways, and communications. However, one of the most relevant sections for modern-day office workers is "General Interference with Organizations and Production." Among the many techniques given, here are a few of my favorites for sabotaging meetings:

- "Refer back to matters decided upon at the last meeting and attempt to re-open the question of the advisability of that decision."
- "Insist on doing everything through 'channels.' Never permit shortcuts to be taken in order to expedite decisions."

- "Bring up irrelevant issues as frequently as possible."
- "Haggle over precise wordings of communications, minutes, resolutions."

Remember that this is from a manual developed by the precursor to the CIA to help foreign agents sabotage enemies of the United States during World War II. And yet, if you've attended enough meetings in modern companies, you can see these techniques employed, consciously or unconsciously, every single day.

Anything that hinders decision-making is sure to demoralize and undermine a team; that's why those techniques are such effective means of sabotage. We all know all too well the scream-out-loud frustration of a team or leader who can't (or won't) make a decision.

SOMETIMES FASTER ISN'T BETTER

Let me leave you with one final thought about Directors. Too often people think that what distinguishes a Director is making the *speediest* decisions. But there are cases where the difficult decision is the slow one, not the fast one. I once consulted with a manufacturing executive team whose company was facing a safety issue in their flagship product. The executive team's instinct was to issue an immediate recall.

That wasn't a terrible instinct. Most of the executives had gone to business school, where they read cases about the 1982 Tylenol recall. In short, seven people died in 1982 after taking Tylenol capsules that had been maliciously laced with cyanide. Johnson & Johnson didn't dither or obfuscate; they quickly recalled thirty-one million bottles. Because they took such swift action, and with a shocking level of transparency, the company preserved and even enhanced its brand.

In this case, however, the CEO wasn't convinced that the safety issue rested solely with their product. Even though the rest of the executives thought immediate action, like that afternoon, was necessary, this wasn't a small decision. Lives could be at stake if they didn't act, but a premature recall could bankrupt the company.

He decided to take a beat. He and I grabbed dinner and, followed by an unhealthy amount of coffee, wrestled with his options. As he walked through all of the potential root causes of the problem, I paused the conversation and asked him a simple question: "Have you hit the elbow point where additional analyses have stopped delivering new information?" "Hell no," he said. "We haven't even pinpointed the exact part that's the root cause. We've got suspicions, but it'll take another two days of hardcore digging to nail down the answer."

By morning, he had a plan. He announced a partial recall of the most at-risk units while fast-tracking testing on the rest. The plan worked, and, just as importantly, the team learned a lesson. Decisional procrastination is bad, but so too are knee-jerk reactions. Sometimes, the Director has to make swift decisions because their team is mired in analysis paralysis, anxiety, or fear of being wrong. Other times, the Director needs to say, "Hold your horses, we're about to walk off a cliff."

Months later, when the crisis had passed, the CEO told me, "That night changed how I lead. I realized that being decisive doesn't always mean being the fastest to act. Sometimes it means having the guts to slow people down while forcing them to think harder and dig deeper."

CHAPTER REFLECTION GUIDE

- Think of a time when you—or someone on your team—had to make a critical decision. How was the decision made, and what was the outcome? Did the process reflect the traits of a strong Director?
- Reflect on a recent decision you've been a part of. Can you identify where the elbow point occurred—where additional analysis stopped delivering new insights? How did your team handle that moment?
- Reflect on a time when a decision was met with resistance or backlash. How was the situation handled, and what could have been done differently to address team concerns while maintaining decisiveness?
- Can you recall a time when indecision stalled your team's progress? How might a strong Director have helped resolve the issue more effectively?

Visit **www.leadershipiq.com/teamplayers** to find more resources, such as exercises, assessments, and additional tools.

CHAPTER 3

THE STABILIZER

I N 2011, ERIC SCHMIDT STEPPED DOWN AS CEO OF GOOGLE. WHEN he was recruited in 2001 by Google cofounders Larry Page and Sergey Brin, the company had $90 million in annual revenue. When he stepped down, revenues were nearly $38 billion.

What was it that compelled Google's founders to take a pass on every other person interested in the job, many with stellar qualifications, and target Eric as their choice for CEO? In addition to Eric's obvious business acumen, Larry, Sergey, and even Eric jokingly referred to him as the "adult supervision." And it's a description that fits quite a few Stabilizers.

Here's how Eric described his job as CEO: "These two young men [Google founders Larry Page and Sergey Brin] are brilliant, crazy, and unreliable, and we need a CEO that can manage them....I had a list of things they needed to do, and we went and did them. Almost all small companies are full of energy and no process. My list was straightforward: internationalization plans, sales plans, product plans, accounting, etc. My first meeting at Google was like being at a graduate school full of interesting people with no deadlines or deliverables."[1]

When he was asked to describe his role as CEO, he again gave a very Stabilizer-like answer: "My role was to manage the chaos. You need to have someone to run fast and have a good product sense. That was Larry and Sergey. My job was to organize the world around them."

WHO IS THE STABILIZER?

Stabilizers are the people on your team who bring order, planning, and predictability. Firmly convinced that careful planning leads to better outcomes, they'll be the ones to ensure your group makes and adheres to both short-term and long-term plans.

If you've ever been on a team that failed to hit its deadlines (like half of all teams, by the way), it's probably because there wasn't someone like Eric Schmidt creating and ensuring adherence to schedules, processes, details, and "dotting the i's and crossing the t's."

Psychologically, Stabilizers tend to have high levels of conscientiousness, attention to detail, and a strong need for order and structure. Their innate drive for consistency and reliability manifests in their meticulous approach to tasks and adherence to established processes.

Sometimes that adherence to precedent can show up as risk aversion. Not only do they derive satisfaction from maintaining stability and predictability, but they've often got a heightened sense of responsibility to ensure nothing goes wrong. The tech startup ethos of "move fast and break things" that sometimes gets bandied about is about as far from the Stabilizer personality as you can get. Of course, that's precisely why smart teams make sure there's a Stabilizer present.

Cognitively, Stabilizers excel in systematic thinking and have a strong capacity for long-term planning. They possess a natural inclination toward analytical problem-solving and are adept at identifying potential issues before they arise. Put more simply, Stabilizers are the motivational force behind strategy tools like scenario planning.

In its most exaggerated form, the Stabilizer role can squelch creativity, free-flowing debate, and conversation that falls outside accepted times and parameters; there are situations in which adhering to a process becomes more important than achieving good results. But when they're at their best, the Stabilizer's conscientiousness and detail-orientation will do more to ensure a team's effectiveness than trample its creativity. The Stabilizer's attention to detail allows them to identify potential issues early and implement preventive measures. They also tend to have a strong sense of discipline and reliability, as evidenced by their tendency to follow through with plans and commitments.

It's not always easy to be a Stabilizer, especially in fast-moving or chaotic environments. I've worked with more than a few Stabilizers who struggled with the emotional labor of their role. Not only are they expected to remain calm and composed in the face of crises or disruptions, but it can be fatiguing to always be the "adult supervision."

I coached a CEO much like Eric Schmidt. Everyone knew her unflappable demeanor; she was always the voice of reason when things went sideways. But privately, she confided that maintaining this composure was taking a toll. "I feel like I'm always the one who has to be the grown-up," she told me, her voice heavy with exhaustion. "Frankly, it sucks to constantly be the voice of caution when everyone else is caught up in excitement."

This is a crucial aspect of the Stabilizer role that often goes unrecognized: the emotional burden of being the team's anchor. I choose that word specifically for its double meaning. On the one hand, anchors keep ships from drifting out to sea and provide stability. On the other hand, an anchor can be a weight that holds us back and limits progress.

Stabilizers often need to find a balance between providing structure and allowing for flexibility. By recognizing their own stress levels and when the emotional labor feels overwhelming, they can better modulate their approach. And, like the examples in this chapter show, it's important for Stabilizers to communicate the reasoning behind their cautious approach; helping team members understand that their goal isn't to stifle progress but to ensure sustainable success.

STABILIZERS REMEMBER THE KEY

Certainly, you could imagine that on a team disproportionately overpopulated with Stabilizers, an effervescent river of creativity might be dammed and channeled into a monotonous flow, stifling the spontaneous bursts of innovation that once bubbled freely from its dynamic currents. But when your team is sufficiently balanced with Trailblazers and the like, Stabilizers don't eradicate creativity; they ensure that no one drowns in those effervescent currents

The White Star Line's crowning achievement, the colossal *RMS Titanic*, set sail from Southampton on April 10, 1912, a floating palace of unprecedented scale and luxury that the company believed represented the pinnacle of human engineering and technological invincibility. Unfortunately, the steamship company's hubris didn't extend to more quotidian notions of plans, processes, and "dotting the i's and crossing the t's."

Shortly before the Titanic's launch, bosses at the White Star Line initiated a capricious management reshuffle. The scheduled second officer, David Blair, was reassigned and transferred to another ship. Disappointed, he wrote to his sister-in-law, "Am afraid I shall have to step out to make room for the chief officer of the Olympic. This is a magnificent ship, I feel very disappointed I am not to make her first voyage."[2]

During the rushed transition, apparently absent robust or even adequate processes, a key detail was missed: making sure that David Blair handed over the key to the crow's nest locker.

A small, barrel-shaped enclosure positioned high up on the ship's forward mast, the crow's nest served as a lookout post for the ship's crew, offering a panoramic view of the surrounding seas. Inside the crow's nest locker sat a pair of glasses (we call them binoculars today), but without the key to access those binoculars, the lookouts resorted to scanning the horizon with nothing but their naked eyes.

The Titanic was almost nine hundred feet long. To give you some comparison of just how long that is, an American football field measures 360 feet from the back of one endzone to another. The night the ship hit the iceberg was abnormally calm, making it even harder to see floating obstacles because there were no waves breaking around the objects. And, of course, it's pretty dark on the open water.

With the dark distance and calm waters, it's not surprising that the Titanic didn't see the iceberg in time. As we all know, the ship sank, killing more than 1,500 people.

During an official inquiry, a United States senator asked one of the surviving lookouts, "Suppose you had glasses....Could you have seen this black object [at] a greater distance?" "We could have seen it a bit sooner," answered the crewmember. The senator followed up: "How much sooner?" to which the lookout responded, "Well, enough time to have gotten out of the way."[3]

There's a thirteenth-century proverb you've probably heard before: "For want of a nail, the shoe was lost. For want of a shoe, the horse was lost. For want of a horse, the rider was lost. For want of a rider, the battle was lost. For want of a battle, the kingdom was lost. And all for the want of a horseshoe nail." We'll never know if the Titanic was lost all for the want of a crow's nest key. But we do know that when a team boasts a Stabilizer, there will almost certainly be a checklist or protocol that guarantees they'll have that key.

Stabilizers are the backbone of a team when it comes to organization and adherence to processes. They're the ones who ensure that the keys to the binoculars don't walk off the boat. They're the ones who focus brilliant, crazy creators and harness their vision to deliver products in a timely and profitable manner.

Again, sometimes the responsibility for ensuring processes are followed and deadlines are met can become overwhelming, potentially leading to burnout. When a group isn't sufficiently aware or appreciative of all five roles, it can feel isolating, especially when there's only one Stabilizer to corral an entire team.

Occasionally, Stabilizers can also find it difficult or stressful to prioritize tasks driven by conflicting demands from various stakeholders. Stabilizers often have to balance their inclination toward stability with the need for innovation and change, especially when those needs are driven by demands from bosses, boards, investors, and the like.

Without mutual appreciation of all the roles on the team, the Stabilizer's role in enforcing rules and ensuring compliance can put them at odds with colleagues who prioritize speed or innovation. Left unaddressed, this can create interpersonal tensions and leave Stabilizers feeling isolated or undervalued. This is particularly unfortunate given the stakes.

LIFE AND DEATH AND STABILIZERS

Willie King's life changed forever in a Florida hospital. The fifty-one-year-old diabetic went in to have his diseased right leg amputated. But when he awoke, he was missing his left leg. Still groggy, he told the surgeon, "Doctor, that's the wrong leg."[4]

The operating room schedule and the hospital computers showed surgery for the left leg. When the surgeon entered the operating room, it was King's left that was draped and prepped for surgery. But it wasn't until the surgeon was already amputating the left leg that an operating room nurse glanced again through King's chart and, shaking and sobbing, told the surgeon.

By then, it was too late to stop the surgery. As horrifying and catastrophic as the error was, the Butterfly Effect of errors started with a clerk hitting the wrong key in the computer system, marking the left leg instead of the right.

While Willie King's story might sound like a once-in-a-million event, studies show that "wrong-site surgeries" are the fourth most significant preventable problem in the healthcare field.[5] Protocols abound for stopping these catastrophes, yet they still occur.

A former New York state health commissioner noted that wrong-site surgery is difficult to eradicate because it involves "getting doctors, who typically prize their autonomy, resist checklists, and underestimate their propensity for error, to follow standardized procedures."[6]

On effective teams, Stabilizers are not passive bystanders, relegated to the shadows with their checklists and Gantt charts, silently praying for a moment of recognition; they are vital architects of order, commanding respect through their mastery of structure and foresight.

Simply having a checklist doesn't obviate the need for having a Stabilizer on your team. For example, surgical safety checklists have proven effective in reducing complications and improving patient outcomes, but only when implemented with high fidelity. The success of checklists is often compromised by inconsistent application, inadequate training, and lack of team buy-in. Despite the introduction of checklists, the overall incidence of surgical errors has remained largely unchanged over the past two decades.[7] And that's why high-performing teams have a Stabilizer who forces a timeout, pre-procedure site verification, and everything else required to prevent wrong-site surgeries.

THE PROCESS OF PROCESS

Dwight D. Eisenhower entered the White House with more Stabilizer expertise and gravitas than any president before or since. As the former Supreme Allied Commander in Europe in World War II, Eisenhower knew structure and process better than anyone.

He created rules and policies that fostered stability and predictability. Eisenhower chose his people carefully, monitored and evaluated their performance, and made adjustments as warranted. But he wasn't a mere plodder, hidebound to antiquated policy; he was a process innovator. The esteemed presidential historian, the late Fred Greenstein, revealed that Eisenhower created the first White House chief of staff, the first congressional relations office, and the first presidential assistant for national security affairs (what we today call the national security advisor).[8] There were roles, processes, and structures.

Early in his administration, Eisenhower enlisted three groups of experienced national security analysts in a yearlong deliberation to rethink our national strategy to achieve "security without paying the price of national bankruptcy." Using a highly disciplined process, with each group providing drastically different strategies, he availed himself of the best possible thinking, and arguably, he honed and modernized the discipline of scenario planning.

Eisenhower's genius for structure and organization permeated the White House. But perhaps Eisenhower's Stabilizer acumen can be seen more clearly in this vignette unearthed in Jean Edward Smith's wonderful biography: "When Eisenhower returned to the White House after the inaugural parade—his first entrance into the Executive Mansion as president—he was presented with a teaching opportunity. Howell Crim, the chief usher, handed him a sealed envelope. 'Never bring me a sealed envelope,' said Ike. 'That's what I have a staff for.' To Eisenhower, a sealed envelope was concrete proof the White House was badly organized. Letters to the president must be screened, and only those that were essential for him to read should be placed before him. A smoothly functioning staff system was long overdue."[9]

For all of the obvious benefits of stability, process, and protocols, Stabilizers do need to mind the emotional needs of their team. Take, for example, Eisenhower's response to the Soviet Union's successful Sputnik launch in 1957. Americans went into a panic over a perceived technological gap between the United States and Soviet Union. Eisenhower's response was to send out his press secretary to undermine the Soviet's accomplishment—followed by his Secretary of Defense—and then his Chief of Staff. Eisenhower himself didn't respond until five days later. Because of his military acumen, he knew that Sputnik was a much smaller threat than the average citizen imagined, but his deliberative nature and steady calm failed to convince the American people that they had nothing to fear.

I've worked with countless Stabilizer executives facing similar challenges in their companies. One such CEO led a healthcare organization. The industry was abuzz about a competitor's new AI-powered product that seemed to leapfrog everyone else. Employees were panicked, fearing job losses and the company's obsolescence.

The CEO's initial response was textbook Stabilizer. He calmly analyzed the situation, knowing that the competitor's product, while flashy, was deeply flawed and largely hype. He offered a measured response, refusing to stoop to the competitor's level. Like with Eisenhower, however, the CEO's deliberate approach and lack of immediate, visible action left the team feeling even more anxious.

My message to the CEO was, "While your analysis is spot-on, your team needs reassurance. They can't see the steady hand on the wheel that you do."

He agreed, and without giving undue weight to the competitor's largely hype-driven product launch, he engaged with, and assuaged, his team's fears. The CEO held open forums where he invited employees to share their concerns, acknowledging their fears about the competitor's AI product. He explained his analysis, pointing out flaws in the competitor's approach and reinforcing the company's focus on reliable, sustainable advancements. And leaning into his Stabilizer talents, he painstakingly detailed the specific steps they were implementing to stay competitive. "I always thought my job was to be the calm in the storm," he told me after. "Now I see that sometimes the team needs me to acknowledge that there's a storm at all."

A sealed envelope, like the one handed to President Eisenhower, might seem a picayune detail, but remember that keys to a binocular locker and confirming surgery sites could appear similarly banal. And depending on the context, a sealed envelope can literally be the difference between life and death.

In the winter of 1776, the American Revolution was on the brink of collapse. George Washington's Continental Army, battered and demoralized, faced a seemingly insurmountable British force. In a desperate gambit, Washington planned a surprise attack on Hessian mercenaries stationed in Trenton, New Jersey. The night before the attack, a crucial piece of intelligence arrived at the home of Colonel Johann Rall, the Hessian commander. A letter containing details of the impending American assault was handed to Rall while he was engrossed in a game of cards. Distracted, he tucked the sealed and unopened envelope into his pocket, where it remained forgotten.[10]

This small oversight proved catastrophic. The next morning, Washington's forces caught the Hessians completely unprepared, securing a pivotal victory that revitalized the American cause. The unopened letter was found in Rall's coat pocket after he fell in battle, another poignant reminder of how a moment's inattention to a seemingly insignificant detail—an unopened envelope—can alter the course of history.

Stabilizers will generally eschew risk and prefer stability over uncertainty. This doesn't mean they're inflexible, but rather that they see structure as a means to achieve efficiency and effectiveness. Stabilizers are often the ones who bring a sense of calm and predictability to a team, counterbalancing more spontaneous or innovative personalities.

The Stabilizer role is best fulfilled by people who have a natural inclination toward organization, planning, and process-oriented thinking. They are the steady, reliable force within a team, providing the structure and consistency that allows other team members to operate effectively within a well-organized framework.

CHAPTER REFLECTION GUIDE

- Think about a Stabilizer you've worked with. How did their attention to detail and focus on planning impact the team's performance? Were there moments when their presence prevented potential mistakes or oversights?
- Have you been part of a team where strict adherence to processes stifled creativity, or where a lack of structure led to chaos? How can a Stabilizer strike the right balance between maintaining order and allowing for flexibility?
- Stories about the Titanic and surgical mishaps highlight the importance of seemingly minor details. Can you recall a situation where a small oversight caused significant issues? How might a Stabilizer have helped prevent it?
- If you've taken on the Stabilizer role in a team, how did you manage conflicting demands for stability and innovation? What lessons did you learn about maintaining balance while ensuring progress?

Visit **www.leadershipiq.com/teamplayers** to find more resources, such as exercises, assessments, and additional tools.

CHAPTER 4

THE TRAILBLAZER

THE VOICE ON THE OTHER END OF THE ZOOM CALL WAS REDOLENT of the actor Sam Elliot, deep and smoky, with a soothing Texan drawl. And when the man's camera came to life, I was struck by his fiercely intense eyes, weathered visage, and long gray hair, a halo of hard-won insight. This was James P. Allison, Nobel Prize winner and pioneer of a revolutionary cancer treatment that unleashes the immune system to fight tumors.[1]

Dr. Allison discovered that a protein found on the surface of T cells (part of the immune system that attacks abnormal cells like cancer, bacteria, and viruses) serves as a braking mechanism, stopping the immune system from becoming overactive and attacking everything. This braking mechanism protects us from autoimmunity; without it, our immune systems might attack all healthy cells and wreak havoc in our bodies. But Dr. Allison also developed an antibody to stop that braking mechanism and allow T cells to attack cancer. This development led to Ipilimumab, the first in a class of drugs called checkpoint inhibitors, which has led to unprecedented results for cancer patients.

It's brilliant, but as Dr. Allison shared with me, "From very early on, even immunologists, certainly cancer biologists, had scorn for immunotherapy, manipulating the immune system as a way to actually treat cancer. The words I heard were snake oil, things like that."

Even though the idea of using the immune system to treat cancer had existed for a century, skepticism ruled the day. Part of the problem was that little present-day progress had been made in harnessing the immune system to fight cancer. There were previous attempts, but because Dr. Allison hadn't yet made his discoveries, the treatments were harsh (requiring ICU stays) and delivered fairly unimpressive results.

When Dr. Allison started unraveling the mysteries of immunotherapy in the 1990s, however, he found that "we could cure almost any kind of tumor in mice because we were treating the immune system, not the tumor. Even the ones that everyone said couldn't be cured, we managed to cure."

Yet the scientific proof wasn't enough. "For three and a half years," he told me, "I looked around, just kept going to company after company after company, showing the data. And, a few times, people would say, 'Oh, that's nice, but it'll never work in humans.' And to that I'd say, 'You're a scientist, right? How come you're so closed-minded?'"

One of the nastiest attacks an out-of-the-box innovator can receive is, as Dr. Allison describes, "It's never worked before, so it'll never work." The point of innovation is, by definition, to do things that have never been successfully done before. Science and technology would be stuck on finding ways to make fire if everyone accepted the types of criticisms that Dr. Allison received.

Eventually, he was able to break through the closemindedness, get a drug developed and approved, save untold lives, and pioneer new immunotherapy frontiers at MD Anderson Cancer Center's James P. Allison Institute.

WHO IS THE TRAILBLAZER?

Jim Allison is a Trailblazer, an innovative and dynamic force within a team. With a natural flair for creativity and a penchant for thinking outside the box, Trailblazers often spearhead new ideas and unconventional solutions to problems. Not bound by traditional approaches, the Trailblazer is willing to take risks and experiment with different strategies. They have a visionary quality and are able to anticipate trends and see possibilities that others might overlook.

Trailblazers aren't afraid to challenge the status quo; they're instrumental in driving change and transformation. But as wonderful as that sounds, if a team doesn't intentionally seek and enable Trailblazers, it's not uncommon for them to experience the type of resistance that antagonized Jim Allison.

In one study, my team and I asked managers to identify the characteristics most associated with innovators.[2] At the top of that list were characteristics like taking risks, challenging conventions, and pursuing audacious goals. Then, those same managers were asked to rate the characteristics of their favorite employees. At the top of that list were qualities like dependability, being a team player, and being easy to get along with: essentially, the characteristics that managers considered to be the least typical of innovative employees. Put simply, managers' favorite employees often have the characteristics of the least innovative employees.

When a team needs innovation, adaptability, and creative problem-solving, Trailblazers shine. Their ability to think differently makes them excellent when a team requires developing new solutions to complex problems. In the most severe scenarios, the Trailblazer can knock a team off-kilter and focus its energies on one wild goose chase after another. But the epitome of the Trailblazer unlocks opportunities that would remain hidden to groups without such an innovative thinker.

Psychologically, Trailblazers typically have high levels of openness to experience, creativity, and a higher tolerance for risk. That also correlates with their generally strong need for novelty and stimulation, seeking out new challenges and unconventional ways to solve them.

Their thinking style is divergent and nonlinear, which helps drive their ability to make unexpected connections and generate innovative ideas. Trailblazers typically score high on measures of curiosity and have a natural inclination toward exploration and experimentation.

We humans have a strange relationship with truly original thinkers and innovations, vacillating between reverence and resistance. On the one hand, we genuflect at the altar of great innovators. Centuries after their deaths, we (rightfully) marvel at the novel innovations and creations of Michelangelo, Copernicus, Thomas Edison, Isaac Newton, Charles Darwin, Galileo, Mozart, and Beethoven.

But one reason we so admire iconic innovators is that we implicitly understand that it takes some measure of audacity, courage, and perseverance to surmount the resistance Trailblazers typically face in order to achieve something groundbreaking. The histories of business, science, art, and more are replete with stories about people like Jim Allison, innovators who had to fight relentlessly against doubters and skeptics to achieve what others thought infeasible.

For decades, Spanish physicist Juan Miguel Campanario has compiled dozens of instances where future Nobel Prize winners encountered resistance from the scientific community and were even rejected by scientific journals. Discoveries like magnetic resonance imaging, lasers, and the Krebs cycle (a series of reactions that convert nutrients to energy in cells) were all initially rejected in one form or another. Paul Lauterbur, who won the Nobel Prize for magnetic resonance imaging, put it bluntly: "You could write the entire history of science in the last fifty years in terms of papers rejected by *Science* or *Nature*."[3]

In a darkly funny twist, *Nature* publicly congratulated Lauterbur after he won the Nobel Prize, only to have him point out that the journal had actually rejected his work initially. (It took significant work on Lauterbur's part to successfully appeal that rejection.)

BEING BOLDER

The Netflix story began in 1997 when Marc Randolph and Reed Hastings, two entrepreneurs with a shared vision, decided to revolutionize the video rental industry. Hastings ran a company that had just acquired one that

Randolph helped found. In a happy twist of fate, they carpooled to work. During these drives, they would brainstorm business ideas, eventually landing on the concept of DVD rentals by mail.

Randolph took the lead in the early days, becoming Netflix's first CEO and guiding the company through its initial launch and growth. Hastings, while heavily involved in the strategic direction and funding of the company, initially took a backseat role as chairman of the board. This arrangement worked well in the beginning, but as Netflix grew and faced increasing challenges, it became clear that a shift in leadership was necessary.

Randolph had nurtured the company from a wild idea into a fledgling startup. But as Netflix grew, it became clear that the company needed something more—a bolder vision and more aggressive leadership.

It was a sweltering day in mid-September when Reed Hastings swept into the Netflix headquarters. Dressed formally in black linen pants and a gray turtleneck, he carried his laptop like a weapon. As he approached Randolph's office, tension filled the air.[4]

"Got a minute," Hastings said, his tone making it clear it wasn't a question. His laptop screen glowed with a PowerPoint presentation; this wasn't going to be a casual chat.

In Randolph's memoir, he candidly shares what Hastings told him: "I'm losing faith in your ability to lead the company alone. Your strategic sense is erratic—sometimes right on, and sometime way off." Hastings didn't mince words, telling Randolph, "I don't think you're a complete CEO. A complete CEO wouldn't have to rely on the guidance of the board as much as you do."

Hastings pitched a drastic change; he would serve as CEO and Randolph would be President. It was a gut-wrenching moment for Randolph, who had poured his life into building Netflix. But he also recognized the truth in Hastings' words. Netflix was entering a new phase that required a different kind of leader: someone bolder.

Randolph loves the chaos of early-stage companies; working on hundreds of things at once, making countless decisions, clearly relishing the Director role.[5] He is the cofounder of Netflix, after all. But he describes

Hastings as more of a Trailblazer, someone who "had a track record of solving seemingly unsolvable problems. Investors and venture capitalists knew this even then. They definitely know it now. That's why the second he walks into a room, people whip out their checkbooks. They know that what he does isn't teachable, isn't reproducible—hell, it's barely even explicable. He's just got it. That's what great entrepreneurs do, in the end: the impossible. Jeff Bezos, Steve Jobs, Reed Hastings—they're all geniuses who did something that no one thought was possible."[6]

Apropos Jeff Bezos, at Amazon he made the Trailblazer part of his job explicit. He is not only a Trailblazer but he has pushed more Amazonians to embrace the Trailblazer mindset: "One of my jobs is to encourage people to be bold," he said. "It's incredibly hard. Experiments are, by their very nature, prone to failure. A few big successes compensate for dozens and dozens of things that didn't work. Bold bets—Amazon Web Services, Kindle, Amazon Prime, our third-party seller business—all of those things are examples of bold bets that did work, and they pay for a lot of experiments."[7]

For some roles, like Stabilizers, the high risk of failure is anathema to a team's functioning. But Trailblazers aren't just comfortable with some risk; they understand it's the fountainhead of breakthrough success. "I've made billions of dollars of failures at Amazon.com," says Bezos. "Literally billions of dollars of failures. You might remember Pets.com or Kosmo.com. It was like getting a root canal with no anesthesia. None of those things are fun. But they also don't matter. What really matters is, companies that don't continue to experiment, companies that don't embrace failure, they eventually get in a desperate position where the only thing they can do is a Hail Mary bet at the very end of their corporate existence."

TAKING THE MORE AUDACIOUS PATH

I got a call one day from a CEO who was struggling mightily to strike a balance between encouraging his Trailblazers while simultaneously keeping daily operations profitably on track.

"I don't have a shortage of creative ideas," he told me, "the problem is that all I see are high-risk projects. Everyone makes SMART Goals (specific, measurable, achievable, realistic, and timely), so I want to make sure that our ideas are achievable and realistic. But all my supposed innovators keep giving us goals and projects that are too unrealistic."

"Okay, I hear you," I replied. "Now let me ask, what's your SMART Goal? What's the achievable and realistic target you've set for yourself and pitched to your board?"

Silence. "You still there?" I asked. Sigh. "Yeah, I get your point," he finally said, probably between gritted teeth. "My goal as CEO is for us to be number one in our space, and it's a stretch goal to be sure. It's pretty audacious, and it sure as heck doesn't meet our 'realistic' criteria.'"

SMART goals have been a fixture in corporate life for decades, but you'll rarely see successful CEOs set SMART goals. Chief executives typically eschew an achievable goal or realistic goal in favor of BHAGs (big, hairy, audacious goals) or HARD goals (heartfelt, animated, required, and difficult). In fact, one of my studies found that top executives are about 64 percent more likely to set difficult or audacious goals than middle managers or frontline employees. Apparently, what's good for the goose is not always seen as good for the gander.

Innovating something truly novel and original may be riskier; there is undoubtedly ambiguity and uncertainty about its success. However, riskiness is not the same as infeasibility. Novel innovations and audacious goals have a higher chance of failure, it's true, but they also have a much greater chance of delivering game-changing and disruptive results. I'm not saying you have to throw out SMART Goals or whatever else, but there's a reason I've spent the past few decades teaching teams and leaders to embrace more difficult or audacious goals: The comfort zone is a deceptively dangerous place to live.

Back in 1997, Jeff Bezos spoke to students at Harvard Business School.[8] After his talk, the students pretended Bezos wasn't there while they dissected Amazon's prospects. As noted Amazon chronicler Brad Stone recounts, the students "reached a consensus: Amazon was unlikely to survive the wave of established retailers moving online. 'You seem like a really nice guy, so don't take this the wrong way, but you really need to sell to Barnes and Noble and get out now,' one student bluntly informed Bezos."

Bezos responded, "You may be right. . . . But I think you might be underestimating the degree to which established brick-and-mortar business, or any company that might be used to doing things a certain way, will find it hard to be nimble or to focus attention on a new channel. I guess we'll see."

Bold trailblazing has long been an integral part of Bezos' DNA. As one of Amazon's early executives remarked: "He is not tethered by conventional thinking. What is amazing to me is that he is bound only by the laws of physics. He can't change those. Everything else he views as open to discussion."[9]

A DOSE OF SOFT INSANITY

Notwithstanding that comment, perhaps a true Trailblazer, someone with what one Nobel laureate calls a "dose of soft insanity," actually can break some of the tethers to the laws of physics, or at least the conventional wisdom.

In 2019, Didier Queloz and Michel Mayor were awarded the Nobel Prize in Physics for the discovery of an exoplanet orbiting a solar-type star. The idea of planets outside our solar system orbiting a star like our Sun has long been common in science fiction; Star Wars would hardly exist without the idea of exoplanets (that's the term for these types of planets). But it wasn't until 1995 that these two Swiss astronomers provided testable proof.

Science fiction notwithstanding, prior to 1995, astronomers who asserted the discovery of an exoplanet were dismissed and often attacked. "It is quite hard nowadays to realize the atmosphere of skepticism and indifference in the 1980s to proposed searches for exoplanets," noted one famous astronomer.[10] There are even stories of astronomers standing up and striding out of the room when talks concern searching for planets.

What Queloz told me is that "it seems like it should be easy to find a planet. You take a telescope, point to a star, and find a planet. But this is not effective because the star is extremely bright; you really don't see the planet. So you have to use tricks and machinery that help you to see better. And the trick we have been using is to try to detect not the planet itself, but the effect the planet is making on the star. You look at the star to find something that tells you there is a planet. In our case, we were looking for a tiny change of speed, called the radial velocity of the star."

While Queloz did, in 1995, detect a change in speed, it was so rapid that he worried he had made a mistake. Queloz wrestled with the discovery. "I came to this conclusion after more than four months of battling with the data," he says. "It didn't come in a day. I identified the object, and I was battling with myself. One part of my brain said, 'No, this isn't possible,' while the other part is saying, 'Well, it's strange because I do see something.' And then you do something, which we're taught not to do in science, and that is why we have to start considering that the prevailing theory is wrong."[11]

Notwithstanding his and Mayor's thoroughness, much of the scientific community was skeptical. Some critics alleged overreading of the data, while other attacks were more insidious, asserting that this wasn't a new kind of planet but rather some unknown effect.

The skepticism wasn't always easy to take. "I must admit that for a couple of years, it was not an easy position to be in when you believe you are doing something right, but much of the community doesn't trust," Queloz told me.

How did he survive those years? "This is what I call the 'soft insanity of success'," he told me. Rather than becoming embittered, ruminating about his critics, and dwelling on the past, he pressed on. He's noted that when people ask him to name his best or favorite planet, his response is, "The best one is the next one."

"It's like a drug; it's an addiction to the novelty, to seeing a bit further, to be the first one to see something that nobody else has seen. It's an emotional drug, and when you've experienced that, you want to experience it again."

TRAILBLAZING REQUIRES MORE THAN BIG IDEAS

The Trailblazer's high tolerance for risk and appetite for change can sometimes clash with cultures that prioritize stability and predictability. They may face resistance from more conservative team members or leaders who are wary of disrupting established processes. Without a team mutually appreciating one another's roles, this friction can lead to feelings of isolation or misunderstanding. And over time, that can even dampen the Trailblazer's enthusiasm and creative output.

The frustration can get so bad that I've had to run trainings for Trailblazers to cultivate their own "soft insanity," with a toolkit of emotional wellness skills to build resilience, perseverance, self-efficacy, and optimism. In essence, it's developing the psychological muscles that propelled the folks like Didier Queloz, Jim Allison, Jeff Bezos, and Reed Hastings.

While Trailblazers have a high tolerance for risk and a willingness to challenge the status quo, it's their ability and willingness to push forward despite widespread doubt that really sets them apart. Their ability to swim against the current and take frequent stands in the face of strong opposition is often coupled with a deep intellectual curiosity and a genuine excitement for innovation.

It's often this combination of traits that allows them to not only generate groundbreaking ideas but also to advocate for them persistently, even when faced with years of rejection.

And for teams in general, bear this in mind: Trailblazers are just as essential as all the other roles. In fact, I'll put it more bluntly: Trailblazers are necessary to ensure the success of every organization. Companies like Kodak, Nokia, Blockbuster, Yahoo, JCPenney, MySpace, Commodore, Sears, Polaroid, Borders, etc., all failed for lack of, or resistance to, Trailblazers.

Back in 2000, when it was not at all clear that Netflix would become the behemoth it is today, the founders tried to sell the company to Blockbuster for a mere $50 million. They met with Blockbuster's CEO John Antioco and pitched him the $50 million price. His reaction? John Antioco struggled not to laugh. For context, in 2004, Blockbuster had about $6 billion in revenue, and in 2010, Blockbuster filed for bankruptcy.

Each of the aforementioned companies collapsed in similarly precipitous ways. Nobody thinks it will happen to their company, but according to an AEI study, when comparing the Fortune 500 companies in 1955 to the Fortune 500 in 2014, only sixty-one companies appear in both lists. Nearly 88 percent of the companies from 1955 have gone bankrupt, merged, or fallen from the Fortune 500.[12]

CHAPTER REFLECTION GUIDE

- Reflect on a time when someone in your team introduced a bold or unconventional idea. How was it received by the team, and what was the outcome? What lessons did you learn about embracing innovation?
- Have you experienced a situation where taking a risk led to a breakthrough—or a setback? How might a Trailblazer's willingness to challenge the status quo have influenced that outcome?
- Think about a time when you or someone else faced resistance to a new idea. How was that resistance managed, and what strategies might help Trailblazers persevere in similar situations?
- Reflect on how your team or organization treats innovators. Are Trailblazers supported and encouraged, or do they face significant resistance? What could you do to create an environment where Trailblazers thrive?

Visit **www.leadershipiq.com/teamplayers** to find more resources, such as exercises, assessments, and additional tools.

CHAPTER 5

THE HARMONIZER

IF YOU'VE SEEN THE JOHN WICK MOVIES STARRING KEANU REEVES, you know that Mr. Wick is a formerly retired hitman navigating a clandestine underworld teeming with assassins. He's a nigh-unstoppable force cutting through one dangerous assassin after another.

At the start of the third John Wick movie, he confronts a seven-foot-three, 290-pound assassin named Ernest. In the dimly lit corridors of a grand library, John Wick is dwarfed by his colossal opponent. With hands so large they envelop Wick's entire head, Ernest punishes Wick, his grip ironclad and inescapable. In between towering bookshelves, Ernest unleashes a front kick powered by size twenty-seven shoes that sends Wick flying out of the stacks. John eventually prevails—it's his movie, after all. And it's a library, so, of course, he kills the bad guy using a book.

The point of this brief retelling is to highlight the colossal titan and brute force incarnate that is the man playing Ernest: Boban Marjanović. This NBA center, while physically imposing, is generally regarded throughout the league as "one of the most beloved individuals in sports."

He's been around the league (six teams so far as I write this), and he is treasured for his personality wherever he goes. *The New York Times* interviewed nearly thirty of his teammates and coaches, and while most such profiles turn up at least a few skeletons or snarky comments, that was not the case with Boban.

Jon Leuer, his Detroit Pistons teammate, observed, "Pretty quickly, you could tell that he's never had a bad day in his life." Ryan Broekhoff, who played with him on the Dallas Mavericks, noted, "He [will] go make meaningful conversations with anybody. I think he's just looking for someone to talk to. He's great at connecting with people and really getting to know people on a deeper level."

Gregg Popovich, who coached Marjanović on the San Antonio Spurs, described him as "a special, caring, loving, upbeat guy. And he's a better player than everyone thinks. But you couldn't ask for a better professional, a better teammate, for sure."

Anthony Tolliver, another Pistons teammate, praised Boban's supportive nature: "He doesn't just sit on the bench and pout because he's not playing. He legitimately cares about everybody else and everybody else doing well." Maxi Kleber from the Mavericks provided a specific example: "Let's say I got subbed out, and I wasn't happy with myself, (I was) a little bit mad at myself, he would talk to you, like, 'Hey, you did a good job.'"

The impact he has on those around him is profound. Aaron Gray, a former Pistons assistant coach, summed it up best: "Man, I cried when that dude got traded. He just changes you, man. He really does."[1]

Boban is a Harmonizer. The Harmonizer plays a crucial role in team dynamics, serving as the social glue that binds members together. They're adept at fostering collaboration, building relationships, and maintaining a positive team atmosphere. Harmonizers excel in creating an environment where team members feel comfortable, valued, and understood.

Psychologically, Harmonizers are often driven by a high degree of emotional intelligence and empathy. They possess an innate ability to perceive and understand the emotions of others, allowing them to navigate complex interpersonal situations with skill and sensitivity. This emotional acuity enables Harmonizers to anticipate potential conflicts, mediate disagreements, and promote understanding among team members, even those with drastically diverse perspectives and personalities.

With three-point shots, floor-spacing, and more, today's NBA de-emphasizes dominant big men like Boban. But he's still found landing spots, and it's in no small part because he has such a positive influence on everyone around him.

WHO IS THE HARMONIZER?

Harmonizers play a crucial role in enabling their teammates to unlock their full potential and become their best selves. By creating a supportive and psychologically safe environment, Harmonizers allow others to feel comfortable taking risks, sharing ideas, and being vulnerable. They can act as informal mentors or coaches, offering encouragement and constructive feedback that helps colleagues identify and develop their strengths.

Harmonizers are generally characterized by high emotional intelligence and empathy. They possess the talent to perceive and understand others' emotions, which is how they navigate complex interpersonal situations so skillfully. Harmonizers can anticipate potential conflicts, mediate disagreements, and promote understanding among diverse team members. Boban, for example, possesses an innate talent for other awareness (the ability to accurately perceive, understand, and empathize with the emotions, needs, and perspectives of those around us).

Psychologically, Harmonizers are driven by a strong need for social connection and group cohesion. They enjoy fostering positive relationships and maintaining a harmonious team atmosphere. This motivation often manifests as a willingness to prioritize others' needs over their own, sometimes to their detriment. More than a few Harmonizers have struggled with setting personal boundaries; taken too far, this can cause varying degrees of emotional exhaustion. Harmonizers typically score high on personality measures of agreeableness. They're generally skilled communicators, particularly when it comes to active listening and interpreting nonverbal cues.

At its best, you'll see the Harmonizer's impact in the strengthened relationships between other team members and the positive atmosphere that permeates the group. Their influence manifests in increased camaraderie, mutual support, and even communicative effectiveness (a fancy way of saying that everyone else becomes a more tactful and empathic communicator).

HARMONIZING IS NOT TOXIC POSITIVITY

Can team harmony be taken too far? Yes, and we've probably all experienced versions of Midwestern nice, Southern politeness, corporate sugarcoating, the conflict-avoidant workplace, toxic positivity, or any of the hundreds of other euphemisms for groups or cultures that can't or won't express dissent or disagreement.

Harmonizers help enable a team's success. Unfortunately, there are teams where team harmony is seen as the end in itself. Our research regularly uncovers complaints on teams like, "We spend so much time on storming and norming that we don't accomplish anything," or "We're so afraid of disagreeing that we accept bad ideas."

Every so often, I encounter a Harmonizer who has crossed the line from emotional intelligence to toxic positivity. Toxic positivity is, at its core, an excessive and distorted form of positive thinking. It's the act of putting a positive spin on all experiences, regardless of how grave or severe they might be. For example, when leaders regularly say, "This is a blessing in disguise," or "All things happen for a reason," they're likely heading into toxic positivity.

The consequences of toxic positivity can be dire, creating a stifling work environment where genuine concerns are ignored or suppressed. This fosters a culture of mistrust, where employees feel unheard and invalidated. Over time, this erodes team cohesion, decreases morale, and drives burnout. And by continuously disregarding genuine challenges and issues, the team risks being blindsided by problems that could have been managed or even averted.

Ursula Burns is a former CEO of Xerox and the first Black woman to lead a Fortune 500 company. She also understands the risk when team harmony is weaponized to suppress bold ideas, hard choices, and mandatory deadlines. "The Xerox family suffers from 'terminal niceness,'" she told company leaders. "My basic message was that we had such an overly kind culture at Xerox that we at times supported each other's mediocrity. When someone makes a presentation at a meeting and it's horrible, we actually say, 'Thank you. It was very good.' And when the person leaves, we say to each other, 'That was the worst presentation ever!' We've got to get over that and speak up."[2]

At a recent team effectiveness workshop, the Harmonizer was easy to spot. As the group entered the room, my eyes were drawn to a woman who seemed to float from person to person, offering warm smiles and gentle touches on shoulders. If her affability had been rebuffed, I might have thought she was getting a bit too loose with personal boundaries. But everyone just lit up when she greeted them; this was clearly a Harmonizer.

Throughout the day, I noticed how she skillfully smoothed over tense moments and drew out quieter team members. When a heated debate erupted over a new project, she intervened: "I can see how passionate everyone is about this. Why don't we take a step back and hear from each person individually? I think we all have valuable insights to offer."

Her approach worked wonders in the moment, but as the day wore on, I sensed a growing frustration from some team members. They'd exchange glances when she'd steer conversations away from conflict, or sigh when she'd suggest yet another round of sharing feelings.

After the session, she approached me, both literally and figuratively wringing her hands. "I feel like I'm always the one trying to keep everyone happy," she confessed. "But sometimes I wonder if I'm actually holding the team back. Am I doing more harm than good?"

This Harmonizer's concern highlights a common challenge for those in this role: finding the delicate balance between allowing healthy conflict and ensuring the conflict stays productive. While Harmonizers excel at creating a positive team atmosphere, their natural inclination to smooth over disagreements can sometimes suppress necessary disagreement. There's an old saying that goes, "In business, when two people always agree, one of them is irrelevant." In other words, a team needs to disagree, sometimes vociferously.

In this case, the Harmonizer's constant interventions, while well-intentioned, were preventing the team from engaging in the kind of constructive conflict that often leads to innovation and better solutions. By always steering conversations away from tension, she was inadvertently creating a form of artificial harmony (or terminal niceness in Ursula Burns's parlance) that could stifle creativity and honest communication.

The key for Harmonizers is to recognize that not all conflict is negative. Healthy disagreement can lead to better outcomes, more robust solutions, and stronger team dynamics. The challenge is distinguishing between destructive conflict that needs mediation and productive conflict that should be allowed to play out.

HARMONIZERS CAN SPOT THE SNARLING

Remember Jim Allison, the Trailblazer from Chapter 4? His trailblazing ways led to the development of an antibody allowing T cells to attack cancer. But his trailblazing discoveries don't become an available drug without help from another role, namely the Harmonizer: Dr. Rachel Humphrey, then scientific director of Bristol Myers Squibb. She took the lead in convincing the company to invest millions into what would become Ipilimumab, the first approved checkpoint inhibitor. Humphrey battled hard through innumerable boardroom fights to get the company to keep spending and increasing trials.

At one early but critical meeting, "Rachel made it a point for me to come and sit next to her," Allison said. "I'll never forget because I was sitting there and there were some people that had very little understanding of immunology, and they were making comments.... I would just be going under my breath 'oh my God' and obviously getting agitated. Rachel kept looking at me and afterwards she says, 'Okay well I wrote down every time you started snarling, and so what about this, and what's wrong with that, and what's wrong with this... we went over her notes for a while, and it was really a lot of fun."[3]

As a Trailblazer, Allison was predictably agitated by those who didn't get or misunderstood the game-changing potential of immunology. But Humphrey's harmonizing approach bridged the gap between Allison and the Bristol Myers Squibb executives. She was fluent in the language of science, but she also spoke corporate investing, risk management, and big company politics. A Harmonizer par excellence, Humphrey had the interpersonal savvy to smooth ruffled feathers, whether Allison's or those of her Bristol Myers Squibb colleagues.

The company doesn't get Ipilimumab without Jim Allison, and vice versa. Allison got the Nobel Prize, and the company got the cancer-treating drug. But the linchpin that fostered and maximized this life-saving partnership was a Harmonizer who brought everyone together for the greater good.

RESTORING A CULTURE

If you've ever been part of a toxic workplace, you've probably already got an innate appreciation for Harmonizers. For years, Abercrombie & Fitch was not an especially harmonious or welcoming work environment. Known for a leadership style simultaneously autocratic and controversial, former CEO Mike Jeffries once described his company thusly: "In every school, there are the cool and popular kids, and then there are the not-so-cool kids.

Candidly, we go after the cool kids. We go after the attractive all-American kid with a great attitude and a lot of friends. A lot of people don't belong [in our clothes], and they can't belong. Are we exclusionary? Absolutely."[4] Jeffries stepped down in 2014 after years of declining sales and more than a few scandals.

His successor is Fran Horowitz, a CEO with a decidedly lower profile and far more collaborative and harmonious approach. When asked to describe her leadership style, she answered, "Optimistic, collaborative, curious, and open. I always strive to foster an environment where everyone feels safe and empowered to share ideas and feedback directly with me, whatever their role. I also spend a lot of time listening to our associates throughout our organization, in stores and throughout our international network. That keeps me in touch with what we're doing from different viewpoints."[5]

"I value all my discussions across the entire organization," she says. "Whether I'm in a meeting with our board or walking through a store with a manager, listening is key to learning and understanding." Horowitz's collaborative, inclusive, and harmonizing approach stands in sharp contrast to her predecessor's, and it's been an essential step in the company's rehabilitation.

The Harmonizer is an integral part of a team, acting as the glue that holds members together. They excel in fostering collaboration and camaraderie and building strong relationships within the group. With an innate ability to understand and relate to others, they're often the key to maintaining team morale and cohesion.

There are times when Harmonizers struggle with the emotional burden of constantly mediating conflicts and managing interpersonal dynamics. Being the one shoulder that everyone cries and relies on can lead to some emotional exhaustion and burnout, especially when they're constantly facing frequent or intense conflicts. It's happened more than once where a Harmonizer found it difficult to maintain personal boundaries, sacrificing their own needs for the sake of team harmony.

In areas like giving feedback, it's not unusual for Harmonizers to struggle balancing empathy with objectivity. Harmonizers don't usually enjoy delivering critical feedback or making tough decisions that will upset team members, even when such actions are necessary for the group's success. When a Harmonizer avoids necessary confrontations or difficult conversations, this is often the reason why.

THE HARMONIZER'S RIPPLE EFFECTS

Ken Hicks, president, chairman, and CEO of Academy Sports and Outdoors, Inc., is a good example of the near oxymoron that is the egoless CEO. Academy is one of the leading full-line sporting goods and outdoor recreation retailers in the United States. With 268 stores and roughly $6 billion in sales, Hicks would be forgiven for having a healthy ego, yet he's far more likely to give credit than take it.

In a recent conversation, Hicks told me that "when you become a leader, it's not about you anymore; it's about the organization and your people. My job is to make my people better than me, and if I can do that, then I succeeded."[6]

When he leaves at the end of the day, Hicks asks everyone he sees questions like, "What'd you do today? What'd you accomplish? And do you feel good about it?" Rather than the reflexive, "Everything's fine," Hicks's questions prompt reflection. "They think about it," Hicks told me. "When they tell me that they processed a difficult account or whatever they did, I have the opportunity to let them know that I appreciate what they accomplished and why it's important." And the benefits extend well beyond Hicks's response. As he explains, "After they leave work, they go home and say to their spouse or their friends, 'You know what? I did have a good day.'"

Like many CEOs, Hicks tells a lot of stories, and like a Harmonizer, he credits others for a great many of them. "Our CFO says" or "Our manager of such-and-such says" are common refrains for him. As he visits their hundreds of stores, Hicks notes that "People see that I give them credit for this idea, and they think, 'Maybe I should also be giving people credit, congratulating and thanking them.' If that's what their leader does, then that becomes a guide for them as well."

Hicks's approach shows how Harmonizers can leverage their natural strengths to create a positive and productive work environment, even (or especially) when they're the CEO of a multibillion dollar enterprise. By consistently acknowledging and appreciating the contributions of others, Harmonizers like Hicks foster a culture of recognition and mutual respect. This not only boosts morale but also encourages team members to emulate these behaviors, creating a ripple effect throughout the organization.

It's important, however, that Harmonizers don't take deflecting credit to the extreme. Too much focus on others' accomplishments can sometimes lead to their own contributions being overlooked. On a personal level, this can lead to them being held back in their ambitions and missing out on promotions. Now, in the real world, you're far more likely to encounter credit hogs than credit deflectors, but it's an issue worth noting. While the selfless approach is admirable, Harmonizers need to strike a balance between recognizing others and ensuring their own value is understood and appreciated.

When done well, Harmonizers enable the team's success. Dr. Rachel Humphrey enabled the approval of Jim Allison's breakthrough cancer treatment. Ken Hicks enables the success of leaders across hundreds of retail stores. Among their superpowers are fostering collaboration and camaraderie. And while their work is often less visible to outsiders, make no mistake that they are worth their weight in gold.

Harmonizers care deeply about people and support and cheer their success. They resolve conflicts, quash toxicity, and ensure that important ideas are surfaced and heard. The results speak for themselves.

CHAPTER REFLECTION GUIDE

- Think about a time when a Harmonizer played a key role on your team. How did their actions foster collaboration and improve team dynamics? What specific behaviors stood out?
- Have you experienced a situation where a Harmonizer prevented or resolved a conflict? How was their approach effective, and what could have been done differently, if anything?
- Reflect on a team environment you've been a part of. Was harmony encouraged to the point of stifling necessary conflict or bold ideas? How might a Harmonizer strike the right balance between maintaining peace and fostering productive disagreement?
- Harmonizers often carry an emotional burden as the "glue" in a team. Have you witnessed or experienced this? What can you or your team do to better support someone in this role?

Visit **www.leadershipiq.com/teamplayers** to find more resources, such as exercises, assessments, and additional tools.

CHAPTER 6

THE ACHIEVER

I N THE ANNALS OF TECH HISTORY, EVERYONE KNOWS THE FORCE OF nature that was Steve Jobs—the uncompromising chief executive in a black turtleneck who revolutionized personal computing. But only slightly less well-known is the teddy bear of a man known as Woz, the gentle engineer whose brilliance laid the foundation for Apple's ascent.

Steve "Woz" Wozniak, with his shaggy beard and kind eyes, cut a very different figure from his more famous cofounder. Where Jobs commanded attention with piercing gazes and charismatic speeches, Woz preferred the quiet hum of electronics and the camaraderie of fellow engineers. Clad in comfortable clothes and often sporting a cheerful smile, he embodied the pure joy of making.

Steve Wozniak's journey into the heart of the computer revolution began long before Apple's inception, finding its true spark in the Homebrew Computer Club. This gathering of tech enthusiasts, hobbyists, and visionaries became Woz's sanctuary in the mid-1970s. Here, amidst the whir of makeshift machines and the excited chatter of fellow creators, Wozniak's genius flourished.

During the day, he designed calculators for Hewlett-Packard and built computers at night. "My stuff was probably kind of impressive," he says in typical understated Woz fashion, "but I wasn't expressive enough to even explain to most of the people what this one had the others didn't have, why it was a better direction."[1]

Of course, it was the differences from other computers that made Woz's computers so impressive. A keyboard interface, games, connecting to a television, and a preassembled motherboard were all features that would set the stage for the Apple behemoth we know today.

Woz didn't want power, fame, or any of the other trappings of success we typically associate with giants of industry. In fact, he actually said, "I designed the Apple I because I wanted to give it away for free to other people." As a testament to his purity of spirit, he pitched this Apple I computer idea to Hewlett-Packard five times, and they turned him down each time.[2]

Today's startup ethos would make quitting Hewlett-Packard a no-brainer. But even then, one of his friends told him explicitly, "Steve you could be an engineer, start a company, you can go into management and get rich."

But Woz didn't want to be in charge. "I couldn't be a manager ever in my life," he says. "You know I saw corporate politics and things like that, that was not my life. All I was, was a designer. I wanted to design neat computers, write neat programs."

It wasn't until this friend convinced him that he could start a company and just be an engineer his whole life (while still getting rich) that he decided to quit Hewlett-Packard and cofound Apple. He explains his epiphany: "You can start a company even though you don't want to be a businessman. You don't want to run a company? You can have other people do that. You can simply start a company and if I like and I can still design, I can still do what I love doing, designing good products, writing good programs."[3]

WHO IS THE ACHIEVER?

Woz is an Achiever. Characterized by a hands-on mentality and an unwavering commitment to excellence, Achievers thrive on immersing themselves in the details of tasks, focusing intently on producing high-quality, error-free results. They're not looking to run the team or wield significant power; they're generally driven by the satisfaction derived from a job well done.

People like Woz experience a genuine thrill from completing tasks flawlessly, even if their efforts go unnoticed by others. This intrinsic motivation stems from a deep-seated need for personal achievement and a relentless pursuit of excellence. Achievers tend to set high standards for themselves and derive satisfaction from surpassing expectations, often going above and beyond what is asked of them.

Driven by a strong preference for autonomy, Achievers are most comfortable when they can concentrate on their tasks without the distractions or responsibilities of managing others. They prefer to work independently, honing their expertise and digging deep into the nitty-gritty.

I was post-speech and finishing up the customary thank-yous and handshakes with the crowd after one of my talks when I noticed a guy from the audience agitatedly lurking nearby. He was practically vibrating with nervous energy, slightly swaying side to side in a restless dance. His eyes darted around but kept flicking back to me. Fortunately, he wasn't giving off serious stalker vibes, so I waved him over.

"I've got a bigger problem than what you were just talking about," he blurted sans preamble. "My team isn't disengaged during meetings like you were talking about. I can feel that they're legit mad at me when I hold meetings, and I just want to get everyone together and know what they're up to."

I clearly wasn't going to get away with a quick two-second answer, nor was I going to enjoy my post-speech Diet Coke in peace, so I relocated our conversation to some chairs in the conference center foyer. Notwithstanding his somewhat frantic introduction, once he'd taken a breath, I learned that he was an eager, newly minted vice president at a prominent tech company who'd been put in charge of a sizeable development team.

"I don't feel connected to these folks at all," he divulged. "I'm supposed to be leading the team, but they withdraw whenever I try to get them together or even build some kind of relationship with them. How am I supposed to show my boss that I was the right choice for the job when it's clear that the team barely tolerates me? And how can I even get my people more recognition and visibility when I'm not that close to them?"

Take note of how many emotionally laden words he used (there were more, but I wrote what I was able to clearly recollect). Notice the words like "feel," "connected," "withdraw," "relationship," and so on. Harmonizers will often use that many feeling words, but Achievers? It's uncommon.

The more he told me about his developers, the clearer it became that he was leading a team of Achievers. He wanted emotional responses with personal connections and deep relationships. His team of Achievers, by contrast, wanted a distraction-free zone to produce.

The problem wasn't a bad relationship; it was a lack of mutual appreciation for their respective roles. The "come together" meetings the VP wanted were typically scheduled on days and times when the developers were at peak productivity and focus; it's small wonder they seemed annoyed. Similarly, the developers might not be appreciating the powerful benefits of having such an enthusiastic Harmonizer advocate. Achievers and Harmonizers can work wonderfully together as long as they understand and accommodate one another's goals, needs, and talents. In this particular case, a bit of give-and-take on scheduling the "come together" meetings and protecting focused coding time markedly improved the team's working relationships.

Clarifying and appreciating the diversity of the roles fixes these types of disconnects pretty quickly. For instance, what might look like disengagement or disinterest is sometimes just an Achiever in hyperfocus mode. Achievers thrive in environments where they can immerse themselves in tasks, meticulously focusing on every detail to ensure the highest quality outcome. And interrupting those immersive periods without a darn good reason isn't helpful to them or the team.

This intense focus and commitment to their work often lead Achievers to set exceptionally high standards for themselves, which they consistently strive to exceed. And their satisfaction is derived more from the quality and precision of their work than from accolades or external validation.

REACHING FOR THE STARS

Can you name the first-ever British group to top the US music charts in 1962? If you said the Beatles, sorry, but that's wrong. (They were the second British group to do it, in 1964, with "I Want to Hold Your Hand.")

The Tornados, with their 1962 hit instrumental song "Telstar," was actually the first British group to top the US charts. And here's a bit of weird history you might not know: Their song was named after the Telstar communications satellite launched that same year.

The nicest way I can describe the song is to say that it has what people in the 1960s would consider a futuristic space-age sound. Whatever you think a trippy instrumental sixties song about a space satellite sounds like, you're probably pretty close. Now, I'm not mentioning this to tell you about the song but rather about the satellite that inspired it. And more specifically, I want to tell you about John Pierce, the Achiever who drove its development.

John Pierce, a visionary engineer and scientist, played a pivotal role in shaping modern communications technology. Pierce, with his PhD from Caltech, joined Bell Laboratories in 1936, an institution renowned for its groundbreaking research in telecommunications and electronics. Bell Labs, the research arm of AT&T, was a powerhouse of innovation, responsible for inventions like the transistor and the laser.

Prior to satellites, long-distance telecommunications relied primarily on terrestrial systems and undersea cables. In the early twentieth century, radio waves enabled wireless communication but were limited by the Earth's curvature and atmospheric interference. Telephone networks expanded through a vast network of copper wires and microwave relay towers. The first undersea telephone cable in 1956 enabled transatlantic communication, but it could only carry thirty-six simultaneous calls and was extremely expensive to install and maintain.

Now, here's where John Pierce's Achiever mind comes to the fore. In true Achiever fashion, Pierce was constantly thinking about satellites, and not just at work. He started writing science fiction stories while at Caltech, and it was the stories and space fantasies that led to his satellite fixation. I thought I knew what "nerding out" meant, but Pierce redefined it for me.

In 1952, he wrote an article for *Astounding Science Fiction.* For that article, he calculated the power necessary to transmit signals between the Earth and the moon, planets, and stars. He calculated how much power would be needed to send signals from one point on the Earth's surface to another. And his calculations kept going: "I made calculations for large balloon-type satellites that would merely scatter the radio waves they intercepted so that about a billionth of a billionth of the microwave signal transmitted would be picked up by an antenna on Earth."[4]

This wasn't some unpleasant task assigned by a vindictive manager. Pierce's Achiever mind was fully engrossed and inspired. "I was amazed and delighted at the outcome of my calculations," he said. "By using currently available microwave equipment, any of these sorts of satellites could be used to communicate across oceans."

His Achiever-fueled passion project led him to a startling conclusion: "The truth is that you could order equipment for an Earth-Moon link from any of several manufacturers." By October 1954, Pierce was presenting detailed calculations on communications satellites, envisioning orbiting unmanned spaceships that could relay signals across the globe.[5]

Project Echo was born out of a desire to test the feasibility of satellite communications in a practical, relatively low-cost manner. In 1958, Pierce and his Bell Labs colleague Rudi Kompfner learned about a project to launch a large, lightweight aluminum-coated Mylar balloon into orbit for atmospheric tests. Recognizing its potential as a passive communications reflector, they quickly adopted this design for their satellite project. NASA agreed to launch the satellite, and on August 12, 1960, Echo I, a one-hundred-foot-diameter metalized balloon, was successfully placed into orbit.

On August 12, 1960, Project Echo transmitted President Dwight D. Eisenhower's voice across the United States via satellite. A prerecorded message from President Eisenhower was beamed from California to the orbiting Echo balloon, which then reflected it down to the receiving station in New Jersey. The message came through the loudspeakers so clearly that those present initially didn't realize it had traveled coast-to-coast.

Today, Pierce is considered the father of satellite communications. But even though he drove the heavy lifting behind the scenes, he was not in charge of the project that launched the satellite and sent the message. That was project engineer Bill Jakes.

And that brings us to another distinctive Achiever trait. "To everyone concerned with the Echo project, Jakes' word was final law," says Pierce. "He talked with us and with many others. But, it was up to Jakes to arrive at final work assignments and timetables. He was wonderful at this. His subsequent career showed him to be an ideal project engineer, hard-working, ingenious in overcoming obstacles, extremely well organized, and universally liked by those who worked with him."[6]

One day, Jakes was chatting with Pierce, expressing empathy for Pierce not having the fun of running the Echo Project himself. But Pierce didn't and wouldn't have wanted that particular role. "The Echo ground terminal would never have gotten built or worked had I been project engineer," he said. "Through a mixture of ineptitude and boredom, I would have flubbed. There may be people of universal capability, though I haven't met any. Mostly, the talents of talented people are very different. It is of great importance that people undertake what they can do and like to do."

Pierce, an Achiever, wanted to live in the details of designing the first communications satellite. But managing the entire project? Dealing with the personalities and timelines and myriad decisions? That was not for him.

Where does Telstar come in? Echo I was a passive communications satellite; it essentially reflected messages from one point on Earth to another. After John Pierce successfully created Echo, like a true Achiever who only cared about digging into the nitty-gritty details of the next project, he turned his attention to the development of the more sophisticated Telstar satellite. Unlike Echo, which merely reflected signals, Telstar was an active satellite capable of receiving, amplifying, and retransmitting signals. This leap in technology allowed Telstar to carry multiple phone calls and television broadcasts, significantly enhancing the potential for global communication. Pierce's work on Telstar culminated in its launch on July 10, 1962, marking a pivotal moment in satellite communications history, and the inspiration for a very popular hit song.

INTO THE WEEDS WE GO

There are fantastic minds on teams with zero desire to be in charge; instead, they want to burrow into the details of a project. Achievers' thorough analysis and precision make them particularly effective in projects requiring creative problem-solving and meticulous execution. Fighting for control of a team? That's not them. But doing the nitty-gritty work that makes the project possible? That's where they shine. Achievers are the people who ensure that the team's goals are not just conceptualized but actually realized with a high degree of excellence and precision.

A disproportionate number of business books and podcasts exhort readers to take charge, grab the reigns, climb the ladder, and all the rest. But the reality is that far more people would rather focus on doing great work and avoid the innumerable hassles and stresses attendant to any sort of management role. And that's okay!

In fact, my data from more than a million professionals shows team members are nearly three times more likely to be Achievers than Directors. Achievers are the most populous role on teams, and unlike some of the other roles, when teams are overloaded with Achievers, the group is less likely to suffer negative consequences. It can be hard for people in other roles to understand, but it's not uncommon for Achievers to resist taking on leadership roles, even when their expertise would seem to make them ideal candidates.

ROUNDING THE RECTANGLES

The late Steve Jobs is rightly lauded for his decisions that redefined and transformed the technologies to which we're all addicted. Yet underlying Jobs's transformative decisions were a group of Achievers behind the scenes who made those trailblazing moves possible. And their successes show what happens when Achievers are directed appropriately.

Apple's design has always set the company's products apart, and much of the impetus for beautiful design came from Steve Jobs. Something as simple as displaying rounded rectangles on a screen (rather than the boxy squares we merely tolerated) was the result of Jobs's demanding vision. But he couldn't make them; the making fell to Bill Atkinson, an early Apple employee and genius developer of graphics for the Macintosh.

As recounted in his biography, Jobs asked the Macintosh team about drawing rectangles with rounded corners. "'I don't think we really need it,' said Atkinson, who explained that it would be almost impossible to do. 'Rectangles with rounded corners are everywhere!' Jobs said, jumping up and getting more intense. 'Just look around this room!' He pointed out the whiteboard and the tabletop and other objects that were rectangular with rounded corners. 'And look outside, there's even more, practically everywhere you look!' He dragged Atkinson out for a walk, pointing out car windows and billboards and street signs."[7]

Finally, Atkinson relented. And the next day, presumably after a night of nonstop coding, Atkinson walked into the office with a big smile on his face and his computer drawing rounded rectangles at blazing fast speeds.

Without clear direction and guidance, it's possible for Achievers to spend their efforts on work that's misaligned with the group's needs. Driven by their intrinsic desire for excellence and, occasionally, an unhealthy dose of perfectionism, I've seen Achievers engineer solutions that far exceeded what was required to actually solve the problem.

I was working with a promising startup that, notwithstanding their immense talent and brainpower, was struggling to meet investor milestones. One of the roadblocks was their brilliant but perfectionist CTO and cofounder.

"He's amazing," the CEO shared, "but we're missing deadlines and our investors are getting antsy." I watched the CTO during their next executive team meeting. At one point, he proudly presented their new analytics model; apparently it was twice as fast as had been promised and was blowing away the benchmarks. Predictably, the CEO snapped: "We needed a basic prototype two weeks ago. We're burning through cash."

The CTO isn't the first Achiever in history to struggle with perfectionism or overengineering. Their focus on delivering flawless results may cause them to spend excessive time perfecting details, potentially leading to missed deadlines or delaying the team's progress. This perfectionist mindset can make it difficult for them to accept "good enough" solutions, particularly in situations where compromises are necessary for the team's overall success.

After the meeting, the CEO and I chatted about what it means to be an Achiever. "That's your CTO to a tee," I said. "He's driven by excellence, often at the expense of practicality. You need to channel that energy, not fight it."

There are dozens of ways to do this. In this case, guided by research showing that constraints can channel and improve innovation, this CEO opted for a time-constrained, rapid engineering challenge: five days for the working prototype. Like a lot of Achievers, the CTO took to the challenge, immediately working out features that could be implemented within the constraints while still showcasing the model's performance. "It's like I'm speaking his language now," the CEO would later tell me. "He's still pushing boundaries, but in a way that's aligned with, and not at odds with, our success."

Achievers, by their nature, aren't typically clamoring to sit at the head of the conference room table. They're unlikely to make lengthy speeches or dominate discussions. And they'd typically prefer to avoid being put in charge of the group. But make no mistake, they are vital to the success of every single team.

CHAPTER REFLECTION GUIDE

- Think of an Achiever you've worked with. How did their meticulous attention to detail and high standards contribute to the success of your team or project? Was their work recognized appropriately?
- Have you encountered misunderstandings between Achievers and other team roles, such as Directors or Trailblazers? What strategies could improve mutual appreciation and collaboration between these roles?
- If you're managing or collaborating with an Achiever, how can you create an environment that respects their need for focus while channeling their talents toward team goals? Are there constraints or challenges you could introduce to inspire their best work?
- Achievers sometimes prefer to work independently. How can teams strike the right balance between providing Achievers with autonomy and ensuring they remain aligned with broader team objectives?

Visit **www.leadershipiq.com/teamplayers** to find more resources, such as exercises, assessments, and additional tools.

CHAPTER 7

CURATING YOUR TEAM

I<small>T WAS A FREEZING</small> D<small>ECEMBER MORNING IN</small> K<small>ANSAS.</small> A <small>GROUP OF</small> massive guys—we're talking 300 pounds each—trudged across a frosty parking lot. They were all on edge, excited but nervous. Someone had hinted at a surprise gift, and they couldn't stop wondering what it might be. Then, all of a sudden, there it was: a line of bright red golf carts. But these weren't just any golf carts. Each one had been customized with the man's name and number.[1]

These were no ordinary guys in a parking lot; they were the offensive line of the Kansas City Chiefs. And the mastermind behind this yuletide gesture? Their quarterback, Patrick Mahomes. As each player discovered his personalized cart, they looked like kids on Christmas morning. One by one, they climbed aboard and floored their new rides, their faces lit up with laughter.

Each year in the NFL, a tradition unfolds that highlights both gratitude and a deep understanding of the importance of each and every role on the team. Quarterbacks and running backs present their offensive linemen with extraordinary gifts, recognizing the unsung heroes who play a pivotal role in their success. These quarterbacks understand that without a robust offensive line, they wouldn't have the protection needed to execute a formidable passing attack or to shield themselves from the injuries that relentless defenders would likely inflict. Similarly, running backs rely on these powerful blockers to carve out the lanes essential for a dynamic rushing game. Though these linemen may not bask in as much limelight as their more visible teammates, their contributions are essential. These gifts are more than just tokens; they're acknowledgments that every yard gained and every game won is built on the foundation of a variety of roles.

This isn't a pitch for the people on your team to buy each other custom golf carts, expensive watches, Louis Vuitton duffle bags, or any of the other lavish gifts that offensive linemen have famously received. The specific gifts aren't important; the underlying appreciation of each other's contributions is what really matters.

Sports teams, rock bands, surgical teams, film production crews, symphony orchestras, pit crews, emergency response teams, and airline crews are just a few of the innumerable groups that recognize and value the diverse roles and talents that make groups successful. You can't be a quarterback without appreciating the linemen in the trenches, a lead singer without valuing the bassist's foundational pulse, or a surgeon without acknowledging the life-saving roles of anesthesiologists and nurses. But in corporate settings, the allure of the singular star can be blinding.

SINGLE STARS DON'T SHINE SO BRIGHT

Remember the Harvard study from Chapter 1 about the negative impact of having too many star stock analysts? A related study from the same researchers analyzed what happens when those stars change firms.

Companies have been waging talent wars for decades, so it's no surprise when stars get poached by a competitor. But contrary to the popular belief that star talent transfers easily, these stars quickly faded when transplanted to a new environment.

The study of more than one thousand star stock analysts discovered that a staggering 46 percent of the star analysts performed poorly in the year after they changed companies. Even more alarming, their performance dropped by an average of 20 percent after switching firms, and the numbers failed to recover to previous levels even five years later.[2]

Ponder that for a moment. These are stars; they're outperforming their peers, and yet, as soon as they change employers, their performance drops. This decline wasn't isolated to a few unfortunate cases. No matter how many millions of dollars companies paid to poach those stars, the drop in their performance was consistent across different types of analysts and firms. Whether they were covering large-cap stocks or niche industries, whether they moved to more prestigious firms or lateral ones, the pattern held true.

So what happened? These companies and star analysts overlooked the cohort of diverse roles and talents that underpinned the stars' success. When a quarterback switches teams, their standout offensive line and receivers don't usually accompany them, and when those star stock analysts change firms, they're doing so without the Stabilizers whose procedures ensured that reports were delivered ahead of rivals, Harmonizers whose collaborative talents allowed analysts to smoothly work across sectors, Achievers who helped rigorously evaluate research, Trailblazers whose cutting-edge technology gave analysts a competitive edge in information gathering, and Directors who smartly allocated resources and determined coverage areas.

These star analysts may have seemed like solo performers, but in reality, they needed the teams around them as much as quarterbacks and running backs need a strong offensive line. And given how many resources they left behind when they changed companies, it's small wonder that the stars' performance declined.

The impact even extended beyond individual performance. When a star analyst was hired, not only did their individual performance plummet, but there was also a sharp decline in the functioning of their new team. The stock prices of investment banks fell by an average of 0.74 percent upon announcing the hiring of a star analyst, translating to an average loss of $24 million in market value per hire. It seems investors knew the risks of hiring stars without the rest of the team, and they priced the company's stock accordingly.

If 46 percent of star analysts perform poorly after changing firms, and their performance drops by an average of 20 percent, how much of their previous success was due to individual talent, and how much of each star's performance was actually due to all of the other people and roles on their teams? Whatever the percentage, it's clear that neither the stars themselves nor the companies hiring them fully appreciated the extent to which other roles and talents are vital to a star's success.

RECOGNIZING THE ROLES

The first task in unlocking your team's potential is creating an appreciation for the diversity of roles and talents that drive a group's success; your team needs to grasp the importance of Directors, Stabilizers, Achievers, Trailblazers, and Harmonizers. Ideally, your team should think like quarterbacks who value their offensive line, not like the star stock analysts who believed too strongly in their own self-sufficiency.

Explain the concept of the five roles to your group. Start by having them read this book. Once they've got a handle on the five roles, conduct the following exercise:

ROLE APPRECIATION

Ask everyone on your team to answer these three prompts:

1. Describe a time when you worked with someone amazing in each of the five roles (think of the best Harmonizer you ever worked with, a great Stabilizer, etc.).
2. For each of those roles, describe how that person helped you or the group achieve success.
3. Describe what the team would've been missing without someone fulfilling that role.

The goal here is simply getting everyone on your team to start appreciating the importance and value of Directors, Stabilizers, Achievers, Trailblazers, and Harmonizers.

Nearly a decade ago, well before my research identified the five team roles, Microsoft CEO Satya Nadella wrote this about his Senior Leadership Team:

"I like to think of the SLT as a sort of Legion of Superheroes, with each leader coming to the table with a unique superpower to contribute for the common good. Amy is our conscience, keeping us intellectually honest and accountable for doing what we committed to do. Kurt pushes us on being rigorous about our strategy and operations. Product leaders like Terry, Scott, Harry, and more recently Rajesh Jha and Kevin Scott push for alignment on product plans, knowing that when we are an inch apart on strategy at the leadership level, our product teams end up miles apart in execution. Brad helps us navigate the ever-evolving legal and policy landscape, always finding just the right position on important global and domestic issues. Kathleen constantly channels the voice of our employees. Peggy does the same for partners, and Chris, Jean-Philippe Courtois, and Judson Althoff for our customers. They are the true heroes of our continuing transformation."[3]

His language is different, but he clearly appreciates the talents the five roles represent, even calling them a "Legion of Superheroes." Amy seems to fit the Stabilizer role, described as "our conscience, keeping us intellectually honest and accountable for doing what we committed to do," matching the Stabilizer's focus on planning, adherence to processes, and ensuring follow-through on commitments.

Brad could fit the Trailblazer role, as he "helps us navigate the ever-evolving legal and policy landscape." Parenthetically, phrases like "ever-evolving" are often used to describe someone who's on the cutting-edge and pushing out-of-the-box ideas; in other words, a Trailblazer. Nadella further bolsters the Trailblazer case for Brad, a former partner at the white-shoe law firm Covington and Burling, noting that he's "remembered to this day as the first attorney in the nearly century-old firm to insist as a condition of his employment in 1986 that he have a PC on his desk."

Kathleen, Peggy, Chris, Jean-Philippe, and Judson could be Harmonizers, as they channel the voices of employees, partners, and customers, ensuring all stakeholders' voices are heard. And so on.

It won't take much effort to get your team to value the importance of each unique role. Drawing on their own experiences to deepen their appreciation, they should quickly grasp the essentiality of Directors, Stabilizers, Achievers, Trailblazers, and Harmonizers. Once people grasp the five roles, they're typically able to spot who's who on every team—like seeing the trick in an optical illusion, once you know it's there, you'll recognize it instantly every time.

THE POWER OF META-PERCEPTION

Once your group starts appreciating the value of the different roles, you're ready to assess the roles currently represented on your team. Before we start, there are two critical points to bear in mind. First, you could be part of wildly different teams, and you need to figure out the role you (and others) play in each of those potentially disparate groups. You'll want to conduct this exercise for each team; for instance, you might be on a team where you're the one making all the tough decisions while simultaneously participating on a team where you're the designated peacemaker.

Second, people often struggle to objectively assess themselves, but they evidence good insight into how others view them. For instance, one study asked employees to rate their own job performance and then predict how their supervisor would rate them. The researchers then compared both types of employee ratings to the supervisor's actual ratings.

Employees were generally inaccurate when rating their own performance, especially for things like teamwork and going above and beyond their core job duties. However, when asked to predict how their supervisor would rate them, employees were literally twice as accurate. Put simply, people are better at predicting how others see them than they are at seeing themselves objectively.[4]

Armed with those two insights, you can now take stock of your team. The key to this is not asking everyone what role they think they fulfill on teams; rather, it's asking what role your teammates would say that you're currently fulfilling on the team.

It might seem like a subtle difference, but considering how your team-mates see you taps into a capacity known as meta-perception—the ability to view one's self from the perspective of other people. It's a well-studied phenomenon, and it doesn't just work for positive characteristics, like roles on a team; it even holds up for personality disorders. If you just ask random people whether they're narcissistic, dependent, avoidant, antisocial, etc., the responses might not be perfectly accurate. But if you ask them to assess to what extent their colleagues see evidence of those characteristics, they'll surprise you with their perceptivity.

For instance, one study examined personality pathology among Air Force recruits. After six weeks of training, recruits were asked to describe themselves and their fellow flight members on personality pathology traits. They then gauged how they would be rated by their fellow flight members on those traits. It turned out that their predictions closely matched the actual feedback from their peers. Inquiring about how they believed their peers perceived them turned out to be a reliable predictor of how their peers actually saw them.[5]

We recently conducted an experiment much like the Air Force study, but instead of measuring personality disorders, we assessed team roles. In a study encompassing more than fifty executive teams, we asked each executive to pinpoint the role they believed their colleagues perceived them playing most often. Subsequently, the executives assessed one another, providing a measure of how they genuinely viewed each other's roles. Just like in the Air Force study, the executives' assessments of how they thought others saw them were incredibly predictive of how their teammates actually did see them. And it was far more predictive than simply asking people to identify the role they see themselves fulfilling.

ASSESSING THE ROLES ON YOUR TEAM

Ask each person on your team to answer the following questions:

1. What role would your teammates say that you are currently fulfilling on the team? (Brief descriptions of the roles have been included for reference.)

   - The Director assumes a leadership role within the team, guiding the direction of the team and making important, difficult, and even unpopular decisions.
   - The Achiever immerses themselves in the details of accomplishing tasks and getting things done, with a keen eye for delivering error-free work.
   - The Stabilizer keeps the team on track with meticulous planning, processes and procedures, clear timelines, and organization.
   - The Harmonizer brings collaboration and camaraderie, builds relationships, and resolves conflict.
   - The Trailblazer brings innovation, creativity, and out-of-the-box thinking, along with the courage to challenge conventional wisdom.

2. Describe a few reasons why you think your teammates see you fulfilling that role.
3. If there's an additional role you'd like to fulfill, what is it?

You'll notice that the last question in this exercise asked about additional roles that people might like to fulfill. As we'll see shortly, you may need people to switch roles, develop new talents, or provide backup, so you'd like to know if someone has an inclination to one of the other roles.

Alternatively, there is an online assessment available at www.leadershipiq .com/teamplayers. And given everything we've just covered, it uses meta-perception so people have to consider how others see them.

CHARTING YOUR TEAM'S ROLE COMPOSITION

Now that you've explored the five essential roles—Director, Stabilizer, Achiever, Trailblazer, and Harmonizer—and your team members have considered how they're perceived in these roles, it's time to create a visual representation of your team's composition. This "Team Role Map" will help you identify your team's strengths and potential gaps.

Here's how to make the map:

1. Gather the role assessments from each team member. Remember, these should be based on how they think others perceive them, not necessarily how they see themselves.
2. Draw six columns on a large piece of paper or whiteboard. The first column is for the names of the people on your team. Label the rows with team members' names and the columns with the five roles.
3. For each team member, place a checkmark in the column corresponding to their primary perceived role. This is the role they believe others see them fulfilling most often.
4. Use smaller dots to indicate any secondary roles that team members would like to fulfill or develop.
5. Finally, step back and look at your completed map. Are all roles represented? Are some roles overrepresented while others are lacking? This visual representation can quickly highlight your team's composition and potential imbalances.

NAMES	DIRECTOR	STABILIZER	HARMONIZER	ACHIEVER	TRAILBLAZER
Pat	✓				•
Chris		✓		•	
Sam			•	✓	
Alex	•			✓	
Taylor	•		✓		
Jordan		✓	•		
Riley	•			✓	
Quinn	•				✓
Jamie				✓	•

RECOGNIZING AND AFFIRMING THE ROLES

Picture a high-stakes business competition in which teams of young professionals are tasked with running virtual companies. They have four weeks to make critical decisions about marketing, finance, human resources, and more. The pressure is on, the clock is ticking, and their results will be graded. This isn't just a hypothetical scenario; it's the setting for a fascinating study that reveals deep insights into what makes teams truly excel.

Researchers at the University of Groningen in the Netherlands set up this complex business simulation with 39 teams. Each team had to work together intensively, making decisions that would determine the success or failure of their virtual company. But the researchers weren't just interested in which teams won; they wanted to understand why some teams performed brilliantly while others struggled.

Here's where it gets interesting. The researchers introduced a concept called "reciprocal expertise affirmation." In simple terms, this means the extent to which team members mutually recognize, respect, and value each other's unique expertise.[6] The key here is that it's not just about liking your teammates or thinking they're generally competent; it's about truly appreciating the specific skills and knowledge each person brings to the table. This is Wynton Marsalis appreciating that the bass guitar is responsible for making sure the drummer doesn't rush or drag. It's Patrick Mahomes valuing his offensive line. And not to put too fine a point on it, but this is exactly what we accomplished with our previous exercise.

Teams with high levels of reciprocal expertise affirmation worked together much more smoothly. They coordinated their actions better, made fewer mistakes, and ultimately performed at a higher level.

When team members understand and appreciate each other's expertise, something powerful happens; they start to use each other's knowledge more efficiently. Wynton Marsalis's band is made up of talented musicians, but it's their appreciation for each other's talents and roles that really makes them swing. In the Dutch business competition, the teams that grasped this concept worked together brilliantly, smoothly leveraging each person's strengths to drive the virtual company forward.

There's another benefit: People who feel that their talents are truly appreciated by others are more motivated to go the extra mile. They put in more effort and engage more deeply with their work, and as a result, they perform better. It's the difference between someone who's just going through the motions and someone who's fully invested in the team's success because they know their role is valued.

Most know that Tom Brady began as a backup at the University of Michigan, but you might not have heard this particular story. Brady recalls a teammate, fullback Chris Floyd, whose primary job was to block linebackers and create openings for the running back. It's a physically demanding role that often goes unnoticed by spectators and media. However, Brady observed how quarterback Brian Griese, who was then starting ahead of Brady, publicly acknowledged Floyd's contribution.

"Brian Griese made a point to tell people: 'There's nobody I'd rather have in the backfield with me than Chris Floyd.' The recognition meant everything to Chris. After hearing that, he walked around like he was ten feet tall."[7]

This experience made a lasting impression on Brady, shaping his approach to team leadership throughout his career. "I began making a habit of giving credit to players in those underappreciated roles," he says, "not just because they deserved it but also to point out to others that no player should go unnoticed."

Brady saw in real time what it meant to appreciate and recognize everyone's role, especially those in often underappreciated positions. In his world, roles have names like fullback, guard, and tackle. In ours, we're looking for Directors, Stabilizers, Achievers, Trailblazers, and Harmonizers. But whether you're more inspired by the story of a legendary quarterback or the science of reciprocal expertise affirmation, the lesson is the same: Teams need to do more than just combine their efforts. They need to acknowledge and appreciate each other's talents.

Recognition and appreciation are where the magic starts to happen. When each member's knowledge is not only pooled but also fully recognized and appreciated, the team can achieve results that far exceed what any individual could do alone. It's like creating a knowledge network within the team that's stronger and more effective than any one person's contribution.

THE IDEAL MIX OF ROLES

At this point, everyone is learning to appreciate each other's talents, and you've assessed the roles on your team. But I've purposefully left unanswered a critical question: What's the ideal mix of roles on a team?

To answer that all-important question, we asked thousands of executives and managers to measure their "best" and "worst" teams. And we uncovered some fascinating patterns.

First off, let's talk about balance. We found that the best teams had a much more even distribution of roles than the worst teams. Specifically, a whopping 97 percent of the best teams had all five roles filled. On the flip side, only about 21 percent of the worst teams filled every role.

It's hard to imagine a team where you don't need someone who takes the lead on making decisions, somebody who produces work and achieves results, another who keeps the group on track and on schedule, yet another who keeps the relationships healthy, and someone who challenges the group with ideas outside the norm.

There's a reason why great teams have someone in every role: It's tough to be successful without each of those talents being represented. You've probably experienced teams with a bunch of Directors, all competing with each other to be the decision-makers, and no Achievers to actually do the work. You might have experienced the opposite: a team with no Directors and a striking inability to make any decisions. Maybe you've seen a group without a Trailblazer, a team where creative ideas go to die. And the list goes on.

Of course, not every team is going to contain exactly five members, so where can you have more people and still be wildly successful? The short version is that the best teams in our research were able to easily handle more Harmonizers and Achievers, and too many Trailblazers was rarely a problem. And here's more detail about the distribution of people for all five roles:

Harmonizers

Having more than a few Harmonizers, a role that focuses on fostering collaboration and resolving conflicts, can help a team with improved communication and teamwork, reducing internal conflicts and enhancing cooperation. As long as all of the other roles are covered, having too many Harmonizers isn't typically a problem. Without coverage of the other roles, however, having a group that prizes interpersonal harmony over achieving results, hitting deadlines, etc., could quickly become a recipe for what former Xerox CEO Ursula Burns called "terminal niceness." You might experience a lack of healthy debate, potentially leading to groupthink or a failure to consider diverse perspectives. While cohesion is important, too much emphasis on harmony could hinder the team's ability to innovate or tackle challenging problems effectively.

Achievers

When it comes to an abundance of Achievers, again assuming that all the other roles are covered, having a bunch of people who want to do great work without needing to be in charge seems like a dream. More people identify as Achievers than any other role, so it's likely your team will have more than a few. If you've got a team of Achievers and nothing else, you'll likely excel in executing tasks but lack in other areas like decision-making, innovation, or interpersonal dynamics. There's also a risk of competition rather than collaboration, as multiple Achievers vie to demonstrate their individual productivity, potentially at the cost of overall team cohesion and effectiveness. But when balanced with the other roles, loading up on Achievers won't typically be much of a problem.

Trailblazers

It's not hard to imagine the problems that would occur with a team re-plete with Trailblazers and no one else: brilliant, out-of-the-box ideas and absolutely no execution. Such a team might struggle with follow-through, jumping from one innovative concept to another without fully developing or implementing any of them. And an excess of Trailblazers might create an environment that's too chaotic or unpredictable, lacking the stability needed for consistent performance. In reality, however, there just aren't that many Trailblazers walking the halls of the typical organization, so you're more likely to struggle finding one than you are to grapple with an overabundance.

Stabilizers

That brings us to Stabilizers, a role that appears frequently in most orga-nizations, so you do face some risk of overload. The risk you face concerns, well, risk—specifically the avoidance of it. A team with too many Stabi-lizers might become overly rigid, focusing excessively on processes and procedures at the expense of innovation and quick responses to changing circumstances. This could lead to a team that's highly organized but slow to adapt, potentially missing opportunities or failing to address evolving challenges in dynamic environments. Many innovations require some risk-taking and deviating from existing protocols, not something that Stabilizers love, so you'll need a Trailblazer to offer some counterweight to the Stabilizer's natural risk aversion.

Directors

This is another role that appears often in organizations. Too many Directors can result in power struggles, conflicting decision-making processes, and a lack of unified direction. This can create an environment where there are "too many cooks in the kitchen," leading to constant debates over strategy and leadership, potentially paralyzing the team's ability to move forward effectively. The absence of followers in a Director-heavy team can also mean that decisions, once made, may lack the necessary support for successful implementation.

The takeaway here is clear: diversity in roles is key to providing the right balance. You need a mix of skills and perspectives to really make your team shine. All things being equal, on a team of eight people, you might want one Director, one Stabilizer, one Trailblazer, two Harmonizers, and three Achievers. Of course, all things are rarely equal, so if your Director and Stabilizer are a bit meeker, you can have two of each and be fine. The same goes for your Trailblazer.

Ultimately, it's less about the number of people in each role and more about ensuring that the talents and voices of the Director, Stabilizer, Achiever, Trailblazer, and Harmonizer are well represented.

ASKING PEOPLE TO SWITCH ROLES

You will inevitably encounter a team that is out of balance, and when that happens, you've got two options. First, you can recruit some new members to join your team. This isn't always possible, and when it is, it requires a bit more discussion, so I'll cover this in Chapter 12.

Your other option, and the one that's more common inside companies, is to encourage a bit of role switching. Remember in the "Assessing the Roles on Your Team" exercise (page 97) when you asked people to indicate any secondary roles they would like to fulfill or develop? This is where those details on your Team Role Map come into play.

If someone has a strong desire to play a different role on the team, it can be a terrific chance for them to grow. The classic case is someone with leadership aspirations taking on more of a Director role on the team, especially if they want to improve their decision-making. Alternatively, you might have someone who knows they need to develop some Stabilizer talents, or at least a better appreciation of the Stabilizer's organizational capabilities. Or the textbook example where someone a bit rough around the edges knows they need better Harmonizer skills if they want to expand their career options.

While some roles align closely, enabling a relatively seamless transition, others may require significant adjustments in approach and mindset. Fortunately, we have data on tens of thousands of team members that can serve as a guide.

Director → Stabilizer

Directors are generally most comfortable switching to the Stabilizer role, which isn't too surprising given the compatibility between leading and organizing; both require a big-picture mindset and strategic thinking. Conversely, transitioning to the Harmonizer role can be challenging for Directors, as it requires a shift from decision-making to diplomacy, which may not always align with a Director's more directive style.

Harmonizer → Director

Harmonizers typically find it easiest to step into the Director role; while the contexts are different, both roles involve a high level of interaction with team members. Harmonizers' ability to understand and manage group dynamics positions them well for leadership. The hardest role for

Harmonizers to assume is often the Achiever role. The solitary focus on task completion can conflict with their preference for collaboration and consensus-building.

Stabilizer → Achiever

Stabilizers tend to find switching to the Achiever role most natural, as there's an overlap in the systematic, methodical approach both roles bring to their work. They can find it more challenging to adopt the Director role, where there's a need for a more dynamic and less structured approach than what Stabilizers are accustomed to.

Trailblazer → Director

Trailblazers show a strong tendency to switch to the Director role, given the innovative and forward-thinking qualities required in both roles. However, they characteristically find it most difficult to switch to the Stabilizer role, as the structured and often routine nature of a Stabilizer can feel stifling, given their drive for creativity and new ideas.

Achiever → Trailblazer

Achievers often find it easiest to switch to the Trailblazer role. It's not hard to picture that change, especially when you think back to folks like Steve Wozniak and John Pierce; they were Achievers who also happened to create truly groundbreaking technologies (Apple computers and communication satellites). And the hardest switch for Achievers is often moving into the Director role; there's a fundamental difference in the leadership demands between the two roles. Just remember Steve Wozniak's comment, "I couldn't be a manager ever in my life."

Notwithstanding all the data, not only are there exceptions, but the ambitions and desires of your team should take priority.

If you've got a Stabilizer who's eager to develop their Trailblazer talents or a Director keen on learning how to be a Harmonizer, you'll want to at least consider their requests. If your team needs more Trailblazers and

Harmonizers, it could be worth a shot, assuming these are folks who've evidenced a willingness to learn and step outside their comfort zone.

It may take some coaching to develop those talents, but there's a good chance it will pay off in the long run. And the leader of a team will always face a balance between solving today's challenges and setting up the team to solve tomorrow's.

BUILDING TEAMS FOR NOW AND THE FUTURE

At the heart of the 2024 Paris Olympics, Coach Steve Kerr of the US men's basketball team encountered a challenge most leaders think they would relish. "We have an embarrassment of riches on this roster, that's the best way to put it," Kerr remarked. "I mean, these guys are all champions, All-Stars, Hall of Famers. However, you want to put it."[8]

An embarrassment of talent on a team might not seem like much of a challenge, but in basketball, there's only one ball. You can only put five players on the court. Each member of the team has wildly different strengths and weaknesses. And every opponent presents a drastically different challenge.

Kerr's first job, then, was to rotate the lineups, game by game, to field the mix of players best suited to beat each unique opponent, even when that meant putting future Hall of Famers on the bench.

This ethos was put to the test in Team USA's opening matches. Against Serbia, a powerhouse in its own right, Kerr opted for a robust front line to counter six-foot-eleven, 284-pound two-time NBA MVP Nikola Jokić. This meant making all of his centers available and relegating superstar and reigning NBA champion Jayson Tatum to the bench.

The next game, against the lightning-fast South Sudan team, recent NBA MVP and seven-foot, 280-pound center Joel Embiid was on the bench. "The whole game today was going to be about switching and staying in front of people," Kerr said. "That's why Joel wasn't in the lineup. We just wanted to make sure we matched up with the smaller, quicker team and all their three-point shooting."

Team USA beat Serbia by twenty-six points and South Sudan by seventeen on their way to a gold medal, lending credence to Kerr's approach. And the all-time greats on the team also understood that winning requires finding the right mix of roles and players.

Kevin Durant, playing in his fourth Olympic games and the all-time leading scorer for Team USA men's basketball, put it simply: "With the amount of talent, IQ and skill in the States, we can mix and match like that. Last game, we had a champion and an All-NBA guy not play any minutes, and tonight, we had an MVP not play any minutes. They didn't complain. We had guys who stepped up and filled those roles perfectly."[9]

But here's where the problems started to emerge. Kerr solved the present challenge, winning gold in 2024, but some argued he might not have positioned the team perfectly for the 2028 Olympics.

The stars of the 2024 Olympics, Steph Curry, Lebron James, and Kevin Durant, have expressed doubts about playing in 2028, so it will likely fall on the next generation to secure gold. Jayson Tatum, who you'll recall spent some time on the bench, should be part of that crew.

Tatum entered these games riding high on an NBA Championship and signing the biggest contract in NBA history. The social pressure to see him play was intense. When he was on the bench, much of the subsequent media coverage boiled down to incredulous rants of, "How do you bench one of the best players in the world?" Tatum's father took to social media: "As a coach, I would have no reservations of playing him. As a coach I would find a way to play him. Why hasn't he played? I don't see it." Even NBA legend Charles Barkley chimed in, "There's no reason for him not to play Jayson Tatum....Come on man, that wasn't right, that wasn't fair. If you're going to the Olympics you want to play, you want to play."[10]

Given how Jayson Tatum entered the 2024 games, the outrage was predictable. The problem isn't the outrage itself; it's how those hurt feelings affect Tatum. He's human; he's going to hear the noise from the media, the frustrations from his father, the disappointment from Boston Celtics fans.

After winning gold in Paris, Tatum was asked whether he would play in 2028. "It was a tough personal experience on the court, but I'm not going to make any decisions off emotions," he said. "If you asked me right now if I'm going to play in 2028, it's four years from now. I'd have to take time and think about that. So I'm not going to make any decision based on how this experience was, or how I feel individually."[11]

He's smart and classy, so he offered the company line: "We won a gold medal, and that was most important." But if USA Basketball is counting on Tatum to be a leader in 2028, this isn't quite the level of excitement you'd hope to see.

Balancing present needs and future considerations is complicated and, contrary to what hot media takes would suggest, there aren't easy answers. We'll never know if the team would still have won a gold medal in 2024 if the less experienced players got more time on the court. But there is a universal lesson here: Building adaptability within your team today increases the likelihood of success in the future.

Maybe the challenge your team faces today is so intense that there's just no room for experimentation and development; you'll need superhuman performances from your most experienced players just to scrape by. But perhaps tomorrow's challenge is a bit less daunting; there might be an opportunity for the players further down the depth chart to get some time in the game. The best teams actively look for chances to grow and develop, encouraging people to grow their skills and even try out some new roles. It might not happen every day or on every project, but if you look hard enough, you'll undoubtedly find opportunities to balance the needs of today with the aspirations of tomorrow.

BE TRANSPARENT WITH ROLE SWITCHES

When you've identified a need for role switching on your team, transparency is key. You don't want to play coy with this; instead, respect their intelligence and commitment to the team.

Start by clearly explaining the team's current composition and why you're asking them to take on this role. You can use your Team Role Map as a visual aid to illustrate the imbalance or gap you're trying to address. This will help you frame the request as a strategic move for the benefit of the entire team.

For example, you might say: "As you can see from our Team Role Map, we have an abundance of Achievers but we're lacking in the Harmonizer role. Given your strong interpersonal skills and your expressed interest in developing in this area, I think you'd be an excellent fit for this role."

Acknowledge the value of their current contributions while also explaining why their talents could be even more impactful in a new role. You'll also want to highlight how developing the skills needed for this new role could benefit them.

Finally, don't diminish the challenges they might face in the new role. If you're asking an Achiever to step into a Director role, for instance, be honest about the leadership demands and decision-making pressures they'll encounter. At the same time, express your confidence in their ability to grow into the role and offer support for their development.

Sometimes, even seemingly small switches can feel significant. Changing something as simple as the way we walk through a doorway can be unexpectedly difficult, thanks to our ingrained habits. Studies show that most people have a natural directional bias; around 70 to 80 percent of us tend to favor the right side when we navigate narrow spaces.[12] It's the reason so many of us instinctively veer right in store aisles or on crowded sidewalks.

Try veering left the next time you go to someplace with crowds, like an amusement park or a concert. There's a tangible benefit; with most people veering to the right, you'll typically find thinner crowds by turning left. And yet, even with the prospect of shorter lines, most of us find it tricky and necessitating a fair bit of conscious effort.

Some people will find playing a different role as difficult as veering to the left or using their nondominant hand; those folks will require more coaching and support. But others will see taking on a different role as an opportunity to express a side of themselves that has heretofore been suppressed or unrecognized.

ROLES AS MASKS

I'm sure you've seen ancient Greek theater masks—those exaggerated face coverings with dramatic expressions, big eye holes, and open mouths that look like they're frozen mid-shout or mid-cry.

In ancient Greek theater, masks weren't just decorative props; they were actually sophisticated tools that transformed the actor's voice and relationship with the audience. And as you'll see, the roles we play in teams are like those ancient masks, amplifying certain aspects of our talents and abilities while allowing us to reach different parts of our "audience" (our teammates and stakeholders).

Greek theater masks covered the entire head, fitting closely with small openings for the eyes and mouth. Typically made from linen or light woods, these masks were acoustic devices that altered the actor's voice and its projection across vast, open-air amphitheaters.

Recent acoustic studies have revealed some fascinating properties about these masks. For instance, the masks tended to amplify the actor's voice for angles greater than 90 degrees from the front. In other words, they boosted the sound projecting from the sides and back of the actor's head. When you consider the semicircular layout of Greek amphitheaters, this ensured that audience members seated at the far sides of the theater could hear just as well as those in the center.[13]

When we step into a role like Director, Harmonizer, or Trailblazer, we're essentially donning a mask that amplifies certain aspects of our abilities and personality. Just as the Greek masks helped actors project their voices to different parts of the amphitheater, our roles allow us to "project" different aspects of ourselves.

When an Achiever steps into a Director role, they're putting on a mask that amplifies their decision-making and leadership qualities. This mask helps them project these aspects of themselves more strongly, reaching team members who respond well to decisive leadership or those who didn't know this "doer" could also be a "decider." Similarly, when a Trailblazer takes on a Stabilizer role, they're donning a mask that amplifies their ability to create structure and maintain consistency, projecting these qualities to team members who thrive on predictability and clear processes.

The Greek masks also altered the actor's tonal qualities. The masks imposed what acousticians call a "comb filtering effect," which changed the timbre of the actor's voice. In essence, the mask gave each character a distinctive vocal signature.

Similarly, our team roles don't just amplify certain traits; they can fundamentally alter how we're perceived and how we communicate. A typically quiet, introverted team member might find that the Harmonizer role gives their voice a new timbre, allowing them to mediate conflicts and build relationships in ways they never thought possible. A usually brash, outspoken individual might discover that the Stabilizer role modulates their communication style, helping them deliver clear, calm instructions that resonate with the whole team.

The Greek masks also amplified the actor's voice in their own ears—measurements show an amplification of up to 18 decibels, particularly in the higher frequencies. This self-perception effect forced actors to adapt their vocal technique, leading to a heightened awareness of their own performance.

When we take on a new role in a team, we often become hyperaware of our own behavior and communication. This self-awareness might be uncomfortable at first; like the Greek actors, we might feel that our own voice is too loud in our ears. But that discomfort often precedes growth and adaptation. It pushes us to refine our approach, to modulate our performance until we find the right pitch for our new role.

And just as Greek actors would switch masks to play different characters, we too can switch between roles as the needs of our team evolve. This flexibility allows us to reach different audiences within our organization, amplifying different aspects of our skills and personality as needed.

Just remember that, like the Greek masks, roles aren't meant to completely obscure who we are. The Greek word for "mask," *prosopon*, was the same word used for "face." The mask wasn't seen as concealing the true face, but as another face of the same actor. Similarly, our team roles shouldn't be fake personas we adopt but authentic expressions of different parts of ourselves.

Just like those ancient masks transformed both the audience's and the actor's perception, our roles can be transformative tools for self-discovery and development. The next time you ask someone to adopt a new role, remember the Greek theater masks. Encourage your teammates to allow the role to amplify aspects of themselves they might not usually express. Let that role help them reach parts of the audience with whom they might not otherwise have connected.

I spent a few months working with a startup CEO who'd built his company from nothing into a two-hundred-person operation. He was a classic Achiever—the kind of leader who would rather roll up his sleeves and code alongside his engineers than make the big strategic calls. "I just want to build great products," he'd tell me. "All this decision-making stuff just doesn't feel like me."

The breaking point came during a critical pivot in their business model. Their biggest competitor had just slashed prices, and the executive team was gridlocked. The sales team wanted to match the price cut. The product team proposed doubling down on premium features. The CFO was pushing to acquire a smaller competitor. The CEO's response? He created a complex spreadsheet modeling all scenarios and kept tweaking the variables, searching for the perfect answer.

Three weeks passed. The company bled customers while the CEO refined his models. Finally, his CTO cornered him after a particularly circular executive meeting. "You know what's worse than making the wrong choice?" she asked. "Not making one at all."

That night, I got a call from the CEO. "I feel like I'm supposed to become a different person," he admitted. "Everyone's waiting for me to be this commanding, decisive CEO, but that's not who I am. I solve problems by diving deep, by understanding every angle."

"Tell me about how often you make tough decisions while coding," I asked. He sounded surprised. "Well, constantly. Architecture choices, tradeoffs between performance and maintainability, when to scrap a feature and start over—those decisions can make or break the product."

"And how do you make those decisions?"

"I analyze the options, understand the tradeoffs, then..." He stopped, realization dawning. "Then I make a clear decision and move forward, because the team needs direction to build the right thing."

"You're not pretending to be someone else," I suggested. "You're just bringing those same decisive instincts from engineering to the boardroom. The Achiever in you doesn't have to disappear when you step into the Director role. It's just that when the team wants you to don the Director mask, they're asking you to emphasize your final decision and spend less time in meetings discussing every nitty-gritty detail behind it."

The next morning, he found his voice as a Director, but in his own way. Instead of trying to mimic some stereotypical CEO, he drew on his analytical strength. He walked into his executive meeting and said, "I've examined every scenario, and here's where we land: We're going to focus on premium features. Sales, I need a plan to retain our top fifty customers. Product, you have two weeks to demonstrate our value proposition. If anyone sees a critical flaw in this analysis, please speak now."

Was it the perfect decision? Perhaps not. But it was a decision that came from an authentic place—his natural drive to deeply understand problems. Months later, when the dust had settled, he told me, "I always thought being decisive meant becoming someone else entirely. But I've learned that good leadership isn't about putting on a fake persona—it's about learning to express different facets of who you already are."

The company ultimately retained around 80 percent of their key accounts and launched several features their competitor couldn't match. But the real transformation was in the CEO. He discovered that stepping into the Director role didn't mean abandoning his Achiever tendencies—it meant channeling them in a new way. He was still the same analytical, thorough leader; he'd just learned to use those traits to drive decisions rather than delay them.

EVERY ROLE MATTERS

If you take away nothing else from this chapter, take this: Your team isn't a collection of interchangeable parts; it's a delicate ecosystem where every role matters. Like a quarterback who knows his success hinges on his offensive line or a lead singer who understands the bassist keeps everyone in rhythm, you need to recognize and value the unique contributions of each team member.

Don't fall into the trap of chasing solo superstars or trying to build a team of clones. Instead, strive for a balance of Directors, Stabilizers, Achievers, Trailblazers, and Harmonizers. And remember, the magic isn't just in having these roles; it's in everyone appreciating what each role brings to the table. When your Trailblazer's out-of-the-box thinking is as valued as your Stabilizer's meticulous planning, when your Harmonizer's people skills are as celebrated as your Achiever's task completion, that's when you've got a team that's firing on all cylinders.

In the world of scientific research, we often celebrate the lone genius or the superstar scientist who churns out groundbreaking papers. But a study by Alexander Oettl from Georgia Tech suggests we might be overlooking the unsung heroes of scientific progress.[14]

Oettl analyzed the acknowledgments in immunology papers since 1950, focusing not just on how productive scientists are, but also on how helpful they are to their colleagues.

To measure helpfulness, Oettl counted how often a scientist was mentioned in the acknowledgments of other researchers' papers. These acknowledgments often thank colleagues for providing advice, feedback, or assistance (in other words, for being helpful).

Using this data, scientists were classified into four categories. All-stars are both highly productive and very helpful, representing the ideal combination of individual achievement and team support. Lone wolves are highly productive but not particularly helpful, embodying the traditional notion of the isolated genius. Mavens, on the other hand, may not be as productive individually, but they're very helpful to others, while Non-stars are average in both productivity and helpfulness (and this is where most of the scientific workforce falls).

Here's where it gets interesting. Oettl looked at what happened to the productivity of a scientist's collaborators after the scientist died unexpectedly. It's a bit morbid, but it provides a natural experiment to see how much impact these different types of scientists had on their peers.

The results were eye-opening, though perhaps not shocking. When an "all-star" or a "maven" died, their collaborators' research quality dropped significantly, by 20 percent or more. But when a "lone wolf" died? There was no noticeable impact on their collaborators' work.

Here's a simple way to think about it: Imagine that Pat is a super helpful scientist; lots of authors thank them in the acknowledgements section of their papers. If someone asks for their help, Pat reads their paper, gives constructive feedback, makes recommendations, and even offers new ideas. If Pat dies unexpectedly, all those authors who relied on their help will suffer. Not only will they mourn Pat's passing, but the quality of their papers will decline. They might not get published in the top-tier journals, or their articles won't be cited as frequently.

In the nonacademic world, all of the roles on a team can be helpers. In fact, one of the reasons the star stock analysts from the beginning of the chapter saw such noticeable declines in their performance was that they quit the firm employing all of their Director, Achiever, Stabilizer, Trail-blazer, and Harmonizer helpers.

The paradox of teams lies in a surprising truth: While conventional wisdom emphasizes creating team cohesiveness, the most critical factor in a team's success is actually the diversity of individuals with complementary talents and skills to fill the necessary team roles. And while some of those roles will be visible to casual observers, others require more discernment to recognize and appreciate.

We often think that the key to a great team is getting everyone on the same page, fostering a sense of unity and shared vision. And while these elements are undoubtedly important, they're not the whole story. The real magic happens when you curate, recognize, and appreciate a diverse group of individuals, each harnessing their unique strengths and helping each other succeed.

Each of the roles—Director, Stabilizer, Achiever, Trailblazer, and Harmonizer—brings a distinct perspective and set of skills to the team. When team members not only recognize but genuinely value each other's unique contributions, they can leverage their distinctiveness to achieve extraordinary results.

Your team's success doesn't just come from everyone getting along or sharing the same mindset. It comes from bringing together the right mix of talents and roles and fostering an environment where these diverse contributions are recognized, valued, and leveraged to their fullest potential.

CHAPTER REFLECTION GUIDE

- Reflect on a team where certain roles were overrepresented or missing entirely. How did this imbalance impact the team's ability to achieve its goals? What could have been done differently?
- How do you think your teammates would describe the role you currently play on your team? Is this role aligned with your own perception, and does it match where you feel you can contribute most effectively?
- Has there been a time when you, or someone else on your team, stepped into a new role to address a team gap? What challenges or growth opportunities arose from this experience?
- Based on the chapter's insights, how would you describe the ideal role composition for your current team? Are there specific steps you can take to fill any gaps or adjust imbalances?

Visit **www.leadershipiq.com/teamplayers** to find more resources, such as exercises, assessments, and additional tools.

CHAPTER 8

LEARNING TO THINK LIKE ALL FIVE ROLES

I DEALLY, YOU'LL GET YOUR TEAM APPROPRIATELY BALANCED WITH an effective mix of Directors, Stabilizers, Achievers, Trailblazers, and Harmonizers, and each role will be filled by someone naturally inclined to that style of thinking and working.

In an imperfect world, however, you might find that it takes an extra step to curate the ideal team. You might find that your team is missing key roles and the folks on your team just aren't ready to try on new roles. Or you might have a team so set in its ways that introducing new roles seems like an utterly insurmountable challenge.

This does not, however, mean that your team is doomed to underperform. There's another approach that helps teams thrive, even when they can't achieve the perfect role balance: teaching everyone on the team to think like each of the five roles.

This is an approach that I regularly use as an introductory teambuilding exercise. It trains every team member to understand and adopt the mindset of each role, regardless of their natural inclinations.

Picture a team where everyone can step into the shoes of a Director when tough decisions need making, channel their inner Stabilizer when processes need refining, tap into their Achiever mindset to get things done, unleash their Trailblazer spirit for innovation, and embody the Harmonizer to keep the team cohesive. This is the kind of mental flexibility that teams need when they can't switch roles or add new members.

Do you remember what I wrote in the previous chapter about ancient Greek theater masks? When we adopt different roles, we're effectively donning a mask. I might not naturally be a Harmonizer or Stabilizer, but I can put on a Harmonizer or Stabilizer mask. I can learn to embrace and embody that role, even if it's just for a brief period.

This exercise will give each member of your team the ability to see situations from multiple perspectives and adapt their approach as needed. It's also going to increase empathy and understanding within your team. When your natural Achiever learns to appreciate the Harmonizer's perspective, or when your Trailblazer understands the Stabilizer's concerns, you'll see smoother collaboration and more effective problem-solving.

Finally, this approach is a powerful tool for individual growth. The people on your team may discover latent talents they didn't know they had, or develop new skills that enhance their career prospects. A Stabilizer who learns to think like a Trailblazer might find they have a knack for innovation they never knew existed. An Achiever who practices the Director's mindset might uncover leadership potential.

THINKING WITH THE FIVE ROLES

When I'm conducting this exercise with an executive team, board of directors, project team, or basically any group facing a challenge or decision, the role-thinking exercise is conducted as a full-team activity, with everyone adopting each role's perspective in turn.

ROLE-THINKING EXERCISE

1. Start by choosing a decision or challenge the group is facing.
2. Introduce the concept of the five roles: Director, Stabilizer, Achiever, Trailblazer, and Harmonizer. Start with one role—for example, the

Director. Provide a brief overview of the Director's typical mindset and priorities (or better yet, take a few minutes and have everyone read the Director chapter).

3. Ask the entire team to adopt the Director perspective and discuss the issue from that viewpoint. Depending on the issue and the stakes involved, this could take five minutes or twenty. Challenge everyone to fully embrace and embody that role's thinking style, regardless of their natural predilections.

4. After the discussion, take a few minutes to summarize key points and insights from the Director perspective.

5. Next, move on to the Stabilizer role and repeat the exercise. Then the Harmonizer, and so on.

6. After all five roles have been explored, you'll want to lead a final discussion where your team members can speak from any perspective they choose. This allows them to apply the insights gained from each role to develop a comprehensive solution or decision.

NOTE: If your team is really entrenched in its thinking, and you're hesitating to push them too hard, start with the role with which everyone is most comfortable. If you want to provide more of a "jump in the deep end" feel, start with the role least represented on your team.

Having a variable rotation ensures that each role gets a chance to be considered first, when the team's energy and creativity is often at its peak, and last, when the team has the benefit of insights from all other perspectives.

You might also find that changing the order reveals new insights, as each role's perspective often builds on different preceding viewpoints. Or you can experiment with completely randomizing the order or letting team members vote on which role to consider next.

The point of the exercise is to force everyone on the team to see through the eyes of each of the five roles. This skill is called perspective taking, and it's often thought to be the cognitive dimension of empathy.

It's the cognitive ability to consider the world from viewpoints other than your own. Atticus Finch, the moral guide in Harper Lee's *To Kill a Mockingbird*, describes it thusly: "You never really understand a person until you consider things from his point of view…until you climb into his skin and walk around in it." Legendary psychologist Carl Rogers said perspective taking is the ability to "perceive the internal frame of reference of another with accuracy, and with the emotional components and meanings which pertain thereto, as if one were the person, but without ever losing the 'as if' condition."[1]

What you're after here is getting every team member to think from each role perspective. And as you progress through the five roles, you'll notice team members becoming more adept at switching perspectives and seeing issues from different angles. This exercise leads to increased empathy, more creative problem-solving, and a deeper understanding of how the different roles contribute to the team's success. It will also identify potential blind spots in the team's approach and lead to far more balanced thinking about the issue at hand.

Occasionally, I'll work with a team that is "almost" balanced; they've got all the roles well covered except for one. In those cases, the team will proceed through their discussions and decision-making as normal, involving all the roles they've got in the room. Once that's done, they'll collectively put on the metaphorical mask of the missing role. The group will embrace and embody that missing role, surfacing the sorts of issues that would otherwise have been missed.

SCENARIOS TO GET YOU STARTED

Sometimes a team will need a little help with fully taking the perspective of the five roles, and that's where this section comes into play.

We'll look at three different situations that could conceivably confront a team. I'll share what each role might be thinking about each scenario and the types of questions each role might ask during a frothy debate. These aren't exhaustive descriptions or lists of questions. This is just to help you get started because you want to give your team just enough help to get the ball rolling but not so much that it prevents them from engaging their brains and internalizing the ideas.

You don't have to give all three scenarios to your team; you can start with the one that most closely resembles whatever your team is facing. Once or twice through this and you'll typically find that your team gets more imaginative and creative as they don the five metaphorical masks.

Scenario #1: Working Remotely

Imagine that a company has a large percentage of employees working remotely. Your team has to decide whether to continue this remote working, force a return to the office, develop a hybrid model, or something else entirely. Each of the five roles will consider widely different aspects of this decision, and they'll ask very different questions.

Seeing Through the Eyes of Achievers

Achievers will typically focus on maintaining and improving productivity and quality of work across different work models. They're considering how to measure and benchmark performance in remote, in-office, and hybrid settings. The Achiever will be concerned with identifying and implementing the right tools and technologies to facilitate effective collaboration and workflow, whatever model is chosen. They're also thinking about how to ensure fair performance evaluations and provide equal opportunities for career growth, regardless of an employee's work location. They'll want to optimize project management processes in potentially distributed teams. Achievers will also consider how to provide necessary training to help employees excel in new work environments.

Achievers could pose questions like:

1. What metrics should we use to compare productivity and job satisfaction across different work models?
2. How can we ensure consistent performance evaluation and career growth opportunities in different work models?
3. How has our team's productivity and output quality been affected by remote work?

4. What tools or technologies could we implement to improve remote collaboration and efficiency?

5. What skills or training do our employees need to excel in a remote or hybrid work environment?

6. How can we measure and improve work-life balance across different work models?

7. What benchmarks should we set to evaluate the success of our chosen work model?

8. How can we optimize our project management processes for the work model we choose?

9. What innovative ways can we use to foster creativity and innovation in a remote or hybrid setting?

10. How can we ensure that our chosen work model allows us to attract and retain top talent?

Seeing Through the Eyes of Directors

The Director is likely evaluating the work model decision from a strategic and financial perspective. They're considering how each option aligns with the company's long-term goals and vision. They're weighing the financial implications of different models, including real estate costs, technology investments, and potential productivity impacts. They're also thinking about how the decision might affect the company's competitiveness in the job market and its ability to scale or enter new markets. The Director might also be concerned with legal and compliance issues, especially for distributed workforces. They're contemplating how different work models might impact company culture, brand image, and relationships with clients and stakeholders. Of course, the Director is also considering potential risks and opportunities associated with each model and thinking about contingency plans if the chosen approach doesn't work as expected. And as you might expect, they're considering how, and by whom, the final decision is going to be made.

When the remote working issue is discussed, Directors might ask questions like:

1. How quickly do we need to implement our chosen work model, and what are the steps for a phased rollout?
2. Who are the key decision-makers for each aspect of our work model (HR, IT, Operations, etc.), and how do we align their input?
3. How does our work model decision align with our long-term strategic goals and company vision?
4. What are the financial implications of each work model in terms of real estate costs, technology investments, and potential productivity changes?
5. How will our decision impact our ability to compete for talent in the job market?
6. What legal and compliance issues do we need to consider for each work model, especially for employees in different states or countries?
7. How might our decision affect our company culture and brand image?
8. What are the potential risks and opportunities associated with each work model?
9. What are the implications for our leadership and management strategies under different work models?
10. What contingency plans should we have in place if our chosen model doesn't work as expected?

Seeing Through the Eyes of Harmonizers

The Harmonizer is likely to be concerned with maintaining team cohesion, employee engagement, and a positive company culture across different work arrangements. They'll want to ensure that employees have a voice and that all employees feel equally valued and included, regardless of their work location. They'll be thinking about strategies to prevent isolation, support mental health, and create opportunities for spontaneous interaction in remote or hybrid settings. They'll also want to surface the diverse needs and concerns of different employee groups, ensuring fair and equitable treatment across various work arrangements. The Harmonizer is also contemplating effective team-building activities and communication practices for different work models. They're thinking about how to support managers in leading potentially distributed teams and how to address the conflicts or resentments that might arise between employees with different work arrangements (e.g., remote vs. in-office).

Expect your Harmonizers to ask questions like:

1. How can we ensure that all employees feel equally valued and included, regardless of their work location?

2. What concerns have different groups of employees (e.g., parents, young professionals, long-time employees) expressed about each work model?

3. How can we maintain team cohesion and social connections in a remote or hybrid work environment?

4. What strategies can we use to prevent isolation and support mental health in a remote work setting?

5. How can we ensure fair and equitable treatment of employees across different work arrangements?

6. What team-building activities would be effective in our chosen work model?

7. How can we create opportunities for spontaneous interaction and collaboration in a remote or hybrid setting?

8. What communication channels and practices should we adopt to keep everyone informed and connected?

9. How can we address potential conflicts or resentments between employees with different work arrangements?

10. How can we support managers in leading teams effectively in our chosen work model?

Seeing Through the Eyes of Stabilizers

The Stabilizer is focused on maintaining operational consistency, security, and efficiency across different work settings. They're considering how to ensure uniform application of company policies and procedures, regardless of where employees are working. The Stabilizer is thinking about necessary changes to IT infrastructure and security measures to protect company data in remote or hybrid environments. They'll want processes for monitoring and maintaining productivity, as well as onboarding new employees in different work models. Your Stabilizers will be concerned with adapting performance review processes and establishing clear guidelines for each work arrangement. They're likely also thinking about how to handle equipment and technology needs for employees in various settings and developing contingency plans for potential disruptions (like power outages or internet issues for remote employees).

Expect Stabilizers to ask:

1. How can we ensure consistent application of company policies and procedures across different work settings?
2. What security measures do we need to implement to protect company data in a remote or hybrid work environment?
3. How will our IT infrastructure need to change to support our chosen work model?
4. What processes should we put in place to monitor and maintain productivity in different work settings?
5. How can we ensure smooth onboarding and integration of new employees in our chosen work model?
6. What changes to our performance review and feedback processes might be necessary?

7. How can we maintain a consistent company culture across different work arrangements?

8. What guidelines or policies do we need to establish for each work model (e.g., core hours, meeting protocols)?

9. How will we handle equipment and technology needs for employees in different work settings?

10. What contingency plans should we have in place for potential disruptions (e.g., power outages, internet issues) in a remote or hybrid model?

Seeing Through the Eyes of Trailblazers

Expect Trailblazers to see the work model decision as an opportunity for innovation and reimagining how the company operates. They're apt to think about how to create a cutting-edge work environment that could give the company a unique competitive advantage. The Trailblazer could even be thinking about radical changes to the organization's structure that could better support a distributed workforce, or how to leverage a global talent pool in unprecedented ways. They might be thinking about unconventional benefits or perks that could make the company's work model more attractive. The Trailblazer might also consider how the work model could drive innovation and creativity in unexpected ways. And don't be surprised if they're excited about the possibility of not just adapting to future workplace trends but setting them.

Questions that Trailblazers might ask include:

1. How can we use this opportunity to completely reimagine the way we work and collaborate?

2. What innovative technologies or practices could we pioneer to create a truly cutting-edge work environment?

3. How might we create a work model that gives us a unique competitive advantage in our industry?

4. What radical changes to our organizational structure could better support a distributed workforce?

5. How can we leverage a diverse, potentially global talent pool in ways our competitors haven't considered?

6. What unconventional benefits or perks could we offer to make our work model more attractive?

7. How might we use our work model to drive innovation and creativity in unexpected ways?

8. What bold experiments in work arrangements could we try that no one else is doing?

9. How can we use our work model to positively impact broader societal issues (e.g., urban congestion, climate change)?

10. How might we create a work environment that not only adapts to future trends but sets them?

Scenario #2: New Technology

Your team is divided on whether to invest heavily in developing a new technology product that could redefine the company's market position but also carries high risk and may deviate from the company's core competencies.

Seeing Through the Eyes of Achievers

Expect Achievers to zero in on the technical challenges and quality aspects of developing the new technology product. They'll be pondering how to make the most of existing skills while acquiring new expertise to deliver top-notch results. You'll find them setting ambitious benchmarks and rigorous testing protocols. Don't be surprised if they're also excited about the personal and professional growth opportunities this project could offer them and others on the team. They'll think about how to measure progress and success. And if the team takes on this challenge, Achievers will want to ensure that the team can knock it out of the park and deliver a product that exceeds the company's standards.

Achievers could ask:

1. What specific technical challenges do we anticipate in developing this new product, and how can we overcome them?
2. How can we ensure that this new product meets or exceeds the quality standards of our existing offerings?
3. What skills or expertise do we need to acquire to excel in this new area?
4. How can we measure our progress and success throughout the development process?
5. What benchmarks should we set to ensure we're creating a top-tier product in this new space?
6. How can we optimize our workflow to ensure efficient development without sacrificing quality?
7. What testing protocols should we implement to guarantee the reliability and performance of the new product?
8. How does this project align with our team's strengths, and where might we need to improve?
9. What opportunities for personal and professional growth does this project offer our team members?
10. How can we leverage our existing expertise while pushing the boundaries of our capabilities?

Seeing Through the Eyes of Directors

Directors are likely viewing this scenario through a strategic (and maybe a financial) lens. They're considering how the new technology fits into the company's long-term vision and goals, and how it might shake up the company's market position and competitive edge. Directors will often crunch the numbers on potential returns, comparing this opportunity to others, and assessing both short-term and long-term financial impacts. Resource allocation, risk management, and stakeholder impacts will probably also be on their radar. They're also contemplating exit strategies in case the project doesn't meet expectations, ensuring that the company is prepared for various outcomes.

Directors could ask about:

1. What specific criteria should we use to make the final decision on whether to invest in this new technology?
2. By what date do we need to make this decision, and what are the consequences of delaying?
3. Who should have the final say in this decision, and how do we ensure they have all necessary information?
4. How does this new technology align with our overall strategic vision and goals?
5. What's the projected return on investment, and how does it compare to other potential investments?
6. How will this decision impact our market position and competitive advantage in the long term?
7. What are the financial implications of this investment, both in the short term and long term?
8. How will pursuing this new technology affect our resource allocation across other projects and initiatives?
9. What are the most significant risks associated with this venture, and how do they compare to the potential rewards?
10. What's our exit strategy if the project doesn't meet our expectations or market demands?

Seeing Through the Eyes of Harmonizers

Harmonizers are thinking about the people side of this potential change. They're considering ways to make sure everyone on the team feels heard and valued as decisions are made. The Harmonizer is thinking about how to keep the team united, morale high, and communication flowing throughout the process. And they're likely pondering how to support team members who might need to switch roles or learn new skills if the project gets the green light. Expect them to address emotional and psychological support systems to help navigate this potential change. Among their goals will be keeping the team unified and motivated, no matter what decision is made, and making sure the company culture stays strong through any transitions.

Harmonizers might want to know:

1. How can we ensure that all team members feel their voices are heard and valued in this decision-making process?
2. What concerns have different team members expressed about this new direction, and how can we address them?
3. How might pursuing this new technology affect team dynamics and morale?
4. What strategies can we employ to maintain team cohesion if we decide to move forward with this project?
5. How can we ensure clear and open communication throughout the decision-making process and potential implementation?
6. If we decide to pursue this new direction, how can we support team members who may need to transition to new roles or acquire new skills?
7. How can we celebrate and recognize contributions from all team members, regardless of their stance on this decision?
8. What team-building activities might help us navigate this potential significant change?
9. How can we create an environment where team members feel comfortable expressing concerns or dissenting opinions?
10. What support systems can we put in place to help team members adapt to the changes this new direction might bring?

Seeing Through the Eyes of Stabilizers

The Stabilizer is likely to focus on maintaining operational stability and managing risks associated with venturing into this new technological area.

They're mapping out new processes and procedures to keep the development of this new technology from disrupting existing product lines and services. You'll see them crafting detailed project plans, complete with clear timelines, milestones, and who's responsible for what. They're probably also considering how to make sure the company stays on the right side of regulations and industry standards in this new area. Stabilizers could also think about whether and how the organizational structure might need to change to support this new direction.

Your Stabilizers could ask questions like:

1. How can we maintain operational stability while venturing into this new technological area?
2. What new processes and procedures will we need to establish to manage the development of this new technology?
3. How can we ensure that this new venture doesn't disrupt our existing product lines and services?
4. What risk management strategies should we implement to mitigate potential negative impacts on our current operations?
5. How can we create a detailed project plan with clear timelines, milestones, and responsibilities?
6. What quality control measures do we need to put in place for this new technology to maintain our standards?
7. How can we ensure compliance with relevant regulations and industry standards in this new technological area?
8. What changes to our organizational structure might be necessary to support this new direction?
9. How can we maintain consistent performance metrics across both our existing and potential new product lines?
10. What contingency plans should we develop in case the project faces significant challenges or setbacks?

Seeing Through the Eyes of Trailblazers

Trailblazers are probably feeling some excitement about the innovation and disruption potential of this new technology. It's probable that they're already dreaming up ways this product could turn the industry on its head or even create brand new markets. You might find them brainstorming innovative features or applications that no one's thought of yet, and pushing the envelope of what's possible with this technology. They might even see this as an opportunity to redefine the company's image and brand in bold, innovative ways. Some Trailblazers will be thinking about how this technology might evolve and how the company can lead that charge. And don't be surprised if the Trailblazer wants to set audacious, visionary goals that go beyond just product development to truly transform the company and industry.

A Trailblazer might pose questions such as:

1. How could this new technology revolutionize our industry or create entirely new markets?
2. What innovative features or applications of this technology haven't been explored yet by our competitors?
3. How can we push the boundaries of what's currently possible with this technology?
4. What unconventional approaches could we take in developing or marketing this product?
5. How might this technology evolve in the future, and how can we position ourselves to lead that evolution?
6. What potential disruptive impacts could this technology have on our industry, and how can we capitalize on them?
7. How can we use this opportunity to redefine our company's image and brand in bold, innovative ways?
8. What creative partnerships or collaborations could enhance our development and implementation of this technology?

9. How can we foster a culture of innovation and calculated risk-taking throughout this process?

10. What audacious, visionary goals can we set that go beyond just product development to truly transform our company and industry?

Scenario #3: Competing Projects

The team has been given limited resources to complete two important projects. They need to decide how to allocate these resources effectively, and how or whether to prioritize one project over the other.

Seeing Through the Eyes of Achievers

Achievers will want to squeeze every ounce of efficiency and quality out of those limited resources. They could be crunching the numbers, trying to figure out which project packs the biggest bang for the buck. They're likely pondering ways to juggle both projects at once, including rooting out any inefficiencies lurking in the current processes, applying lessons from past projects, and implementing systems to quickly address resource bottlenecks. Their primary goal is to ensure the highest quality deliverables, regardless of which project(s) are chosen, while also stretching the limited resources as far as possible.

An Achiever might ask:

1. How can we measure and compare the potential impact and success of each project?

2. What specific skills and expertise are required for each project, and how can we best utilize our team's strengths?

3. How can we optimize our workflow to potentially handle both projects simultaneously?

4. What performance metrics should we establish to ensure efficient use of resources on the chosen project(s)?

5. How can we identify and eliminate any inefficiencies in our current processes to stretch our limited resources further?

6. What innovative approaches or technologies could help us complete both projects with the given resources?

7. How can we ensure the highest quality output regardless of which project(s) we choose to pursue?

8. What lessons from past projects can we apply to improve our efficiency in these projects?

9. How can we create a system to quickly identify and address any resource bottlenecks during project execution?

10. What opportunities for skill development and team growth does each project offer?

Seeing Through the Eyes of Directors

Directors are thinking about how each project fits into and aligns with the big picture, including the company's long-term goals and vision. Expect them to raise tough questions about how choosing one project over the other will shake up the company's market position or competitive edge. They're assessing the risks associated with each project and considering the potential opportunity costs. The Director is likely also thinking about how this decision might affect future project opportunities and considering contingency plans. And of course, they're thinking about how the team is going to make this decision, what happens if opinions are split, and how to overcome procrastination or bottlenecks.

A Director could ask:

1. What are our top three priorities in making this resource allocation decision, and how do they rank against each other?

2. What is our deadline for finalizing resource allocation, and how does this impact our project timelines?

3. Who needs to be involved in the final resource allocation decision, and how do we resolve any disagreements?

4. How does each project align with our long-term strategic goals and vision?

5. What are the potential returns on investment for each project, both in the short and long term?

6. How might prioritizing one project over the other affect our market position and competitive advantage?

7. What are the risks associated with each project, and how do they compare?

8. How will our decision impact key stakeholders, including clients, investors, and partners?

9. What are the opportunity costs of choosing one project over the other?

10. What contingency plans should we have in place if the chosen project(s) don't meet expectations?

Seeing Through the Eyes of Harmonizers

Harmonizers are checking the group's emotional temperature to keep the team unified and engaged even as resources are being divvied up. They're thinking about how to make sure everyone feels heard and valued in the decision-making process. If resources end up split between projects, Harmonizers are considering ways to keep the team feeling united and how to ensure fair recognition and opportunities for all team members. They're thinking about effective communication strategies to keep everyone aligned and informed, and how to support team members who may need to shift focus or take on new responsibilities.

A Harmonizer might want to know:

1. How can we ensure that team members feel their input is valued in this resource allocation decision?

2. What concerns have different team members expressed about each project, and how can we address them?

3. How might our resource allocation decision affect team morale and job satisfaction?

4. What strategies can we use to maintain team cohesion if we need to split resources between projects?

5. How can we ensure fair recognition and opportunities for team members, regardless of which project(s) we choose?

6. What communication strategies should we employ to keep everyone aligned and informed throughout the process?

7. How can we support team members who may need to shift focus or take on new responsibilities due to our decision?

8. What team-building activities might help us navigate the challenges of limited resources?

9. How can we foster a collaborative environment that encourages resource sharing and mutual support between project teams?

10. How might we turn this resource challenge into an opportunity to strengthen our team's problem-solving skills and resilience?

Seeing Through the Eyes of Stabilizers

Stabilizers will be focused on creating and implementing structured processes to manage the limited resources effectively across the projects. They're considering how to develop a detailed resource allocation plan that accounts for all project aspects and includes contingency buffers. Expect that they're thinking about implementing systems to monitor and control resource usage in real time, and how to maintain consistent standards if resources are split. Don't be surprised if they're concerned with risk management strategies and maintaining operational stability. And they're probably considering how to modify the team's standard project management processes to accommodate the resource constraints.

Stabilizers might ask about:

1. How can we create a detailed resource allocation plan that accounts for all aspects of both projects?
2. What processes should we put in place to monitor and control resource usage throughout the project(s)?
3. How can we ensure consistent quality and performance standards across both projects if we split resources?
4. What risk management strategies should we implement to mitigate potential resource-related issues?
5. How can we maintain operational stability while potentially juggling multiple projects with limited resources?
6. What clear guidelines and procedures need to be established for resource sharing or reallocation during the projects?
7. How can we ensure compliance with any relevant regulations or contractual obligations while managing our resources?
8. What systems can we put in place to track progress and resource utilization in real time?
9. How should we modify our standard project management processes to accommodate our resource constraints?
10. What contingency buffers should we build into our resource allocation plan to account for unexpected challenges?

Seeing Through the Eyes of Trailblazers

It wouldn't be shocking for a Trailblazer to see the resource constraint as an opportunity for innovation and reimagining project approaches. They could be exploring unconventional ideas like leveraging unique partnerships, adopting cutting-edge technologies, or fundamentally restructuring work processes to overcome resource limitations. They might even be considering how to create innovative solutions that could potentially accomplish the goals of both projects simultaneously or how to turn the resource constraint into a competitive advantage. Some Trailblazers might encourage a shift in perspective from scarcity to abundance, exploring how this mindset change could lead to transformative approaches to resource allocation and project management.

Trailblazers might pose questions like:

1. How could we fundamentally reimagine our approach to these projects to require fewer resources?
2. What unconventional resources or partnerships could we leverage to expand our capabilities?
3. How might we create a new, innovative solution that accomplishes the goals of both projects simultaneously?
4. What radical changes to our work processes or team structure could help us overcome our resource limitations?
5. How could we turn this resource constraint into a unique selling point or competitive advantage?
6. What cutting-edge technologies or methodologies could we adopt to dramatically increase our efficiency?
7. How might we involve our clients or end-users in the projects to augment our limited resources?
8. What bold, out-of-the-box ideas could transform how we approach resource allocation in the future?
9. How could we use this challenge to pioneer a new way of working that sets us apart in our industry?
10. What if we viewed our resources as abundant rather than scarce? How would that change our approach to these projects?

A FINAL THOUGHT

The ability to think from multiple role perspectives isn't just an interesting exercise; it's a crucial skill for modern teams. When your team members can step into each role's mindset—whether it's the Director's decisive lens, the Stabilizer's organizing viewpoint, the Achiever's detail-oriented perspective, the Harmonizer's people-focused outlook, or the Trailblazer's innovative vision—they develop a deeper appreciation for how each role contributes to the team's success. This mental flexibility allows your team to navigate challenges more effectively, even when you can't achieve perfect role balance. The scenarios and questions provided here are just starting points; the real power comes when your team develops the habit of considering problems from all five perspectives. This leads to better decisions, more creative solutions, and ultimately, a more cohesive and high-performing team.

CHAPTER REFLECTION GUIDE

- Think of a recent challenge or decision you faced. How might your approach have changed if you had consciously adopted the mindset of a Director, Stabilizer, Achiever, Trailblazer, or Harmonizer? Which role was the hardest to imagine yourself fulfilling, and why?
- Reflect on a team discussion or meeting where the outcome could have benefited from considering multiple perspectives. How might incorporating the viewpoints of all five roles have improved the decision-making process?
- How has understanding the five roles increased your empathy for team members with different work styles or priorities? Can you recall a time when this understanding helped resolve a conflict or improve collaboration?
- How might you incorporate role-thinking exercises into your team's processes to foster a deeper appreciation of each role's value? What specific team challenges could benefit from this practice?

Visit **www.leadershipiq.com/teamplayers** to find more resources, such as exercises, assessments, and additional tools.

CHAPTER 9

HIERARCHY IS NOT A BAD WORD

M ORE THAN A CENTURY AGO, JUST OUTSIDE KRISTIANIA (NOW modern-day Oslo), stood an old country estate. Peaceful, quiet, it was the kind of place where you'd expect time to stand still. But not with young Thorleif Schjelderup-Ebbe running around. This six-year-old was a bundle of energy, always up to something. And what caught his attention more than anything else? The chickens.

While other kids might've been off playing games or getting into trouble, Thorleif was fascinated by those clucking, pecking birds in the barnyard. It was like he had his own little kingdom right there on the estate grounds.

He began giving the chickens names, discerning their unique characteristics, and treating them with the same affection and attention one might reserve for cherished friends. As Thorleif got older, he couldn't shake his fascination with those chickens. It wasn't just kid stuff anymore; he started looking at them with a more curious, scientific eye. By age ten, he was meticulously documenting the interactions among the chickens. Through hours of observation, he discovered that not all chickens were equal.

There was a hierarchy, a discernible order. He termed it the *Hackliste*, which in German roughly means "pecking order." The dominant hen, the "despot," commanded respect and submission, ensuring her superiority with assertive pecks. Lower in the hierarchy, hens acknowledged their status, yielding to those above them.

Thorleif's observations weren't just childish pastimes. They laid the groundwork for a significant breakthrough in our understanding of animal behavior. The "pecking order" concept he developed became a cornerstone in the field. By 1922, drawing from the notes he'd kept throughout his childhood, he published his observations. The work soon reverberated through academia, gaining recognition and sparking a flurry of research. Thorleif's "pecking order" wasn't just for chickens. The same hierarchies, he posited, manifested across various species, painting a universal theme of dominance and submission throughout nature. It spoke to a deeper, primal instinct present across species.[1]

ARE WE BETTER THAN CHICKENS?

You might be thinking that, of course, chickens have hierarchies; they're simple barnyard creatures. They can't write symphonies, invent medicines, build skyscrapers, create artificial intelligence, and all those other uniquely human accomplishments.

Hierarchies feel outdated, maybe even primal or primitive; they're millions, if not hundreds of millions, years old. You've probably never seen someone jump up in a modern-day office and exclaim, "We need more hierarchy!" Hierarchy is one of the least appealing words in the English language (it's not as off-putting as "moist," but it's close). Humans have evolved beyond the need for pecking orders, right?

As we'll see in this chapter, humans are wired for hierarchies. Toddlers can spot hierarchies with incredible accuracy. Boards of directors and NBA teams perform better with hierarchies.

But, and I cannot stress this enough, *humans perform at their best with a hierarchy that's much more evolved than a barnyard pecking order.* There are legitimate reasons why hierarchies rub some people the wrong way; at their worst, they're inflexible, undemocratic, and unmeritocratic.

That's why this chapter is all about adaptive hierarchies. Adaptive hierarchies deliver the clarity and order of traditional hierarchies while moving faster, producing better results, and harnessing the unique talents of everyone on your team.

First, however, we need to understand why hierarchies have been such an enduring feature of human organization.

HOMO HIERARCHICUS

While human beings aren't involved in a literal "pecking order"—with individuals walking around and physically pecking one another to establish dominance—most groups (and even societies) are structured by some type of hierarchy.

From the studious hush of libraries where students vie for the top class rank to the rigid discipline of military ranks, hierarchy is stitched into the fabric of our lives. Recall those childhood moments, sitting in church pews, noticing the distinction between priests and bishops? Or later in life, navigating the corporate ladder, where entry-level employees in cubicles aspire to executive suites with doors, desks, and assistants? Hierarchies can be nuanced, where it's not just about the most expensive car in the driveway but also the brand of one's attire or the number of followers on one's social media.

Even futuristic science fiction is replete with hierarchies. The world of Star Trek is a post-scarcity society in which humanity has evolved beyond the need for money; people work to better themselves and their community. And yet, there are admirals, captains, first officers, chief medical officers, and all the rest. Captain Kirk and Captain Picard are legends and heroes, but make no mistake, they have bosses.

Homo sapiens, along with many group-living species, display an inherent inclination toward hierarchies. With our beautiful art, advanced medicine, and jaw-dropping technology, we are, in many ways, truly deserving of the label "wise humans" (that's what *Homo sapiens* means). But as we'll see, our predisposition and receptivity to hierarchies make us just as deserving of the term *homo hierarchicus.*

Imagine you're at a corporate networking event when, out of the corner of your eye, you notice someone looking intently in a particular direction. Will your gaze follow theirs?

In the wild, our primate cousins instinctively follow the gaze of their pack's alpha figures more than those lower in the pecking order. But do humans do the same? One group of researchers put the idea to the test with some modern tech magic. They crafted images of male and female faces, dialing up or toning down facial features typically associated with dominance (dominant faces had larger jawlines, heavier brows, etc.).[2]

Here's where it gets interesting. In a rapid-fire test, these dominant and nondominant faces flashed briefly on a screen (a mere 200-milliseconds), followed by a target either in the direction the face was gazing at or the opposite direction. When the dominant faces were on the screen, people were significantly faster to spot the targets than when the nondominant faces appeared.

In other words, just as with our primate cousins, humans followed the gaze of dominant faces. It's a little nod from evolution, reminding us that regardless of how we consciously view hierarchies, we're deeply wired to respond to them.

It's not just adults that recognize hierarchies. Picture a nursery school: bustling rooms of lively kids, all between the ages of three and five. Now imagine them sitting in front of a little stage, eyes wide, as they're introduced to two identical puppets. Crafted by a team of researchers, the puppets look like twins, but one puppet proudly flashes a box with just two colored pencils, while the other flaunts a box boasting six pencils.[3]

Now, the million-dollar question these tots were asked: Does one of these puppets seem like the "boss"? A whopping three-quarters of the kids identified the puppet with six colored pencils as the dominant one. Any toddler can identify the boss when one puppet is significantly bigger than another. Or when one of those puppets speaks more loudly and assertively than their quieter counterpart. Or if the puppets are shaped like chickens and the bigger chicken puppet pecks the smaller chicken in the head.

But this study was notable because it asked kids to detect a far more subtle hierarchy, that of resource inequality. Even at preschool age, children can infer that not only is it more desirable to have a great number of colored pencils, but that having more puts people (or puppets) higher in the hierarchy. And that speaks to just how hardwired our hierarchy-detecting mechanisms really are.

WE KEEP FIGHTING AGAINST HIERARCHIES

Roughly every decade, a new managerial fad sweeps through the management cognoscenti, promising to upend hierarchies. In the early days of Google, founders Larry Page and Sergey Brin grappled with the idea of the conventional management hierarchy. Inspired by their time in graduate school and their engineering backgrounds, they envisioned a company without the traditional managerial layer, hoping to foster rapid idea development and maintain a collegial atmosphere. By 2002, this vision led them to experiment with a completely flat organizational structure. However, the initiative quickly proved problematic.

Employees, lacking guidance and clarity, frequently approached Page with mundane issues, from expense report queries to interpersonal conflicts. Additionally, a Google research team, seeking to validate the hypothesis that manager quality doesn't affect team performance, concluded the exact opposite. Their data demonstrated that teams led by competent managers were not only happier but also more productive, sparking a quick return to managers and hierarchy.

Another anti-hierarchy movement was the self-governing operating system known as holacracy. There are no managers; instead, there's a system of flexible roles embedded within a series of nested circles representing autonomous teams. There's obviously not an organizational chart for this kind of approach, so think of a bunch of little circles inside a bigger circle, with those bigger circles placed inside a mega circle. It gained popularity sometime around 2014, as companies like Zappos and Medium publicly espoused its benefits.

Jon Wolske, former culture evangelist at Zappos, says, "You answer to your circle. It is self-managed in that if this table here was one circle and they have different roles, you're going to get together and manage, which means you're going to talk about any opportunities or concerns or questions about your work, but there's not that one person managing it."[4]

If you find this circle idea disquieting in its ambiguity and vagueness, you're not alone. By 2016, Medium's head of operations noted that they were moving away from holacracy: "Our experience was that it was difficult to coordinate efforts at scale. In the purest expression of Holacracy, every team has a goal and works autonomously to deliver the best path to serve that goal. But for larger initiatives, which require coordination across functions, it can be time-consuming and divisive to gain alignment."

Zappos found that the self-governing operating system had created its own forms of bureaucracy so severe that some units had stopped using it. Shortly after its implementation, 150 departmental units had ballooned into five hundred circles. And by 2023, *The Wall Street Journal* was reporting that layoffs and other moves by corporate parent Amazon were largely unraveling the version of Zappos envisioned by its late founder, Tony Hsieh (the driving force behind holacracy).

BENEFITS OF HIERARCHIES

Hierarchy, by its very design, is streamlined and simple. It follows a clear order, making it easier for our minds to process and internalize.[5] A minuscule 200-millisecond glance at a face is all it took to determine dominance. Preschool kids sussed out hierarchies based on nothing more than puppets and colored pencils.

Even sophisticated business leaders are influenced by hierarchies. On a board of directors, for example, hierarchies are often subtle and informal;

status isn't just derived from official titles or shares owned. It's about the respect a director commands and their perceived value to the board.

In one study of more than five hundred boards of directors, researchers gauged someone's status in the hierarchy by looking at the number of other corporate board seats each director held. A director on multiple boards, researchers reasoned, likely held more esteem among peers, signaling their elevated status.[6]

If your company recruits a new board member and they're serving on a board for the first time, that's probably less impressive than landing someone like Intuit founder Scott Cook, who's served on such boards as Amazon, eBay, and Procter & Gamble.

A pronounced inequality in board seats indicated a more distinct and clearer informal hierarchy, and that hierarchy brought results. Firms with more hierarchy exhibited higher financial performance, as measured by their return on assets. And in cases where the firm was underperforming or the industry was undergoing rapid changes, a clear informal hierarchy proved even more beneficial. Much like having a star or two on an NBA team increases wins, having some standouts on a board improves the company's financial results.

Apropos the NBA, a study delving into basketball statistics offers a fresh perspective on why hierarchies can be beneficial for teams. Picture an NBA team where all players have the same salary, the same amount of playing time, and shared leadership equally. This sounds fair, and conventional wisdom has long held that massive gaps in pay and playing time foment jealousy and erode teamwork.

But the conventional wisdom was wrong. Researchers from Stanford and Northwestern analyzed a decade of NBA data, focusing on three specific hierarchies: pay dispersion (essentially the unevenness of players' salaries), starting lineup frequency (how frequently a player starts the game), and playing time allocation (the unevenness of minutes played per game). If every player gets the same salary and evenly splits playing time, that would be evidence of little or no hierarchy. By contrast, if a team has a few players with top salaries and those guys play the most minutes, that's a strong hierarchy.[7]

The surprising results revealed that teams with clear hierarchies in terms of salary, starting positions, and playing time consistently outperformed their more "egalitarian" counterparts (even after controlling for average salary and past performance). But why?

It turns out that hierarchy can actually enhance coordination and collaboration. Teams that had clearer hierarchies displayed better teamwork indicators—they had more assists, better shooting accuracy, more defensive rebounds, and fewer turnovers. In essence, when roles were more defined and delineated, players worked better together, leading to more victories.

Now, please do not take this to mean that you can install a rigid hierarchy and your team will magically perform better. While hierarchies provide order, reduce ambiguity, simplify decision-making, and accelerate communication, there's another reason behind their effectiveness: They unlock the powers of everyone else on the team.

In 2013, Lebron James won his second NBA title with the Miami Heat. That year, he led the team in minutes played, points per game, rebounds, and assists.[8] In the eyes of opponents, Lebron James sat clearly atop the team's hierarchy.

But in a discussion with basketball analytics guru Kirk Goldsberry, James revealed how hierarchies benefit everyone else on the team: "When I'm in attack mode, I get a lot of eyes and I know that. I attract a lot of attention. For some odd reason, teams seem to forget that Ray Allen is the best shooter ever created, and so they pay attention to me, and all I need is a split second; and all he needs is a split second, he gets the ball off faster than [anyone] I've ever seen; and once I can see a defender's eyes pay attention to me and come off Ray, I'm going to him."[9]

His teammate Ray Allen was indeed one of the best three-point shooters of all time. And the attention focused on James enabled Ray Allen's deadliness from three-point range (even in his penultimate year in the league), a key factor in their championship victory.

What James understood, that too many miss, is that the best hierarchies are neither inflexible nor static. James led the team in minutes, points, rebounds, and assists, but that didn't mean that he was the only person who could or should score. His position at the top of the hierarchy allowed him to see when someone like Ray Allen was actually the better choice to take the shot. Yes, James was the highest-status player, but there were possessions when one of his teammates was better positioned to score.

In 2017, Lebron James was back on the Cleveland Cavaliers, facing NBA-star Paul George and his Indiana Pacers in the playoffs. In the waning seconds of the game, George had the ball when a double-team forced him to pass. His teammate CJ Miles got the pass, took a shot, missed, and the Indiana Pacers lost the game.

The problem, from Paul George's perspective, was that "In situations like that, I gotta get the last shot. I was asking for it. CJ took it upon himself."[10] George was the team's leader in points by a large margin, clearly atop the team's hierarchy, and felt as though he needed to be the taker of last-second shots.

But here's the problem: Most observers agreed that George was not in the best position to take the final shot. CJ Miles noted, "Obviously, we wanted to get the ball to Paul to be able to get the shot to win the game. I got the ball at four [seconds], so I had to take it myself. I got a good shot. I just didn't make it."

Even Lebron James chimed in: "I can only speak for myself. When you're doubling me, I'm giving it up. That's me. I don't know how everybody else feels about that, but if you get a double, I think we all know math in here: There's two guys on the ball, and that means there's a 4-on-3. You have your numbers. So if you're the best player on the floor, that doesn't mean you have to take the shot. I think he made the right play, and you live with the results."

A clear hierarchy doesn't mean only the top person contributes. Instead, it creates a framework where everyone can excel in their role, like LeBron James's ability to leverage his status to create opportunities for teammates. Hierarchies work best when they streamline processes while remaining adaptable to specific situations and individual strengths.

ADAPTIVE HIERARCHIES

In the early moments of what would become an immense California fire in the early nineties, the urgency was palpable. Merely three minutes after the initial distress call was logged, 65 firefighters, seven engine companies, two water-dropping helicopters, and a bulldozer were mobilized, racing against time to the heart of the blazing inferno. As the hours unfurled in a haze of smoke and desperation, the deployment swelled incredibly, drawing in a remarkable 458 fire agencies spanning 12 states. The skies bore witness to an aerial brigade of 44 units comprised of both helicopters and fixed-wing aircraft. Below, 839 engines stood ground and more than 7,000 firefighters from across the nation convened in a Herculean effort to battle the raging inferno.[11]

Effectively managing a force this large—coordinating thousands of people, millions of dollars of equipment, and a staggering number of local, state, and federal agencies—was possible because of a system called the Incident Command System.

The Incident Command System is a standardized hierarchy that provides a coordinated approach to the command, control, and coordination of emergency response. It looks like a corporate organizational chart on steroids. It defines hierarchies for planning, logistics, finance, air support, demobilization, claims, food, strike teams, supplies, facilities, ground support, and the list goes on.

This hierarchical system was developed after Southern California's disastrous 1970 fire season. That year, in less than two weeks, 16 people died, more than 700 structures were destroyed, 500,000 acres burned, and damages were in the hundreds of millions of dollars. While firefighters' bravery was on full display, there wasn't anything resembling a clear hierarchy or command structure. Fire engines passed each other on the road, literally driving in opposite directions. Different agencies duplicated their efforts. Resources ran dangerously low.

But amidst the development of this quintessential hierarchy, a significant advance in hierarchies emerged. And it's a concept with which Lebron James was already well acquainted.

Here's how one fire chief, a seasoned veteran of California fires, described his approach within the hierarchical Incident Command System:

"As a manager, it is really incumbent on me to recognize my weakness [in a particular area]...and that I don't have as much knowledge as maybe a guy standing here next to me. Maybe I've got one of the premier national urban search and rescue truck captains standing next to me, and this guy knows it like bread and butter. So I'd be a much better manager, and I'd basically build the trust of people better, if I said, "Okay, here's what the overall goal in this incident is: to get this truck off this guy. Okay? And Bob over here on Truck 45, or whatever, is the one that's going to basically direct the point-by-point operation of this."[12]

Even though this fire chief sits atop a clear hierarchy, when there's someone on the team who's better suited to direct a particular piece, that person takes the lead.

That's what I call an adaptive hierarchy. It has a clear structure, but it's not static. Simply put, the hierarchy adapts so that the right person takes the lead.

Sometimes the "right person" is incredibly easy to identify. If we're analyzing a basketball team, there's two seconds left in the game, and everyone is covered except the point guard, it's pretty clear that the point guard should take the shot. If we're looking at a workgroup inside a tech company, the group faces a key decision about a financial calculation, and if there's only one team member with financial expertise, it's easy to spot the best choice to take the lead.

But most of the time, hierarchy decisions are a bit more complex; there's more required than simply having the right technical skills.

For instance, when a team faces a critical deadline and needs to make quick decisions, a Director might step forward to provide clear direction and break through indecision. However, if the team then moves into a phase requiring meticulous planning and process implementation, a Stabilizer could take the lead. When innovation is needed to overcome a challenging obstacle, a Trailblazer's unconventional thinking might be crucial. For projects demanding technical excellence and hands-on expertise, an Achiever could guide the team to deliver high-quality results. And in times of team conflict or when merging diverse groups, a Harmonizer's interpersonal skills could be invaluable in fostering collaboration and resolving tensions.

Let's look at how Adaptative Hierarchies harness the unique powers and talents of each of the five roles.

WHEN THE <u>HARMONIZER</u> SHOULD TAKE THE LEAD

Harmonizers are best suited to lead teams in situations that require strong interpersonal skills, conflict resolution, and building a positive team culture. They excel when a team needs to improve collaboration, navigate difficult personalities, or merge diverse groups. Harmonizers are ideal leaders during times of organizational change, when team morale needs boosting, or in environments where effective communication and relationship building are critical to success.

Sam Walton, the iconic founder of Walmart, revolutionized the retail industry with his unique vision and unyielding drive for customer value. But beyond his business acumen, Walton's magnetic charisma and genuine warmth set him apart in the corporate world. Walton wasn't just the face of a retail behemoth; he was a beloved figure who fostered a deep sense of community and camaraderie among his employees.

When he retired in 1988 at age seventy, the company faced a delicate challenge. How does a team replace a beloved legend? Someone who radiated warmth and charisma? No doubt, a sense of uncertainty would have permeated the Walmart workforce. Employees, who had long thrived under Walton's affable leadership, would have found themselves grappling with a profound sense of loss. For many, Walton wasn't just a boss, but a guiding light and mentor. Who could possibly sit atop the Walmart hierarchy after Sam Walton? And what CEO in their right mind would even want to try?

Enter David Glass. Unassuming and humble, he didn't fill a room with the palpable charisma of his mentor Sam Walton. When *Fortune* magazine asked him how he managed his career in the shadow of a charismatic leader like Walton, he responded, "Most people have enough ego that they want to distinguish themselves from a charismatic leader, and that's what creates the problem. I've never had much ego, and I'm not worried about things like that. I'm more interested in the satisfaction that we are doing the right things and we're getting it done and being a part of it. I like being part of a winning team. I don't have to be the winning team."[13]

Glass couldn't compete with Walton's charisma, nor did he want to. Instead, he cared deeply about people, and supported and cheered their successes. A fellow Walmart executive noted, "He listened to your ideas, and he encouraged you. He let you fail and learn from your failures. Mr. Glass was a person of humility. He inspired you to see the opportunities with open eyes, and he served others from a state of confidence. He led with a humbled heart."[14]

Glass's personable nature and his knack for forging genuine connections shine through in this recollection from a former employee regarding their initial encounter: "I found a smallish man with peppered black and white hair that seemed to have lost a bout with a comb earlier that day. He smiled at me with what I would call a crooked grin, but there was no escaping those eyes: bright, piercing, probing."

Some will argue that a larger-than-life star should be followed by another larger-than-life star, but a Harmonizer like Glass was unquestionably the right choice. During his twelve years as CEO, Walmart's sales surged tenfold, earnings soared by 760 percent, and its stock price increased by more than 1,500 percent.

Filling the shoes of an icon like Sam Walton requires more than just business expertise or a flair for innovation. Being in charge after someone like him demands the ability and desire to connect with people, understanding their apprehensions and assuaging their fears.

A Director, while providing decisive leadership, might focus too heavily on broad strategies, possibly missing Walton's personal connection with employees. Achievers, though diligent and attentive to details, could overemphasize task completion at the expense of worker morale. Trailblazers, despite their creative brilliance, might introduce changes too rapidly, unsettling veteran staff used to Walton's approach. Stabilizers might prioritize process and routine over innovation, potentially hampering Walmart's dynamic growth.

By contrast, a Harmonizer, with their knack for relationship-building, could bridge the gap left by Walton. The Harmonizer role embodies the spirit of unity and camaraderie that Walton championed, ensuring that while business strategies might evolve, the heart and soul of Walmart would remain unchanged.

WHEN THE <u>DIRECTOR</u> SHOULD TAKE THE LEAD

Directors are ideal for leading teams in situations that require quick, decisive action. They excel when the team needs to break through indecision, overcome analysis paralysis, or make tough choices in high-pressure situations. Directors are best suited to lead when clear goals need to be set and a strong vision needs to be established and maintained.

Hitler invaded France on May 10, 1940. Unfortunately, the French, Belgian, and British soldiers sent to counter the German advance were caught by surprise. Instead of attacking the heavily fortified Maginot Line, a nearly impenetrable system of fortifications and weapon installations, the Germans simply circumvented the line and launched a swift campaign through the Ardennes forest (wrongly thought to be impassable).

The strategy effectively split the Allied forces in two, trapping the British Expeditionary Force against the beaches of Dunkirk.

Facing the prospect of a catastrophic defeat, whispers of doubt and uncertainty filled the halls of Westminster. Some Members of Parliament advocated for negotiation with Hitler, seeing it as the only way to spare Britain from utter devastation.

But Winston Churchill, newly appointed prime minister and ever a Director, saw things differently. There were hard decisions to be made, but negotiating with Hitler was not among the options. In his first speech as prime minister to the House of Commons on May 13, 1940, he uttered the following:

"We have before us an ordeal of the most grievous kind. We have before us many, many long months of struggle and of suffering. You ask, what is our policy? I can say: It is to wage war, by sea, land and air, with all our might and with all the strength that God can give us; to wage war against a monstrous tyranny, never surpassed in the dark, lamentable catalogue of human crime. That is our policy. You ask, what is our aim? I can answer in one word: It is victory, victory at all costs, victory in spite of all terror, victory, however long and hard the road may be; for without victory, there is no survival."[15]

The first step to victory was to mitigate the looming disaster at Dunkirk. He knew that to safeguard Britain's future he had to salvage its present, and that meant evacuating the troops across the English Channel.

This wasn't an easy decision. The operation, named Dynamo, would be treacherous. The shallow beaches of Dunkirk made it challenging for large naval vessels to approach, and the threat of the formidable German Luftwaffe loomed in the skies overhead. The logistics alone were a nightmare. Yet Churchill's Director mindset was always two steps ahead. He foresaw the morale boost a successful evacuation could bring to a beleaguered British public. In his mind, the soldiers at Dunkirk were more than men, they were the embodiment of British resilience and determination.

Where other leaders might have hesitated, paralyzed by the gravity of the situation, Churchill took charge. A Director at his core, he was unafraid to make the hard decisions, recognizing that leadership often demanded sacrifice and that not all choices would yield perfect outcomes. It wasn't about finding a flawless solution but rather the best possible one under the circumstances. The retreat wasn't a defeat but a strategic withdrawal, a recalibration to ensure a stronger retaliation.

The eventual success of the evacuation validated Churchill's choice. More than 330,000 troops were rescued from the clutches of the advancing German army, far surpassing initial estimates. The "miracle of Dunkirk," as it came to be known, bolstered British spirits and solidified Churchill's reputation as a decisive leader.

It's worth pondering how a leader less entrenched in the Director's role would have reacted. Would they have dithered, caught in the quagmire of indecision? Would they have capitulated to the overwhelming sense of doom? Perhaps. But Churchill's Director instincts ensured that he took the reins, made a choice when it mattered most, and steered Britain away from the precipice of disaster.

Dunkirk stands not just as a testament to British tenacity but as a shining example of Churchill's Director leadership. He demonstrated that with the courage to act decisively, even the bleakest situations could be transformed into beacons of hope.

Trailblazers, with their penchant for out-of-the-box thinking, might have been too radical, risking more than what was already at stake. Achievers, with their dedication to task completion, could have been too wedded to avoiding defeat. The Stabilizers, though essential in maintaining structure, might have struggled, given the chaotic and rapidly evolving nature of the Dunkirk crisis. Harmonizers, crucial in conflict resolution and team dynamics, might have faltered when faced with making the tough, impersonal strategic decisions needed at the moment.

It was precisely this kind of unprecedented situation where a Director was indispensable. Churchill, in his Director's role, didn't waver or succumb to the paralyzing fear that such a crisis can induce. Instead, he took charge, made the difficult decisions, and orchestrated one of the most significant evacuations in military history.

WHEN THE TRAILBLAZER SHOULD TAKE THE LEAD

Trailblazers are best suited to lead teams in situations that require innovation, creative problem-solving, and challenging the status quo. They excel when a team needs to develop new products, explore uncharted territories, or find unconventional solutions to complex problems. Trailblazers are ideal leaders when the conventional wisdom is both wrong and deeply entrenched.

For much of the twentieth century, the popular belief was that ulcers come from ambition, working too hard, and internalized stress. Sometime in the 1930s, ulcers earned the label the "wound stripe of civilization." And in 1945, an article in *LIFE* magazine reported, "The ulcer rate is highest among white males, and it is notoriously high in the ranks of high-powered executives....Indeed, doctors have been able to portray the typical ulcer patient. He is between 20 and 40 years old, tall and slender rather than stout and probably with a history of ulcer predisposition in the family. He looks not unlike Humphrey Bogart. He is active, intelligent, ambitious, aggressive, independent."[16]

While plenty of studies were conducted to bolster the stress view of ulcers, they were generally poorly designed and executed. So, after a sufficient lack of evidence, the medical community had a new idea. The acid theory held that increased acid secretion and/or decreased resistance to acid produced ulcers. The dictum was "no acid, no ulcer." Like the stress (aka psychosomatic) theory, the acid theory made intuitive sense. Unlike the stress theory, the acid theory was more conducive to laboratory experiments (i.e., the natural strengths of medical researchers). And drugs. We can't forget about the drugs.

The seventies were a time of big interest in ulcers, and especially the acid theory. Drugs to reduce acid secretion took off: SmithKline launched

Tagamet, and Glaxo launched Zantac, which the *1986 Guinness Book of World Records* declared was the bestselling drug of all time.

While these drugs did help with symptoms of ulcers, they didn't cure ulcers. In fact, some studies found that the relapse rate after cessation of treatment is 50 percent after six months and around 95 percent after one year.

Fortunately, there were two guys in Western Australia with a pretty big idea. In the late seventies, a pathologist at the Royal Perth Hospital named Robin Warren identified spiral bacteria-like forms in biopsy specimens obtained from the stomachs of patients with gastritis. These bacteria would later be named *Helicobacter pylori* or *H. pylori*. Shortly thereafter, a physician-in-training named Barry Marshall needed a research project. He was referred to Robin Warren and the Gastroenterology department, and together, these two men successfully cultured the bacterium *Helicobacter pylori*.

This was a very big deal because, back in 1983, no one thought there could be bacteria in the acidic stomach. Warren and Marshall described their findings in letters to the prestigious British medical journal, *The Lancet*. Marshall's letter speculated that the bacteria "may have a part to play in other poorly understood gastritis associated diseases."

But as Marshall himself says, "*The Lancet* had procrastinated with our publication. They had been unable to find reviewers who could agree that our paper was important, general enough and interesting enough to be published." In fact, even after publication, gastroenterologists weren't particularly interested in their findings.[17]

With evidence that ulcers were caused by bacteria, it was possible to eradicate the infection (i.e., cure ulcers) with the antibiotic metronidazole and bismuth. Marshall and Warren just needed money to conduct trials on humans to further make their case. But, as you might imagine, the drug companies weren't exactly excited about funding studies that might replace their highly profitable drugs with cheap generic antibiotics and bismuth (think Pepto-Bismol). And the gastroenterology community was in full skeptic and/or denial mode. Creative ideas can be scary to those who don't think them up, and out-of-the-box thinkers can be downright threatening.

Marshall watched helplessly as patients with bleeding ulcers filled the hospital beds. He knew a simple course of antibiotics could save them, but they weren't under his care. Instead, he witnessed the tragic cycle repeat: Patients would arrive with severe bleeding, receive the standard acid blockers, and vanish overnight to the surgical ward where their stomachs would be removed—a drastic solution that Marshall knew was entirely unnecessary.

So, Marshall ran an experiment on the only human subject available: himself. He took *H. pylori* bacteria from a patient, stirred it into a broth, and drank it. Here's how he described what happened next:

"I had a patient with gastritis. I got the [*Helicobacter pylori*] bacteria and cultured them, then worked out which antibiotics could kill his infection in the lab—in this case, bismuth plus metronidazole. I treated the patient and did an endoscopy to make sure his infection was gone. After that I swizzled the organisms around in a cloudy broth and drank it the next morning. My stomach gurgled, and after five days I started waking up in the morning saying, "Oh, I don't feel good," and I'd run in the bathroom and vomit. Once I got it off my stomach, I would be good enough to go to work, although I was feeling tired and not sleeping so well. After 10 days I had an endoscopy that showed the bacteria were everywhere. There was all this inflammation, and gastritis had developed. That's when I told my wife."[18]

Happily, he lived. But while he had unequivocally proven that bacteria were the underlying cause of ulcers, the establishment still wouldn't listen. It would take another ten years before the majority (especially in the United States) "got it." The psychological, reputational, historical, and financial inertia against *Helicobacter pylori* was almost insurmountable. Almost. Eventually, in 1994, years after the rest of the world had accepted *H. pylori*, the National Institutes of Health held a Consensus Conference and basically said that the key to treatment of duodenal and gastric ulcer was detection and eradication of *Helicobacter pylori*.

And now comes the cathartic storybook ending: In 2005, Barry Marshall and Robin Warren received the Nobel Prize for Physiology for Medicine. And in the understatement of the year, the Nobel committee said the doctors "with tenacity and a prepared mind challenged prevailing dogmas."

In the case of ulcer research and treatment, a Trailblazer like Barry Marshall was the ideal leader. The situation demanded someone willing to challenge deeply entrenched beliefs and pursue unconventional solutions to a complex problem.

A Director might have been too focused on making quick decisions based on existing knowledge, potentially and ironically reinforcing the status quo. A Stabilizer could have been too risk-averse, reluctant to challenge the established medical theories and practices. An Achiever, while excellent at executing known procedures, might not have had the vision to completely reframe the problem. A Harmonizer, focused on maintaining consensus, might have struggled to fight against the entire medical establishment.

A Trailblazer like Marshall brought the perfect blend of innovative thinking, willingness to challenge conventional wisdom, and courage to pursue radical ideas. His ability to think outside the box led him to consider bacteria as a cause of ulcers when practically everyone else dismissed the possibility. Marshall's Trailblazer mindset allowed him to persevere in the face of skepticism and rejection, ultimately leading to a paradigm shift in ulcer treatment that has saved countless lives. This approach ensured that a major medical breakthrough was not only discovered but also eventually accepted and implemented, despite overwhelming resistance from the established medical community.

WHEN THE STABILIZER SHOULD TAKE THE LEAD

Stabilizers are best suited to lead teams in situations that require structure, organization, and careful planning. They excel in environments where consistency, reliability, and processes are crucial. Stabilizers are ideal leaders when a team needs to implement and adhere to processes, manage complex projects with multiple moving parts, or navigate situations where mistakes can have serious consequences.

When Steve Jobs brought Tim Cook to Apple in 1998, shortly after rejoining the company himself, he likely saw in Cook the embodiment of a true Stabilizer; someone who could bring order, planning, and predictability to a company teetering on the edge of bankruptcy. Cook's role at Apple exemplifies the Stabilizer archetype: a team member who ensures adherence to schedules, processes, and details while "dotting the i's and crossing the t's."

From his very first days at Apple, Cook demonstrated the Stabilizer's penchant for structure and efficiency and wasted no time in addressing Apple's manufacturing and supply chain issues. In one memorable instance, upon learning of a problem in Asia, Cook told his team, "This is really bad. Someone should be in China driving this." Thirty minutes later, he looked at one of his executives and asked, "Why are you still here?" The executive immediately left for China without even packing a change of clothes.[19]

This encapsulates the Stabilizer's approach: identify problems, create clear action plans, and ensure swift execution. Cook's focus on inventory management further underscores this trait. He famously declared that inventory is "fundamentally evil," likening it to the dairy business: "You kind of want to manage it like you're in the dairy business. If it gets past its freshness date, you have a problem."

Under Cook's stewardship, Apple's inventory management became comparable to Dell's, then the gold standard for manufacturing computers. This logistical discipline allowed Apple to pull off what seemed miraculous: unveiling revolutionary products that had been kept completely secret until they magically appeared in stores worldwide.

The Stabilizer's role in bringing order and predictability is evident in Cook's approach to Apple's supply chain. In 2005, when Apple introduced the iPod Nano, Cook's team accurately predicted the demand and prepaid

$1.25 billion to suppliers like Samsung and Hynix to corner the market on a specific kind of memory through 2010. As Kevin O'Marah, chief strategist at AMR Research, noted, "That's the sort of thing they wouldn't have thought of in the days before Tim Cook."[20]

Cook's Stabilizer qualities were not limited to operations and supply chain management. He also played a crucial role in product transitions. In 2006, Apple transitioned its entire computer line to Intel processors, a technically challenging feat. Yet, under Cook's leadership, there was "nary a blip in sales." This seamless transition demonstrates the Stabilizer's ability to manage complex changes while maintaining stability and efficiency.

As a Stabilizer, Cook brought a different temperament to Apple's leadership. Described as "cool, calm, and never, ever raises his voice," Cook's demeanor contrasted sharply with Jobs's more volatile personality. This calm, steady approach is characteristic of Stabilizers, who bring a sense of predictability and reliability to a team.

However, it's important to note that Cook's Stabilizer qualities didn't stifle Apple's innovation. Instead, they provided the structure and efficiency that allowed Apple's creative forces to thrive. As *Wired* noted, "Cook hasn't just been a company caretaker during Apple's good years. He's also a product, sourcing and supply-chain visionary. Cook arguably did as much as anyone to turn Apple around after its nearly disastrous fall in the mid-1990s."[21]

Now, for the first decade of Cook's tenure at Apple, Steve Jobs was still alive and very much an era-defining CEO. So, you might ask, was Tim Cook and his Stabilizer mindset the right choice to lead Apple upon Jobs's passing?

Under Cook's leadership, Apple has achieved unprecedented financial success, becoming the first company to reach a $2 trillion valuation, "worth more than six times what it was on October 5, 2011."[22] Cook's Stabilizer qualities have allowed him to expertly navigate the maturing smartphone market, diversify Apple's portfolio with successful products like the Apple Watch and AirPods, and bolster the company's services business.

While some might argue that Apple hasn't produced as many "epoch-shifting" products as it did under Jobs, Cook's steady hand has ensured that Apple continues to innovate incrementally and remains patient with ambitious projects. As one industry expert notes, "Incremental improvements to existing products, after all, were just as key to Jobs's success as the great leaps forward."[23]

In the post-Jobs era, a Stabilizer like Tim Cook was the right choice for Apple. The company needed someone who could maintain its innovative spirit while bringing structure, efficiency, and predictability to its operations. Will a Stabilizer be the best choice in perpetuum? Maybe not; there could certainly come a point when a Trailblazer (or some other role) would make sense. But following Jobs's passing, Cook's stabilizing approach was a smart choice.

A Director could have been too focused on quick decisions without the patience for careful, long-term planning. And given the reverence in which Steve Jobs was held, would someone else get his benefit of the doubt? An Achiever, while excellent at hands-on tasks, might not have had the broad vision needed to lead such a large, complex organization. A Trailblazer could have pushed for constant innovation at the expense of stability and profitability. And perhaps more importantly, could a non–Steve Jobs Trailblazer really have led Apple? A Harmonizer, while great for team dynamics, might not have had the operational expertise to manage Apple's vast supply chain and product lineup.

A Stabilizer like Cook, however, brought the perfect blend of operational excellence, strategic thinking, and steady leadership. His focus on efficiency and process improvement provided the stable foundation upon which Apple could continue to innovate and grow. Cook's Stabilizer mindset allowed him to balance the need for incremental product improvements with ambitious long-term projects, all while turning Apple into a financial powerhouse. This approach ensured that Apple not only survived the loss of its visionary founder but thrived, becoming the most valuable company in the world.

WHEN THE <u>ACHIEVER</u> SHOULD TAKE THE LEAD

Achievers are best suited to lead teams in situations that require hands-on expertise, technical proficiency, and a focus on excellence in execution. They excel when a team needs to deliver high-quality results, solve complex technical problems, or improve specific processes or products. Achievers are ideal leaders for specialized teams working on detailed, intricate projects that require deep knowledge and skill.

Eric Yuan is the creator of Zoom, the video conferencing platform with which we are all intimately familiar. He's also a quintessential Achiever.

Yuan started at WebEx, where his tireless work ethic and technical prowess, (he would often code through the night on Fridays and play soccer without sleep on Saturdays), ultimately elevated him from an early employee to Vice President of Engineering.

Why did he leave? It wasn't a quest for fame or power; it was simply a desire to fix a problem by building something better. "I never thought about leaving WebEx," he says, "because I was a part of the early founding team. I wrote a lot of code, I was a Vice President of Engineering. You feel like, 'That's my baby.' So every day I spent a lot of time on talking with customers, trying to solicit their feedback."[24]

That's where his frustration emerged. "Back then, every morning when I woke up, I really did not want to go to the office because I did not see a single happy WebEx customer. I felt the pain, so I wanted to fix it."

Try as he might, and he tried mightily, he couldn't convince his bosses of the value of solving the underlying problems. "The solution was very old, the architecture was very old, and it didn't support video very well," he notes. "The one way to address those problems was to build a new solution from the ground up. I tried to convince others [at WebEx] to build a new solution and to start over, but nobody listened. They thought I was crazy."[25]

After leaving WebEx and securing funding, he and his newly hired team worked quietly for nearly two years, focusing on creating key differentiators that would set Zoom apart from its competitors. As he told one of his early investors, "Someday someone is going to build something on the cloud, and it's going to kill me."[26] But with Yuan's Achiever focus and hands-on diligence, he got there first.

One of my *Forbes* colleagues tells the story of the technological leap Zoom had made with its lightweight, device-agnostic Web client, browser update-resistant software layer, and ability to function even with 40 percent data loss: "Zoom customer service chief Jim Mercer was then working at competitor GoToMeeting when a colleague opened a Zoom account to see what the hype was about. 'One click, we were in, and there were 25 feeds of participants at the same time,' he says. 'We were like, What is this voodoo? How are they doing it?'"[27]

Even as the CEO of a successful company, Yuan maintains his nitty-gritty detailed approach. He regularly grabs a temporary desk with whatever team he wants to focus on. When Zoom announced a voice product, he moved in with the engineers for months.

Just because Achievers aren't clamoring for leadership roles doesn't mean that they don't sometimes end up in one. A groundbreaking study uncovered that approximately one in five US high-technology firms are led by "Inventor CEOs." These are executives who have been awarded at least one patent in their own name.

The study, which examined high-tech companies from 1992 to 2008, found that firms helmed by Inventor CEOs consistently outperform their peers in innovation metrics. These companies produce 25 percent more patents and receive nearly 16 percent more citations on their innovations. More importantly, the patents filed under Inventor CEOs' leadership tend to be more valuable and scientifically impactful.[28]

What sets Inventor CEOs apart is their ability to leverage their hands-on experience in specific technology areas (usually areas where they were likely to have been Achievers). The research shows that firms produce more patents and higher-quality innovations in technology classes where their CEO has direct inventor experience. In other words, the practical insights gained from being an inventor translate into superior capabilities in evaluating, selecting, and executing innovative projects.

In Zoom's case, an Achiever like Eric Yuan proved to be the ideal leader. The company's success hinged on solving complex technical problems and delivering a superior product in a highly competitive field.

A Director might have been too focused on high-level strategy without the deep technical knowledge needed to revolutionize video conferencing. A Stabilizer could have been too risk-averse, potentially stifling the innovative leaps required. A Trailblazer might have pushed for constant innovation without the patience to perfect the core product. A Harmonizer might not have had the technical expertise to drive the necessary improvements.

An Achiever like Yuan brought the perfect blend of hands-on technical expertise, relentless focus on product quality, and a deep understanding of customer pain points. His experience as both an engineer and a user of video conferencing software allowed him to identify and solve critical issues, leading to Zoom's game-changing technology. Yuan's Achiever mindset ensured that Zoom didn't just enter the market, but redefined it with superior execution and attention to detail.

FOR MOST TEAMS, IT'S SIMPLE

An adaptive hierarchy doesn't require creating a complex, ever-shifting org chart or constantly reshuffling who reports to whom; rather, it's about recognizing that different challenges call for different types of leadership, and then letting the right person take point when their skills are most needed.

Consider an executive team overseeing the acquisition of another company. An adaptive hierarchy approach doesn't require reinventing the executive team structure; it simply involves assigning leadership roles for different aspects of the merger based on each executive's strengths.

The CEO might serve as the Director, pushing the rest of the executive team to make, and not avoid or defer, tough decisions. Maybe the HR chief is a Stabilizer, taking charge of workforce integration, using their talent for creating structured plans and processes. The Harmonizer COO might handle cultural integration, tapping into their strong interpersonal skills. Maybe a Trailblazer CTO leads technological integration, applying their innovative thinking to find synergies. And an Achiever CFO could manage financial aspects, employing their technical expertise and attention to detail. Each executive takes the point in their area of strength, while still working as part of a cohesive team under the CEO's overall direction.

The beauty of this approach is its flexibility and simplicity. As projects evolve or new challenges arise, the same team can realign their efforts without any formal restructuring. Maybe next month, the team faces a different challenge that requires more innovation. The roles might shift, with the team's resident Trailblazer taking more of a leading role, while the group's planning-oriented Stabilizer ensures everything stays on track. The titles haven't changed, but the leadership dynamics shift to meet the new challenge.

This isn't about creating a new management fad or imposing a rigid system. It's about fostering a team culture where everyone understands their strengths and those of their teammates, where there's enough trust and communication for leadership to flow naturally to where it's most effective. Sometimes you lead, sometimes you follow, but you're always contributing where you can make the biggest impact.

The "following" part is where too many teams fall apart and struggle with adaptive hierarchies. Much like an NBA star who struggles to let an open player take the last-second shot, too many team leaders struggle to relinquish even a little bit of control.

"Followership" is the technical term for helping and supporting the decisions of others, prioritizing the team's goals over personal interests, and doing the necessary work to achieve the team's objectives even if that means temporarily relinquishing your position atop the hierarchy. In other words, are you willing to follow someone else when they're in a leadership role? Or going back to the Lebron James example, even though you're on top of the team's hierarchy, are you willing to live with an open player, other than you, taking the last-second shot?

Research has found that followership and leadership are inexorably linked. One study discovered that people who rated their teammates highly on followership also rated them highly on leadership. Team members who were rated highly on followership experienced 72 percent less interpersonal conflict, and teams with high levels of followership had 49 percent lower overall conflict levels. Put simply, team members who are willing to follow and support others are also seen as better leaders, and vice versa.[29]

Remember Ken Hicks, the Harmonizer CEO of Academy Sports, from Chapter 5? Here's how he described followership to me: "A leader has to be willing to get criticized for something that their people did." When you've got a team with different predilections, a balanced mix of Directors, Trailblazers, Harmonizers, Stabilizers, and Achievers, you've got to let them fulfill their roles and unlock their talents.

"You might have made a different decision," Hicks told me, "but they will own it, and they will make it work. If a leader mandates every little thing they do, however, that leader is eventually going to fail. At some point, I can't tell people everything they need to do; they need to be able to take the initiative."

Every business school on earth has courses on leadership, but few, if any, have courses on followership. And yet, learning to take a step back might be the more beneficial skill for today's aspiring and current leaders.

Three days into Apollo 13's lunar mission in 1970, an oxygen tank explosion 200,000 miles from Earth left NASA facing a devastating scenario: three astronauts trapped in a crippled spacecraft with dwindling oxygen, minimal power, and no clear path home. The crisis turned a routine space flight into what would become NASA's "successful failure"—a rescue mission that pushed the limits of engineering ingenuity and exemplified adaptive hierarchies.

Flight Director Gene Kranz faced an unprecedented challenge. With the command module powered down and three astronauts crammed into the lunar module—a spacecraft never designed for extended life support—every watt of remaining power became precious. Their survival hinged on having enough power to restart the command module for Earth reentry.

When Kranz suggested following standard power-up procedures, engineer John Aaron spoke up bluntly: "Well, Gene, we can't do that....We don't have enough power." Instead of pulling rank, Kranz recognized Aaron's expertise and immediately appointed him as the mission's "power broker," declaring, "Anybody that needs to use power in the spacecraft has to get their sequence cleared with John."[30]

Aaron's trailblazing solution was a radical departure from NASA's most fundamental procedures. Standard protocol demanded powering up visibility systems first—all communications, telemetry, and instrumentation—so ground control could monitor each subsequent step. But Aaron realized this approach would drain precious power during the entire startup sequence, as those monitoring systems would stay running while each additional system came online. Instead, he proposed something revolutionary: The crew would power up the command module "in the blind," activating most systems without turning on any monitoring or communication equipment. By leaving the power-hungry visibility systems for last, they could conserve the spacecraft's severely limited battery power through most of the startup process.

The control room was deeply anxious about flying blind during humanity's first cold start of a command module in orbit. But Aaron's gamble paid off. When they finally activated communications, the power readings confirmed his calculations, with only a minor two-amp variance that revealed previously unknown details about the spacecraft's wiring. The team had pulled off what many thought impossible, conserving just enough power to bring the crew home.

The successful splashdown on April 17, 1970, validated more than Aaron's technical strategy—it demonstrated the power of adaptive hierarchies. This shift in command structure, allowing a specialist to take the lead during a critical moment, proved essential to bringing three astronauts home alive.

CHAPTER REFLECTION GUIDE

- Think of a team or organization you've been a part of. Can you identify a moment when the hierarchy adapted to let the right person lead? What was the impact on the team or the outcome?
- Reflect on a time when you supported a teammate who took the lead in a specific situation. How did this experience affect the team's dynamics and your relationship with that person?
- Adaptive hierarchies rely on different roles taking charge depending on the situation. Have you experienced situations where the wrong role led? How could an adaptive hierarchy have improved the outcome?
- Consider a current challenge your team is facing. How could applying the principles of adaptive hierarchies help you address the issue more effectively?

Visit **www.leadershipiq.com/teamplayers** to find more resources, such as exercises, assessments, and additional tools.

CHAPTER 10

MAKING BETTER DECISIONS ON YOUR TEAM

IMAGINE YOU'VE VOLUNTEERED TO TAKE A SIMPLE TEST. YOU AND seven others sit in a room where you're shown two cards: one with a single line and another with three lines of varying lengths. This is an easy test, so don't overthink it; all you have to do is identify which of the three lines matches the length of the line on the first card. There's no trick, and the answer is glaringly obvious: The correct line stands out clearly from the others.

But as the group begins to voice their answers one by one, you notice something odd. The first person selects the wrong line, then the next person does the same, and so on until it's your turn. You know that answer is incorrect, yet seven people have just confidently chosen it. What do you do?

This setup was a legendary experiment in the early 1950s by psychologist Solomon Asch. He wanted to answer a simple but profound question: To what extent would people conform to the opinions of a group, even when those opinions were obviously incorrect?

Unbeknownst to the lone subject in each group, the other seven individuals were confederates—actors instructed to provide the same wrong answer. The purpose was to see if the subject would stick to their perception or conform to the group's obviously wrong consensus. The results were pretty shocking: 75 percent of participants conformed to the group at least once, and overall, about 37 percent of responses across all trials were conforming despite the clear and obvious evidence that the consensus was wrong.[1]

When asked afterward, lots of participants admitted that they knew the group's answers were wrong but chose to conform to avoid conflict or the discomfort of standing alone. Others began to doubt their own eyes and judgment, wondering if the group saw something that they had missed.

In more technical terms, this experiment revealed an interplay between normative social influence (the desire to fit in) and informational social influence (the desire to be correct). As the results showed, the desire to fit in is awfully powerful and drives what we now know as conformity bias.

THE PITFALLS OF TEAM DECISION-MAKING

For all the younger iPhone addicts reading this book, this next sentence will probably come as a shock. In 2007, Nokia produced more than half the planet's mobile phones, and their mobile operating system was on nearly two-thirds of the world's phones.

It's easy to forget about Nokia because, by 2013, they were crushed by Apple, Google, and Samsung. At first glance, the once-dominant company's demise is a story of strategic and technological mistakes. However, investigative research recently unveiled a different root cause. INSEAD professors interviewed seventy-six top and middle managers, engineers, and external experts, discovering that Nokia was destroyed by "a culture of temperamental leaders and frightened middle managers scared of telling the truth." One middle manager interviewed describes how when a colleague suggested that he challenge a top manager's decision, "he didn't have the courage; he had a family and small children."[2]

Nokia's managers recognized the need to develop a more advanced operating system to compete with Apple's. But they were also aware that creating such a system would take years. Despite this, they hesitated to openly admit that their existing operating system, Symbian, was lacking, concerned that it might make them appear pessimistic or defeatist. That fear translated into outright obfuscation.

One manager told the researchers that "top management was directly lied to.... I remember examples when you had a chart and the supervisor told you to move the data points to the right [to give a better impression]. Then your supervisor went to present it to the higher-level executives. There were situations where everybody knew things were going wrong, but we were thinking, 'Why tell top managers about this? It won't make things any better.' "[3]

In theory, teams make decision-making easier and more effective; they bring together diverse perspectives, expertise, and experiences. At their best, teams pool knowledge and insights, navigate complex problems more efficiently, and reach smarter and more thoughtful conclusions. And when your team is assembled with the right mix of Directors, Stabilizers, Trailblazers, Harmonizers, and Achievers, the available acumen is something to behold.

In practice, however, decision-making in teams can be both challenging and fraught. The promise of improved decision-making is often undermined by a host of cognitive and social biases. Teams can fall prey to conformity pressures, where members may feel obligated to go along with the majority opinion to avoid conflict or the discomfort of standing out. Authority bias may lead team members to overly defer to senior voices, regardless of those voices' rightness or wrongness. The desire for consensus can result in premature agreement without thoroughly exploring alternative viewpoints.

That's why it's pretty typical to see some cynicism about group decision-making. One McKinsey study, for example, found that only 20 percent of respondents thought their organizations excelled at decision-making. The majority felt that a significant portion of the time spent decision-making is often used ineffectively. That helps explain why 72 percent of executives believe that bad strategic decisions are as common as good ones in their companies.[4]

Now, I'm not suggesting that you shouldn't use teams to make decisions; individuals also suffer from a host of decision-making biases. You've got about as much chance of finding a perfectly rational and unbiased individual as you do seeing a winged unicorn. I'm not telling you that individuals are better than teams at making decisions; a room of Directors, Stabilizers, Trailblazers, Harmonizers, and Achievers is an incredibly powerful decision-making force. Rather, my point is that in order to unlock the potential decision-making power of a team, we're going to need a very specific way of operating.

NOT EVERY DECISION REQUIRES A TEAM

The first step in unlocking your team's potential decision-making prowess is recognizing that not every decision should be made by a group. Sometimes group decision-making gets a bad rap simply because we're asking a team to make a decision that should have been made by a single person. We need to save group decision-making for situations where the benefits of the group's insights outweigh the time and effort required.

Decisions vary widely in terms of their impact and the level of input they require. Some choices have far-reaching consequences that affect multiple departments or even the entire company. Some decisions deal with complex, high-stakes situations where there isn't a clear path forward. There are plenty of situations where you need innovative and novel solutions, insights outside your area of expertise, or buy-in from multiple stakeholders. And sometimes, a decision is risky enough (for example, the wrong decision could cost us our job) that we'd be crazy not to assemble a team of Directors, Stabilizers, Trailblazers, Harmonizers, and Achievers.

In any of those scenarios, you will absolutely want to involve your team in the decision-making process. You'll want those diverse perspectives to ensure you've considered all angles, analyzed potential risks, involved the right people, and surfaced all of the available innovations and creative solutions.

On the other hand, there are plenty of decisions that are far more routine and familiar. These are decisions that get made every day regarding recurring issues that don't have an especially wide impact, aren't particularly high risk, where the inputs and outputs are well understood, and that aren't all that politically sensitive.

In those cases, it's usually more efficient to delegate the decision-making to a particular individual. When someone with the right knowledge and expertise can handle the matter, it streamlines the process, speeds up execution, and, frankly, saves your team's energy for cases where group input would really make a difference.

In Chapter 9, I covered how various roles could take point on certain types of issues. You can scale that down a bit and apply the same thinking to fully delegating particular decisions.

If there's a minor interpersonal conflict, you might be able to fully delegate that to a skilled Harmonizer. Your Director could handle decisions about prioritizing short-term projects or allocating resources between departments. Your Stabilizer might be able to handle decisions related to updating internal processes completely. When faced with a technical decision about improving a specific feature, could one of your Achievers take that over fully? Your Trailblazer might be able to creatively resolve a nagging customer complaint.

If this all sounds a bit complex, here's an incredibly simple heuristic Amazon uses: one-way and two-way doors. As described in their leadership principles, "A one-way door decision is one that has significant and often irrevocable consequences—building a fulfillment or data center is an example of a decision that requires a lot of capital expenditure, planning, resources, and thus requires deep and careful analysis. A two-way door decision, on the other hand, is one that has limited and reversible consequences: A/B testing a feature on a site detail page or a mobile app is a basic but elegant example of a reversible decision."[5] This provides a simple framework for deciding whether or not you can safely delegate a decision to an individual rather than convening the group.

There's another benefit of delegating some decisions to individuals: You'll develop the decision-making skills of others on the team. Nudging people to become a bit more independent and self-reliant ultimately speeds up decision-making and offers some incredibly valuable learning opportunities.

You can nudge by asking simple questions, like "How are you planning to handle this?" or "Which way are you leaning on this decision?" The goal is to get them to think through the issues. If you tell them what to do or make the decision for them, not much learning occurs. But when they use you as a sounding board and not a crutch, they develop their own decision-making toolkit.

And yes, they might make a different decision than you. They might even fail. But remember, we're talking about two-way doors; these are decisions that, even if they fail, can be reversed. This approach recognizes that failure, when properly managed, isn't a setback but a stepping stone to success.

Giving employees room to fail is not the same thing as encouraging failure. It's about creating a culture of learning, innovation, and personal growth. It's about recognizing that, sometimes, the best way to develop a skill is through hands-on experience, even if that experience includes failure. As a team leader, your role isn't just to direct and decide but to create an environment where your team members can grow, learn, and ultimately succeed. You'll not only develop stronger, more capable employees but also build a more resilient and innovative organization.

By the way, delegating a decision doesn't prevent someone from getting advice or feedback from others. It just removes the need for a collective decision-making process.

Here's one more thought for the hardcore Directors reading this: Just because a Director is great at making decisions doesn't mean that they have to make every decision. Julian Francis is president and CEO of Beacon Building Products, the largest publicly traded distributor of roofing materials and complementary building products in the United States and Canada.

Theirs is a multibillion dollar company, but it's a short cycle business, with rapidly changing markets and orders received and shipped in days.

In a fast-moving business, Francis can't sit at the center of every decision, so he recently told me one of his key decision-making rules: "One of my mantras is that the CEO should make as few decisions as possible. And where I do make decisions, they should be 50/50 decisions. If a decision is 60/40 or 70/30, for or against an issue, then there's already a reasonable business case, the answer is pretty obvious, and someone else should have already made that decision."[6]

Put simply, if one of his leaders is already 70 percent of the way to choosing Option A, Francis isn't going to step in and choose Option B. The leader is already leaning toward Option A; they simply need to channel their inner Director and execute the decision. When Francis does get involved, he tells me, "I want everyone to learn from the 50/50 decisions. Let's talk about the decisions and why they were made. Eventually, I want to get that type of thought process moving throughout the organization so that we can be faster and more responsive."[7]

Yes, he makes decisions like any highly skilled CEO, but he doesn't need to make every single decision. In fact, his approach is cultivating more deciders throughout the company. Ironically, Directors don't need to control every decision to foster great decision-making; they just need to ensure that a good decision is made.

WHEN YOU DO MAKE DECISIONS WITH A TEAM

Now that we're ready to make decisions with our team, our primary goal is leveraging the powerful insights brought by our Directors, Stabilizers, Trailblazers, Harmonizers, and Achievers. We've got them on the team, and now we need to unlock and summon their talents and perspectives.

However, it's not enough to simply have them in the room. We need to empower them to contribute fully, and then, of course, we have to be ready to listen to their ideas fully.

It's darn near impossible for one person to think through each of the perspectives necessary for a great decision. Each role on your team—Director, Achiever, Stabilizer, Harmonizer, and Trailblazer—offers a unique lens through which to view decisions.

Your goal is structuring the decision-making process to ensure you hear and consider each of those unique perspectives. It sounds simple enough, but remember the conformity bias experiment from the beginning of the chapter and the cautionary tale of Nokia. The pressure against surfacing and embracing diverse perspectives is immense.

And, of course, even though the term has been around for half a century, one of the most insidious pressures facing teams is still *groupthink*.

GROUPTHINK

The Bay of Pigs invasion has to rank pretty high on the list of American foreign policy fiascos. The ill-fated 1961 plan was a CIA-sponsored military operation in which a force of Cuban exiles, trained and equipped by the United States, would land at the Bay of Pigs and attempt to overthrow Fidel Castro's communist government.

The data and assumptions driving the plan were both faulty and divorced from reality. The plan assumed that the small force could land at the Bay of Pigs and spark a widespread uprising against Castro. The planners believed they could maintain secrecy about US involvement despite early leaks. They were convinced that obsolete B-26 bombers could neutralize Castro's air force in a surprise attack. Perhaps most egregiously, they grossly underestimated the strength of Castro's military and his popular support. The invasion was a debacle, with the vast majority of the landing force quickly captured or killed.

Organizations have terrible ideas every day, but they're usually not calamitous until they're acted upon. In the case of the Bay of Pigs invasion, groupthink is the mechanism by which a terrible idea transformed from idle musings into a foreign policy fiasco.

Coined by psychologist Irving Janis, groupthink is a phenomenon whereby the desire for harmony in a decision-making group overrides a realistic appraisal of alternatives. In his groundbreaking 1971 article entitled "Groupthink," he introduced the concept using the Bay of Pigs invasion as a prime example of how cohesive groups can make disastrous decisions due to their tendency to prioritize consensus over critical evaluation.[8]

When the CIA presented their plan to President Kennedy, not all his close advisors were fans. Arthur Schlesinger Jr., a respected historian and Kennedy adviser, had serious misgivings about the invasion. But in the heat of high-pressure meetings, he didn't strongly voice his objections. In his memoir, Schlesinger wrote, "In the months after the Bay of Pigs I bitterly reproached myself for having kept so silent during those crucial discussions in the cabinet room." He added, "I can only explain my failure to do more than raise a few timid questions by reporting that one's impulse to blow the whistle on this nonsense was simply undone by the circumstances of the discussion."

This self-censorship wasn't a case of Schlesinger freezing up in a big meeting; there were much deeper dysfunctions in the group. For example, there was a false perception that everyone was in agreement. As Schlesinger observed, "Our meetings took place in a curious atmosphere of assumed consensus." This imagined consensus served to further stifle dissent, creating a feedback loop of acquiescence.

There was also an active discouragement of dissent. At a social event, Robert F. Kennedy, the president's brother and attorney general, took Schlesinger aside and bluntly told him, "You may be right or not, but the President has made up his mind. Now is the time for everyone to help him all they can." And Secretary of State Dean Rusk ensured that the objections of several other key officials failed to reach the president. These "mindguards" (another wonderful Janis coinage) serve to reinforce and exacerbate the groupthink.

With enough assumed consensus and suppression of dissent, the group takes on an illusion of invulnerability, believing their success is inevitable.

This just furthers the groupthink cycle, making dissent even more likely to be ignored. When Senator J. William Fulbright was invited to present his objections to the plan, Janis notes that as soon as he finished speaking, "the President moved on to other agenda items without asking for reactions of the group."

The result of this groupthink was, as Janis put it, a "deterioration in mental efficiency, reality testing, and moral judgment." The proof is in the spectacular failure of the Bay of Pigs invasion.[9]

BRAINSTORMING, BUT BETTER

Have you ever noticed a colleague holding back during a team meeting, their body language suggesting they've got something to say, but they won't speak up? Or witnessed a team leader ask, "Any questions or concerns?" only to be met with awkward silence and averted gazes? Has there been a time when someone raised a valid concern, only to have it subtly brushed aside or not discussed? Have you ever caught yourself thinking, "I don't want to be the only one in the group who isn't on board!"

All of those are examples of groupthink. Every one of us has experienced moments like those, and while the ubiquity of groupthink might seem a bit depressing, there is a solution.

For decades, traditional brainstorming has been the go-to method for surfacing a group's input: People on the team throw out every idea that pops into their heads without criticism or evaluation, no matter how crazy that idea might seem. It sounds nice, but it's still vulnerable to groupthink. And remember that in Solomon Asch's conformity experiments, people knew the correct answer but still wouldn't say it.

There is, however, research that identifies a much better approach. Researchers from INSEAD and the Wharton School discovered that instead of the classic brainstorming approach, where everyone gets together and throws out their ideas spur-of-the-moment, thinking independently before the group convenes delivers far better results.

Through a series of experiments, the researchers compared the effectiveness of traditional group brainstorming with an approach that forced people to think independently for a measly ten minutes before they gathered as a group. The results were striking: Teams where people thought independently for ten minutes before convening as a group generated about three times more ideas than those that only brainstormed as a group.[10]

The ideas from the group that thought independently first were rated as having more business value and more likely to be purchased by customers. The difference in the quality of their ideas was so large that an average idea generated from the independent thinking approach could rank thirty places higher in a list of one hundred ideas when compared to an idea generated from traditional brainstorming. A paltry ten minutes of thinking independently could be the difference between having a good idea and having a great, potentially game-changing idea.

This idea is incredibly simple yet immensely powerful. Why does it work so well? One reason that preliminary independent thinking outperforms traditional brainstorming is that it avoids some of the pitfalls inherent in group discussions. When people express their thoughts at the spur of the moment, some struggle to share their ideas while others speak. This is especially salient if you've got introverted or quieter people on your team who aren't especially comfortable talking over their colleagues. Others are going to censor themselves for fear of judgment from their peers.

But when you've got the time to think independently before you have to share your ideas with the group, you're far more likely to express what you really think. This approach counters a great many of the groupthink effects we discussed regarding the Bay of Pigs invasion. You know going into the sharing portion of the meeting that the folks on your team are likely to have a wide range of perspectives; after all, the team has a broad diversity of mindsets and approaches with its Directors, Stabilizers, Trailblazers, Harmonizers, and Achievers.

There's an important message conveyed to the group when you say explicitly, "We need to hear the full range of perspectives this team has to offer, and that's why we're collectively taking steps to surface each and every one of those diverse perspectives." You're, in effect, telling the group that all of the roles matter and that the team needs to hear each and every one of their voices.

If your team is really struggling to unearth everyone's ideas, you can intensify this approach. Let's say your team has to decide on the pricing strategy for a new project. Each of your Directors, Stabilizers, Trailblazers, Harmonizers, and Achievers brings a unique and valuable perspective, and you need to hear them all.

INSTRUCTIONS FOR BETTER BRAINSTORMING

A day or two before the actual meeting, send out instructions along these lines:

1. At the upcoming meeting, we're going to discuss pricing strategies for the new project. Please write down your thoughts to bring to the meeting.
2. Explain your unique perspective, including the rationale behind your thoughts, opportunities and risks, pros and cons, the whys and the why nots, etc.
3. Rank your top ideas or suggestions by creativity, impact, feasibility, or relevance [or whatever your particular decision requires], and be prepared to explain why you've prioritized them this way.
4. Prepare your points on no more than one piece of paper so they could potentially be read by someone else on the team.

You can modify these instructions to best fit whatever decision your group is currently tackling.

Here are a few important thoughts to bear in mind. You're giving your team advance notice and a clear context to encourage independent thinking. And you want them to dig deep, hence asking for rationales, pros and cons, and all the rest. At the same time, you do not want to turn this into a marathon session of who can make the longest presentation. You're extracting the diverse perspectives of the people on the team, not making this a speechmaking contest or a test of endurance.

Relatedly, the instructions raise the possibility of anonymous sharing (for example, each person's paper could potentially be read by someone else on the team). First, the requirement that people write down their thoughts will generally prevent them from self-censoring or changing their ideas to fit in with the rest of the group. That's the groupthink and conformity bias that we're trying to prevent.

When your team gathers, you've got a few options for how people will share their thoughts. The most common approach is giving each person a minute (maybe even two or three, depending on the stakes of the decision) to share what they've written. But if you're really worried about groupthink and conformity, or you've previously seen your team struggle to share their unvarnished thoughts, you can control the sharing. Ask everyone to pass their papers to you, whereupon you can read them aloud. Here you control the order and attention paid to each person's input. You might have a brilliant but timid Achiever on your team whose valuable ideas are often overlooked, as they're overshadowed by more assertive team members. When you control the sharing, you'll be able to prioritize their ideas, ensuring that they get the attention they deserve.

Controlling where the spotlight shines also gives you a powerful tool for influencing your group via the herding effect.

Everyone knows the free online encyclopedia Wikipedia. What you might not know is that there's an ongoing maintenance function where volunteer editors discuss whether newly created articles should be kept or removed. Ensuring that Wikipedia's sixty-one million pages remain relevant and high quality is not an easy task.

Researchers analyzed more than four hundred thousand of these keep or delete discussions and something profound emerged. Wikipedia users can participate by voting to keep or delete an article and providing their rationale. At first glance, it might seem like a straightforward process: Wikipedia users vote, those votes get tallied, and voila, a decision is made.

But here's the twist: The first few votes dramatically influenced subsequent participants and the final outcome. Strikingly, when the very first vote in a debate was to keep an article, it increased the likelihood of a final keep decision by more than 40 percentage points. And when the first votes were to delete an article, it increased the likelihood of a final delete decision by around 20 percentage points.[11] This is what's known as a herding effect; those initial votes had an outsized impact on the group's final decision because people aligned their opinions with the first few voters.

If you're thinking that this herding effect sounds like it could exacerbate groupthink, you'd be right. Now, Wikipedia has implemented structured policies to mitigate herding, and given what we've covered so far, they'll sound very familiar. Approaches like encouraging independent assessment and allowing administrators to make tough final calls have helped ensure that decisions are based on collective reasoning rather than majority votes driven by herding.

But herding doesn't have to be all bad. If you use the herding effect to bolster the voices of the suppressed or overlooked folks on your team, it can become a powerful tool for balancing debates and surfacing previously unheard ideas.

You might already know if there are underrepresented roles in your team's debates or if certain individuals are frequently overlooked. It could also be the case that you're facing a decision where a particular role's perspective will be especially helpful.

Imagine your team is deciding what features to release in a new product launch. Wouldn't it be a good idea to ensure that your Trailblazers and Achievers are clearly heard? If your group is leading a change that'll impact a large swath of employees, shouldn't you make space for your Harmonizers and Stabilizers to be clearly heard? By simply adjusting the order of whose ideas get discussed first, you can leverage the herding effect and influence the direction of the ensuing conversation.

Parenthetically, if you don't have time to send instructions to your group days before the meeting, you can do it in real time. As soon as everyone is in attendance, pass around sheets of paper, or if it's a virtual meeting, use a web meeting tool that allows people to write responses. Give them the same instructions as on page 184, along with a few minutes to think and write.

IT'S SO INSIDIOUS

There's a point that I cannot stress enough: Even if your team is wonderful, even if you think they're immune to groupthink, the pressure to conform is so insidious that it can happen unconsciously.

It was a sunny day in Northern California as I observed a group of six software engineers chatting amongst themselves. The company where they worked had recently acquired a smaller software firm, and the engineers were debating strategies for integrating the two software platforms.

There was a lot of technical discussion that I couldn't follow. But I did notice something interesting. The engineers were sitting at the table three-to-a-side. And whether consciously or unconsciously, the side where each engineer selected to sit perfectly matched their side of the debate. One side of the table wanted immediate full integration of the two software platforms, while the other side wanted a phased approach.

The seating arrangement was already interesting enough, but then, during their debate, the CEO strolled by. As he slowly walked about twenty feet away from this group, only one side of the table could see him. The three engineers on that side tried to pretend they didn't notice him, and the group kept debating. But then the side that could see him made an emphatic point, and the CEO very subtly nodded in agreement and walked away.

Up until this moment, I would have said that the debate was pretty even. But as soon as the CEO gave that subtle nod, the CEO side of the table became subtly emboldened. All three sitting within view of the CEO sat a little straighter, their voices became the tiniest bit more serious, and the debate started to turn in their favor.

I don't think the non-CEO side took conscious note of their opponents' physical changes, but they sensed something. If I had surveyed the whole table right then, asking, "Which side of this debate has the most convincing argument?" each side would have said, "We do!" But, if I had asked them, "Which side do you think is ultimately going to win this debate?" they would have all chosen the CEO side. Have you ever rooted for a sports team that was winning the game, but then something goes wrong, and you suddenly have this "Oh crap, we're gonna lose" feeling? That's what was happening here.

One by one, the engineers on the non-CEO side disengaged from the debate. First, one engineer fixed his gaze down at the picnic table and nervously rubbed his hands together. Then he just stopped talking altogether. Shortly thereafter, a second engineer followed with the same behavior. The third engineer kept talking, but even he became less emphatic. And just like that, the debate was over.

What I witnessed that day is called a "spiral of silence." Coined by German political scientist Elisabeth Noelle-Neumann, its simplified definition is the tendency of people to not publicly express their opinions when they believe their point of view is in the minority and could subject them to ostracism.[12] It's essentially a variety of groupthink, and it's not a one-time affair; it's a self-reinforcing spiral.

The spiral of silence works like this: First, people generally have an innate fear of being ostracized. Researchers have found that social rejection activates many of the same brain regions involved in physical pain. One study put subjects inside an fMRI scanner where they played an online game of catch with two other players. Eventually, the two other players began throwing the ball only to each other, excluding the subject. Compared with volunteers who continued to be included in the game, those who were rejected showed increased activity in the dorsal anterior cingulate cortex and the anterior insula—two of the brain regions that show increased activity in response to physical pain.[13] As far as your brain is concerned, the pain of a broken heart or rejection of your creative idea is not so different from the pain of a broken arm.

Second, because we humans are afraid of being ostracized for holding beliefs that are unpopular or in the minority, we have what Noelle-Neumann called a "quasi-statistical sense" for assessing the strength of each side in a debate. We may not always know the exact percentages of who's on either side, but we do have a pretty keen eye for detecting shifts. For example, smokers may not know the exact percentage of the American public that's anti-smoking, but they can tell you when the debate shifted against them. And they know when they're in a room where the prevailing sentiment is anti-smoking.

Third, the spiral of silence works because as we sense that our side is losing, our fear of ostracism kicks in, and we start to withdraw from the debate so as not to incur the wrath of the crowd. And when we withdraw, the other side senses this with their own "quasi-statistical sense," and they become emboldened. This causes us to become even more silent, and so on. Hence the spiral.

Imagine attending a meeting where you propose a completely out-of-the-box idea, whereupon a few powerful people roll their eyes at what you just said. This is often more than enough to initiate a spiral of silence. Not only are you likely to withdraw, but anyone else contemplating out-of-the-box ideas will sense the room's dynamics and also withdraw. This, in turn, emboldens the skeptics, and creative ideas abruptly die.

DON'T TAKE MY WORD FOR IT

It's easy to gripe about the preponderance of virtual meetings these days, but they offer a fascinating source of data that wouldn't have been readily available in years past. The vast majority of virtual meeting tools have some type of transcription capability, and these transcripts offer a goldmine of information about your team's decision-making process, participation levels, and potential groupthink issues. You don't have to take my word as gospel; you can perform your own analysis.

ANALYZE YOUR MEETING TRANSCRIPTS

Start by analyzing each team member's speaking time and frequency. This can reveal whose perspectives might be underrepresented and help you correct any imbalances.

- Are all voices being heard?
- Is there a balance in participation, or do certain individuals dominate the conversation?
- Look for patterns over time—are the same people always speaking the most, or does it vary by topic?

Next, examine the content of what's being said.

- Are people building on each other's ideas, or are certain suggestions consistently ignored?
- Look for instances where the conversation shifts dramatically after a senior member speaks—this could be evidence of the herding effect or groupthink.
- Also pay attention to how often dissenting opinions are voiced and how they're received by the group. A lack of constructive disagreement often indicates groupthink is at play.

You can also streamline this analysis process with AI tools (like ChatGPT, Claude, Gemini, or any of the others).

Not all meeting content is suitable for analysis or long-term storage. Before diving into transcript analysis, you'll want to redact any sensitive or confidential information. This might include personal data, proprietary business details, or any information that could be compromising if leaked.

After redactions, upload or paste your transcript and try these prompts:

- "Analyze this meeting transcript and provide a breakdown of speaking time for each participant."
- "Identify instances in this transcript where someone's suggestion was ignored or quickly dismissed."

- "Based on this transcript, are there signs of groupthink? Provide specific examples."
- "Compare the language used by team members before and after the project leader spoke. Are there noticeable changes in tone or opinion?"

NOTE: AI tools are changing and updating so rapidly that there might be prompts that work better than what I've written here. You can find a regularly updated AI toolkit for incorporating AI into your teams at **www.leadershipiq.com/teamplayers.**

With all of the tools available these days, employing a bit of analytical sophistication just makes sense. You'll be able to identify potential issues and ensure that all voices are heard, encouraging dissent and minimizing groupthink. You've built a team of Achievers, Harmonizers, Stabilizers, Directors, and Trailblazers; make sure that you hear what they have to say.

Doing this type of analysis is foreign territory for most teams, but the results can be transformative. The CEO of a tech company client took me aside after I finished teaching their leaders about groupthink. "I don't see any obvious signs of groupthink on our senior team," he started, "but I can't shake the feeling that maybe we have just a little dose of it happening sometimes."

I'm not a mind reader, nor can I travel back in time to spot subtle signs of groupthink. But the executive team had plenty of transcripts. We analyzed their three most recent meetings. The team appeared fairly healthy in terms of speaking time, interruptions, and sentiment, but a deeper look revealed an issue.

The team had recently been discussing a significant investment into a new market. The sentiment about the move was generally positive, but two of the executives raised some concerns. The CMO, a Harmonizer, worried about brand and customer reactions, while the head of R&D, an Achiever, had some technical feasibility concerns. Troublingly, following each instance where they expressed trepidation, their speaking time dropped precipitously for the rest of the meeting.

For instance, they would say things like "I'm a little worried about...," "We need to be careful not to...," "I'm not sure our market will...," "There might be some pushback on...," and "We should probably test this before..." Each time the CMO or R&D head raised a concern, someone else on the team would respond. Following that response, the CMO and R&D head would then say very little for the rest of the meeting.

By now, you can probably guess what was happening. After a concern was shared or an objection raised, the other executives would say things like "I think you're being too pessimistic," "That's not really a major issue," "Let's focus on the positives," and "We can't let perfect be the enemy of good."

The responses weren't nasty or ad hominem, nor was any yelling involved. Yet, just like every other groupthink scenario we've seen, the message was clear: conform, get in line, we don't want to hear your concerns.

What I love about these types of analyses is that once the data pinpoints the problem, the solution is often a fait accompli. Theirs was a simple case of following what we've covered in this chapter.

First, they adopted pre-meeting independent thinking, where each executive would write down their thoughts, concerns, and ideas before coming together. This ensured that everyone, including their Harmonizer and Achiever, had the opportunity to formulate their perspectives without immediate influence from others. Second, they strategically reordered their discussion process, intentionally bringing dissenting voices to the forefront. This "herding" of diverse opinions to the start of the conversation gave greater weight to alternative viewpoints and set a tone of open dialogue.

In some particularly crucial meetings, the CEO even took the step of reading aloud everyone's written responses himself, ensuring each executive's perspective received equal attention and consideration. This not only elevated previously marginalized voices but also signaled the value the team placed on diverse thinking. Finally, using their newfound skills, they continued to analyze meeting transcripts. This helped them monitor their progress, identify any backsliding into old patterns, and continue to refine their approach.

IS THIS PSYCHOLOGICAL SAFETY?

You've probably noticed that there's a bit more structure in my approach than what you might be accustomed to with team building, which involves trust-building and psychological safety. While psychological safety emphasizes creating an environment where individuals feel comfortable taking risks, sharing ideas, and speaking up without fear of judgment, my approach introduces a layer of structure to translate those ideals into actionable practices. It's not that I disagree with the value of psychological safety; rather, I believe that relying solely on an open and trusting environment might not be enough to overcome deep-seated group dynamics like groupthink, conformity bias, or the spiral of silence. That's why the techniques in this chapter have focused on implementing a practical framework to surface diverse perspectives consistently, even in teams that are still building their psychological safety.

One of the primary differences in my approach is the emphasis on structured independent thinking before group discussions. While psychological safety encourages spontaneous sharing and open dialogue, the approach I described earlier in this chapter starts by requiring team members to think and write down their ideas independently before coming together. This small but crucial step reduces the immediate social pressures that can stifle unique ideas or minority viewpoints. Research has shown that this approach can significantly increase the quantity and quality of ideas generated by a team, providing more innovative and well-rounded solutions than traditional brainstorming alone. By setting aside time for individual thought, we create space for all voices to be heard—particularly those who may be more introverted or hesitant to speak up in group settings.

Another key difference is my approach to managing the herding effect—the tendency for initial opinions to disproportionately influence the rest of the group. In a psychologically safe environment, the hope is that all opinions will naturally flow, but in reality, even in safe environments, louder or more assertive voices can still dominate. By controlling the order in which ideas are presented—such as reading anonymous contributions or consciously prioritizing quieter voices—the team can avoid the undue influence of early, dominant opinions. This structured intervention doesn't just create a fairer dialogue; it also ensures that critical but potentially unpopular perspectives aren't drowned out by the majority.

You'll notice that I'm also advocating for a data-driven approach to analyzing team dynamics through tools like meeting transcripts and AI-assisted sentiment analysis. Psychological safety often relies on qualitative assessments, which, while helpful, can suffer from subjectivity and inconsistency. By leveraging data, we can more objectively identify patterns of groupthink, participation imbalances, or instances where valuable dissenting opinions are dismissed. This continuous feedback loop allows teams to make real-time adjustments and ensure that psychological safety isn't just a feeling but a measurable outcome where all voices are genuinely heard.

The bottom line is that harnessing the full potential of your team is going to require structured, tactical steps to mitigate the pitfalls of human dynamics. It's not enough to simply declare that "all voices matter"—we need the structure to guarantee they do.

USING AI TO MAKE BETTER DECISIONS

Since I've already touched on one way that AI can assist your team, let me share one more case that I discovered recently.

I sit on a number of teams myself, including boards, CEO peer groups, and my company team. And this past year, two boards temporarily lost key members. One member, a brilliant Trailblazer, had surgery and required a few months of leave. Another, a gifted Harmonizer, took a bucket list trip around the world with their grandkids.

They both returned, but their absences left a void in our discussions. Now, I'm not going to tell you that we created sentient robot versions of these board members to take their place. We're not quite at a point where AI can lead team meetings in our stead. However, AI was able to channel their roles and offer us a dose of their thinking. AI was able to replicate the types of questions that Trailblazers and Harmonizers (and Directors, Stabilizers, and Achievers) might ask. AI raised objections, poked holes in our thinking, brainstormed new ideas, and, of course, analyzed our meeting transcripts.

For example, during our Harmonizer's absence, we faced a major decision about a fundraising initiative that would significantly reshape our relationships with long-term donors. During each board meeting, we'd feed the proposal details into our AI tool with prompts like "As a Harmonizer focused on relationship-building and stakeholder perspectives, what questions would you raise about this fundraising approach?" The AI, channeling the Harmonizer perspective, surfaced crucial donor-centric questions we might have missed: "How might our most loyal donors feel about this new campaign?" "What personal touches could we incorporate to ensure donors feel genuinely valued rather than merely solicited?" and "To what extent is our campaign conveying the messages of greatest importance to particular donor segments?" It even suggested relationship-nurturing strategies and provided questions about the campaign's potential impact on the organization's employees. While not a perfect replacement for our human Harmonizer, the AI helped ensure we didn't overlook the delicate interpersonal dynamics of donor relationships, just as our absent colleague would have done. The process was simple but effective: As our meetings progressed, we would input questions into the AI asking it to think like our missing Harmonizer, and then integrate those relationship-focused insights into our discussion.

If this all seems a bit far-fetched, you should know that AI's capabilities are expanding rapidly, even into domains that most people would have thought only humans could occupy.

Imagine your friend forgot your birthday after saying they'd go to dinner with you; of course, you're feeling unwanted. It would be great if you could hear some words of wisdom, or empathy, or something, to help you feel better about this lousy situation. Sounds like a job only a human could do, right?

Well, AI (specifically OpenAI's GPT-4 model) was tested against 601 humans in reappraising emotionally difficult scenarios—such as feeling unwanted after being forgotten by a friend. Both humans and AI were asked to reframe the negative situation to help the subject see it in a more positive (or less distressing) light. The responses were then evaluated by another group of human raters to see which response was better. The result? AI significantly outperformed the humans.[14] The AI responses did a better job of reducing negative emotions or increasing positive emotions, expressing empathy, and coming up with novel ways of looking at the situation.

In another study, where participants debated against either an AI or a human, the AI was 87 percent more likely to persuade participants to its assigned viewpoint than a human debater.[15] The AI leveraged data-driven arguments, a nonemotional tone, and adaptive reasoning to craft persuasive points that swayed participants' opinions more effectively than traditional human debate styles.

Yet another study put AI head-to-head with human financial analysts in the challenging task of predicting the direction of a company's future earnings based solely on standardized balance sheets and income statements. AI achieved a prediction accuracy of 60 percent compared to the 53 percent accuracy of human financial analysts, and AI really excelled in cases where human analysts typically struggle, like forecasting earnings for smaller or money-losing companies.[16]

In a study involving 149 simulated patient-doctor consultations, Google's medical AI system, AMIE, was pitted against twenty board-certified primary care doctors. AMIE outperformed the doctors on twenty-eight out of thirty-two metrics assessing diagnostic accuracy, empathy, and clinical judgment.[17] When GPT-4 competed against MBA students from an elite business school to generate startup ideas, external judges consistently rated the AI-generated ideas as superior.[18]

These studies aren't meant to strike fear. This is a book about teams, not fear-mongering about AI's imminent subjugation of humanity. The point I'm making is that if AI can construct empathic statements, forecast financial results, and craft persuasive arguments, it can certainly help your team think through decisions with the mindsets of your Trailblazers, Harmonizers, Directors, Stabilizers, and Achievers.

As I noted earlier, AI tools are changing so rapidly that it's impossible to keep them updated in a book. So visit www.leadershipiq.com/teamplayers for updated prompts, videos, and tools to enlist AI's help with your team's decision-making.

But in the meantime, here are some prompts to get you started. Tell the AI of your choice about the decision you're facing, and then, depending on which role you'd like it to help you simulate, modify one of the prompts below. Parenthetically, if you're a regular user of AI and large language models, you know they can be weird. Sometimes repeating an instruction works wonders. Sometimes changing a word or two is incredibly helpful. So, play around with these prompts and don't view them as immutable.

For the sake of illustration, these prompts assume that your team is deciding whether to invest in a new AI-driven customer service platform that promises to improve efficiency and enhance customer experience but requires a significant upfront investment and comes with some implementation risks.

AI PROMPT FOR THE DIRECTOR ROLE:

"Imagine you are the Director on a team. As the Director, your priority is to cut through the noise and drive swift, impactful decisions. As the Director, your role is to drive the decision-making process regarding whether to invest in a new AI-driven customer service platform. You prioritize decisiveness and strategic alignment with the company's broader goals. What are the most critical factors to evaluate to make a swift, confident decision? What key performance indicators (KPIs) or data would you need to see to justify this investment? Identify potential quick wins or major risks, and outline the immediate actions you would take to ensure the decision aligns with the company's long-term strategy."

AI PROMPT FOR THE ACHIEVER ROLE:

"Imagine you are the Achiever on a team. As the Achiever, you are focused on excellence, attention to detail, and ensuring high-quality results. As the Achiever, your focus is on the quality and impact of the new AI-driven customer service platform. Delve into the specifics: What detailed questions should the team ask to ensure this platform truly enhances efficiency and customer experience? What criteria should be used to evaluate the platform's effectiveness, and how can the team measure success post-implementation? Consider potential issues or bugs that could arise and suggest methods for rigorous testing and quality assurance to ensure the platform delivers high standards without compromising current operations."

AI PROMPT FOR THE STABILIZER ROLE:

"Imagine you are the Stabilizer on a team. As the Stabilizer, you prioritize risk management, consistency, and maintaining smooth operations. Considering the decision to invest in a new AI-driven customer service platform, what are the potential risks—both short-term and long-term—that the team should be aware of? What processes or controls would you suggest to mitigate these risks and ensure a seamless integration with existing systems? Provide a step-by-step plan for implementation that includes risk assessments, contingency plans, and clear timelines to keep the team grounded and prepared for any disruptions."

AI PROMPT FOR THE HARMONIZER ROLE:

"Imagine you are the Harmonizer on a team. As the Harmonizer, your focus is on maintaining team morale, fostering a positive environment, and ensuring everyone feels heard. As the Harmonizer, your focus is on the human impact of adopting a new AI-driven customer service platform. Think through the potential effects on team dynamics and morale: What concerns might employees have about this new platform, and how could these affect the overall workplace culture? What strategies would you propose to ensure buy-in from all stakeholders, including front-line staff and customer service teams? Suggest methods for fostering open communication, addressing fears of job displacement, and ensuring a supportive environment throughout the transition."

AI PROMPT FOR THE TRAILBLAZER ROLE:

"Imagine you are the Trailblazer on a team. As the Trailblazer, you thrive on innovation, bold moves, and exploring uncharted territories. As the Trailblazer, you are excited by the potential for innovation and growth that the new AI-driven customer service platform could bring. From your perspective, what are the most compelling reasons to pursue this bold investment? What unconventional questions should the team consider to challenge the status quo and fully explore the platform's potential? Offer strategies for leveraging this new technology to gain a competitive advantage, and propose ways to experiment and iterate quickly to stay ahead of market trends while balancing the risks of a high-stakes innovation."

SHOULD WE JUST TAKE A VOTE?

The most common question I get when discussing a team's decision-making process is, "Should we hold a vote or let the leader decide?"

I don't want to say that's the wrong question, but it's the wrong question. It seems simple enough, but if you've employed the techniques in this chapter, your initial thoughts about the group's decision have hopefully changed.

Maybe you were fully prepared to cast a vote one way or the other before the meeting started. But after hearing the diversity of perspectives, the hard questions, pros and cons, some well-reasoned objections, and maybe some ideas you didn't even know were available, I sincerely hope you're thinking differently about the decision.

Think all the way back to Chapter 1 where I shared the example of Dr. Shuji Nakamura winning the Nobel Prize for discovering blue LEDs. He beat scores of well-resourced scientists at major semiconductor companies to the discovery because he rebuffed groupthink. Others tried to pressure him into conformity, but he's such a Trailblazer that I think the pressure only served to accelerate his journey down the path less traveled.

His contemporaries, however, were not so constitutionally immune to groupthink or the spiral of silence. He told me stories of scientists at the big semiconductor companies who would see him at conferences and take him aside for private conversations. The other scientists would recount how anyone who considered using gallium nitride was called "crazy" or a "foolish scientist." (Remember that gallium nitride proved to be the key to unlocking blue LED light.)

Disparaging the out-of-the-box thinker is a common first step in groupthink. And it only takes one or two insults before the rest of the group fears ostracism and falls into line.

Imagine, though, if those teams had employed the techniques in this chapter, if they had platformed those dissenting voices and broken through the groupthink. It's likely that the debate would have shifted entirely. Instead of a ten-to-one vote against gallium nitride, it might have turned into a free-flowing discussion about how to solve gallium nitride's dislocation density issues to unlock its potential.

If you're employing the tools to break through groupthink, the ideas and perspectives you'll hear from the team should give you something new to consider. If you leave team meetings without having learned anything new, that's a bad sign. Conversely, if you start a meeting to decide between Choice A and Choice B, and then, after robust discussion and surfacing alternative views, everyone realizes you should be considering Choice C and Choice D or figuring out how to make Choice B work better, that's a win.

So, should you vote or let the leader decide? If you fully embrace the tools in this chapter, what you're likely to discover is that the decision you thought you were making has changed. And not only has the decision changed, but a much clearer consensus has emerged.

CHAPTER REFLECTION GUIDE

- Reflect on a time when you felt the pressure of conformity bias. How did you handle the situation, and what might you do differently in the future?
- Consider a recent team decision. Were all five roles—Director, Stabilizer, Achiever, Trailblazer, and Harmonizer—represented in the discussion? If not, how might including those perspectives have influenced the outcome?
- When leading or participating in team decisions, do you find yourself defaulting to certain behaviors (e.g., speaking first, deferring to authority, avoiding conflict)? How can you use the insights from this chapter to make your approach more inclusive and effective?
- How could you incorporate pre-meeting independent thinking into your team's processes? What specific challenges or decisions might benefit from this approach?

Visit **www.leadershipiq.com/teamplayers** to find more resources, such as exercises, assessments, and additional tools.

CHAPTER 11

THE SCIENCE OF GREAT MEETINGS

I WANTED TO START THIS CHAPTER WITH A FUN AND INTERESTING story that captured the universal meeting experience. But while there are plenty of interesting stories about meetings, in both virtual and in-person settings, they don't feel all that fun. They run the gamut from merely irritating to truly cringe-inducing.

There are stories like infamous WeWork founder Adam Neumann showing up forty-five minutes late to a meeting he scheduled for 2 a.m. Or reports that former Yahoo! CEO Marissa Mayer would consistently arrive more than forty-five minutes late to her Monday direct report meetings.[1] That might not sound terrible, but the meeting was always held at 3 p.m. Pacific Time, with some of her direct reports in New York and Europe. Those executives often couldn't get off the call until 3 a.m. or later.

Then there are the eye-popping stories clients and others have shared with me. One CFO, frustrated in senior meetings, cut holes in his pockets to covertly pull his leg hairs in the hope of suppressing potential outbursts. (He told me the idea came from an episode of *Friends*.) Another leader kept themselves awake by creating a "meeting bingo" card with overused phrases. It worked great until the day she accidentally left the card behind at the meeting's end.

How many virtual meeting fails have we seen go viral? I recall an executive making a Zoom presentation from home while her just-showered boyfriend, thinking the coast was clear, strolled across the room behind her in nothing but a towel. Then there's the "BBC Dad." During a live video call interview with the BBC, political analyst Robert Kelly's two young children invaded his home office. His four-year-old daughter confidently marched in, followed by his nine-month-old son in a walker. A visibly flustered Kelly valiantly kept talking until his wife mercifully burst in, frantically dragging the kids out of frame.

The evidence isn't just anecdotal. One of my studies discovered an inverse correlation between the number of meetings a leader attends and the extent to which they consider that day a success. In other words, the more meetings you attend, the less accomplished you'll feel at the end of the day.

Another study found that employee productivity was 71 percent higher when meetings were reduced by 40 percent.[2] Yet another revealed that nearly three-quarters of executives find their meetings unproductive, inefficient, and often a hinderance to deep thinking.[3]

If the quality of meetings isn't bad enough, the quantity makes things even worse. Estimates vary, but employees can spend more than eight hours per week in meetings. It's even worse for managers, with some exceeding twenty hours per week.[4] In case you were wondering, the number of meetings has increased over time: In fact, according to one analysis, executive meeting attendance doubled between the 1960s and the 1980s.[5]

That's obviously the bad news. The good news is twofold: First, if you follow everything in the previous chapters, you'll fix the vast majority of meeting problems. Your team's Director won't let a meeting end without a clear decision being made. Your Harmonizer is likely to spot frustrated attendees long before they start pulling out their own leg hairs. Achievers will accomplish meaningful work, Stabilizers will keep meetings disciplined, and Trailblazers will ensure your discussions don't grow stale. Putting the right people in the right roles solves meeting problems with shocking alacrity.

The second bit of good news is that, whether your meeting is virtual or in-person, there are a few simple techniques that enhance everything we've covered thus far. That's what we're covering in this chapter.

STATEMENT OF ACHIEVEMENT

Recently I surveyed people coming out of meetings, and one of the survey questions was: "Did the meeting you were just in accomplish its original objective?" Survey participants were given three response choices: "Yes," "No," and "I have no idea." Sadly, "Yes" wasn't the most common response. "No" wasn't either. The most frequent response was "I have no idea." The startling fact is that 90+ percent of meetings fail to produce an identifiable achievement.

The reason why so many folks are sitting in meetings with no idea why they're there is because they lack a clear objective. That's what a Statement of Achievement is. It's one sentence that says, "As a result of this meeting, we will have achieved _____."

STATEMENT OF ACHIEVEMENT

Before your meeting, fill in the blank:

As a result of this meeting, we will have achieved _____.
The blank can be anything; it's your meeting. But before you can proceed with that meeting, you have to be able to fill in that blank.

Once you've got your Statement of Achievement, share it with the people who will be in the meeting. You can do it in an email prior to the meeting or include it in the meeting agenda so people have a chance to prepare.

Alternatively, you can stand up before the meeting starts and say, "Hey folks, as a result of this meeting, we will have achieved _____. And once we achieve that, this meeting is over."

Maybe your Statement of Achievement is, "As a result of this meeting, we will have picked a price for the proposal we're submitting to the Johnson account," or "As a result of this meeting, we will have decided which of the three clinical safety protocols we're going to move forward with," or "As a result of this meeting, we will have decided who is going to be in charge of next week's employee lunch." As long as you can fill in that blank with an intended achievement, your meetings will have a stated purpose and get a lot more productive. Your meetings will also get shorter.

If you remember chemistry class, you'll recall that gases naturally expand to fill any available space. For example, there's not a little pocket of oxygen in the middle of your office right now; the oxygen molecules have dispersed throughout the room, filling it evenly. Well, in more ways than one, meetings are like a gas. They will expand to fill whatever space you give them. And what we find is that when organizations implement a Statement of Achievement in all their meetings, those meetings end, on average, seventeen minutes earlier. This happens because they have a crystal clear objective that says, "As soon as we accomplish this Statement of Achievement, this meeting is over."

That said, time alone is not a good metric for assessing the success of a meeting. Fulfilling your Statement of Achievement is an even better metric. Agreeing on a price for the proposal, or picking a color for the new product, or settling on a new location, or completing ten employee reviews. Your Statement of Achievement tells you exactly when you've achieved success so everyone can leave the meeting having accomplished a meaningful goal.

I'm not a good runner, but I do try. And when I lace up my sneakers and head out the door, I face a choice of running for four miles or forty minutes (I'm not fast, so, theoretically, those are roughly equivalent). On the days when I set out to run four miles, I find myself pushing harder, especially as I approach familiar landmarks that signal the final stretch. My mind kicks into a higher gear, urging me to pick up the pace as I visualize the finish line.

By contrast, when I opt for a forty-minute run, I tend to settle into a steady, almost monotonous rhythm, occasionally glancing at my watch but never feeling that same surge of energy. And it's not just me. Studies generally find that you're more likely to run (or cycle or swim) faster when the goal is a distance rather than a time.[6] One study of cycling workouts found that athletes began distance-based time trials at significantly higher power outputs compared to time-based trials. In other words, when cyclists knew exactly how far they had to go, they started off pedaling much harder than when they were just told how long to ride.[7]

That's what we're doing with a Statement of Achievement; we're giving our meeting attendees something to aim for besides merely running out the clock. It's the specific and achievable goal that explains why groups implementing a Statement of Achievement end meetings about seventeen minutes faster.

The goal isn't to rush meetings simply to say we got done faster; we're after more tightly managed and focused meetings. The longer the meeting drags on, the more fatigued and less effective we become.

RIGHT PEOPLE IN THE ROOM

Writing a Statement of Achievement will tighten up your meeting. It will also force you to answer an all-important question: "Given what I need to accomplish in this meeting, which people and roles need to be in attendance?"

Most people, especially the most productive people, don't want to sit in a meeting where they're not going to add value. Once you know exactly what your meeting needs to accomplish, you should review the list of potential meeting attendees to assess whether each person meets one of these criteria: They play a necessary role, wield the right kind of influence, or have some special insight to help you meet your objective.

Imagine you're planning a meeting where your objective will be finalizing the milestones and deadlines for a new product launch. You certainly wouldn't want to conduct that meeting on a day when your trusted Stabilizer is on vacation. Maybe there's a division head who's not a regular part of your team, but they control some of the staff you need; you'll likely want their input. Perhaps there's a product manager who's survived multiple product launches and has some veteran tricks up their sleeve.

Each of those folks plays a necessary role, wields influence, or has insights that could be immensely helpful. To accomplish your objective of finalizing the milestones and deadlines for a new product launch, you'll probably want their input.

Additionally, don't forget about the concept of adaptive hierarchies we covered in Chapter 9. Various meeting objectives might benefit from different roles taking the lead or even running the meeting.

For instance, when brainstorming innovative solutions, you might want your resident Trailblazer to facilitate that portion of the meeting. When it's time to make tough decisions, your Director could step up. If you're working through complex technical details, your Achiever might be best suited to guide the discussion. For portions dealing with tricky interpersonal dynamics, your Harmonizer could take point. And when it's time to establish processes or timelines, your Stabilizer might be the ideal person to lead. Applying adaptive hierarchies to your meetings not only ensures that the right people are in attendance, but also that you're leveraging each team member's strengths at the right moment.

CHOOSING THE RIGHT NUMBER OF PEOPLE

It's obviously important to get the right people involved; missing a critical role could doom a meeting's chance of success. On the other hand, roping in every single person you can think of isn't exactly ideal either.

You're probably familiar with Amazon's "two-pizza rule." In a nutshell, it means that teams should be small enough to be fed with two pizzas. This typically translates to teams of five to eight people (although the exact number can vary depending on appetites and pizza sizes).

The thinking behind this rule is that smaller teams are more efficient, communicate better, and are less prone to groupthink. Amazon founder Jeff Bezos believed that as teams grow larger, they become less efficient, with more time spent on coordination and communication than productive work. The goal was to keep teams nimble, reduce unnecessary bureaucracy, and maintain startup-like agility even as the company grows.

There is something to that rule, although it's not quite as simple as smaller means better. In general, as teams and meetings grow larger, the marginal returns of adding more people will decrease. You might also experience what's known as *social loafing*: when people put in less effort working in a group than they would if they were working alone because they're expecting others to pick up the slack. But sometimes, getting more people in the room generates bigger and better results.

Researchers at Microsoft and Facebook (now Meta) conducted an experiment where teams of varying sizes (between one and thirty-two people) collaborated on a crisis mapping task for one hour. Crisis mapping is when online volunteers work together to create maps showing what's happening during a disaster, using information shared by people in the affected areas.

The study found that larger teams generally outperformed smaller ones, but their performance increased at a decreasing rate as teams got larger. Simply adding more people didn't yield proportional improvements in output. And as team size increased, individual effort decreased by about 30 percent.[8]

When you're picking people for your meeting, this is your balancing act. You're always trying to find the sweet spot between having enough people to bring diverse perspectives and skills to the table and keeping the group small enough to maintain efficiency and engagement.

This sweet spot isn't a fixed number—it can vary depending on the nature of the task, the complexity of the problem at hand, and the specific individuals involved. For some straightforward decision-making meetings, the two-pizza rule might be spot-on.

Assemble a Director, Stabilizer, Harmonizer, Trailblazer, and Achiever, and voila, you're ready to go. For more complex tasks, like the crisis mapping example, a larger group might be more effective. You might need multiple people to fill some of those roles.

The key is to critically evaluate each person's potential contribution against the potential drawbacks of adding another participant.

QUESTIONS TO ASK YOURSELF WHEN SELECTING MEETING ATTENDEES

1. Does this person bring a unique and necessary perspective or skill set?
2. Will their inclusion significantly improve the quality of the discussion or decision-making?
3. Is their role critical enough that their absence could hinder the meeting's success?

Even if you need someone's input, consider whether a meeting is the best way to avail yourself of their insights. Some people may need to attend only part of a meeting, or it might make better sense to access their knowledge and input by scheduling a private meeting. To be sure, there are some people who absolutely love attending meetings. But many of the bright folks whose input you want and need are in high demand. If you can save them from attending the parts of the meeting where their input isn't necessary, they'll be very grateful.

AGENDAS

Agendas and start times are two of the least sexy topics when it comes to meetings, yet the problems that plague them remain so pervasive that each warrants a mention.

I'm sure you've experienced the sanity-testing frustration of being in a meeting, prepped and ready to start a deep conversation about an important topic, when one lone slacker pipes up: "Can someone remind me what we're talking about today? Oh, I didn't bring those reports with me. Anyone have an extra copy?"

Squandering the first crucial minutes of a meeting to bring unprepared participants up to speed isn't just frustrating; it's one of the most egregious wastes of collective time in the corporate world. So, here's your fix: Whatever form your agenda takes, send it out ahead of time, and put, in bold, something like, "Here's what participants need to have prepared," or "Be ready to discuss." There are innumerable agenda formats, but as long as yours is crystal clear about what participants should have completed as prework or must bring to the meeting, you'll be in good shape.

Armed with an agenda and prepared attendees, you're ready to start the meeting on time. And I really do mean on time. If you arrive late to a Broadway show, you could spend twenty minutes waiting in the lobby until there's a little break in the action or a reasonably unintrusive time to get ushered to your seat. Corporate meetings, unfortunately, tend not to enforce such discipline. I say unfortunately because there's a growing body of research that late starts do real damage to meetings.

In one such study, researchers found that more than half of meetings started late; hardly a surprising discovery. However, they also found that when a meeting started ten minutes late, participants perceived it as less effective when compared to on-time meetings. And in those late-starting meetings, participants engaged in more negative behaviors like criticizing others or having side conversations. Those meetings also produced fewer ideas, and the quality and feasibility of those ideas were rated lower.[9]

Put simply, when a meeting starts late, it's not just irritating; the negative effects impact the group for the duration.

END-OF-MEETING RECAPS

If you find that the to-dos coming out of your meetings aren't getting accomplished, or they disappear into some kind of accountability black hole, you ought to try an end-of-meeting recap.

I'm not talking about meeting minutes; they're common, but they don't often fix accountability issues. While meeting minutes typically document who said what to whom, they commonly fail to include action items, who's responsible for fulfilling those action items, and by when. And even when they do include action items, they're frequently buried so deep in the minutes document that they're easy to miss.

Even executive teams struggle with this. For instance, one of my studies discovered that only 10 percent of executives felt strongly that every meeting ends with clear to-dos, deadlines, and accountabilities.

Fortunately, the fix is simple. Before your meeting ends, ask each person in attendance to answer this question: "What are you personally going to achieve and by when?" Document the responses and distribute them to all meeting attendees. Don't bury those accountabilities in a lengthy minutes document; make it a standalone list with each item clearly outlined. Collectively sharing everyone's accountabilities creates peer pressure that eliminates the excuse, "That got buried somewhere in the meeting minutes, and I didn't know I was responsible for it."

If that approach feels too "old school" for you, enlist AI to do the work (this is especially easy for virtual meetings). Virtual meeting tools are increasingly embedding AI into their platforms, so you might be able to have the platform produce a list of everyone's to-dos after (or even during) the meeting.

Alternatively, take the transcript of your meeting, redact as necessary, and ask your favorite AI tool to produce a list of the to-dos and deadlines for every meeting participant. This could be as simple as telling the AI, "This is a transcript of a recent meeting. Summarize the meeting and create a list of to-dos for each meeting attendee. Attendees will often volunteer to take on certain tasks, or they may be assigned something; look for anything that sounds like someone agreeing to take on or being assigned a specific task or project." (As I mentioned in the previous chapter, AI tools are constantly updating, so check www.leadershipiq.com/teamplayers for the latest AI prompts and recommendations).

If you've ever found yourself having to nudge certain meeting participants to ensure they're working on their post-meeting to-dos, you could also task your AI to "Write a short email that I can send to each meeting participant a few days before our next meeting to check in on their progress. Reference each person's particular to-dos and make the tone friendly but still professional."

DEBRIEFS

These simple techniques, when added to everything else we've covered, will quickly elevate your meetings game. To maintain that progress, however, you'll want to incorporate the occasional team or meeting debrief.

Originally created in the 1970s for military use, debriefs are a simple yet powerful way to keep improving. One meta-analysis, for example, discovered that teams conducting debriefs outperform the ones that don't by more than 20 percent.[10]

The mechanics are simple. At the end of your next meeting, whether in-person or virtual, reserve five minutes to conduct a four-question assessment.

END-OF-MEETING DEBRIEF

Display each question one at a time, and then give attendees one minute to answer each one. (The first time you do this, you might need to give attendees two to three minutes per question.)

Here are the four questions:

1. How well did we meet our Statement of Achievement?
2. What is one thing you'd like to see more of?
3. What is one thing you'd like to see less of?
4. How well did we harness your talents?

Here's why we ask each question:

Question #1: How well did we meet our Statement of Achievement?

It's one thing to have a Statement of Achievement; it's quite another to stick to it. The question provides a quick accountability check to ensure that we're accomplishing what we said we wanted to accomplish.

Question #2: What is one thing you'd like to see more of?

Even in meetings that seem interminable, there's often some part that provided at least a bit of value. And leaders need to know what that piece was.

Asking your team what they'd like to see more of is quite different than asking them to describe their favorite part of the meeting. Their favorite part may have been a one-time random occurrence and thus not a repeatable feature. Maybe my favorite part of the virtual meeting was when Bob's cat jumped onto his desk and stuck her face in his coffee cup. It was funny, sure, but it's not repeatable, nor is it helpful to me as the team leader.

Question #3: What is one thing you'd like to see less of?

Another rapid way to reduce meeting burnout is to identify the least useful pieces of your meetings and stop doing them. Maybe attendees show up late or forget to plug in their headsets beforehand. It could be that too much time is spent doing project updates or sharing screens. As a leader, it's important to know what's not working in your meetings, because at least a few of those things can undoubtedly be quickly fixed or eliminated.

Question #4: How well did we harness your talents?

You've curated a team of Directors, Stabilizers, Harmonizers, Trailblazers, and Achievers. This question is a quick check to make sure everyone is utilizing their talents to the fullest. If your Trailblazer notes that they didn't get a chance to share their big idea, or your Harmonizer says that the group leader rebuffed their attempts at involving more people in the conversation, you've just learned exactly how to elevate the team's performance.

You don't have to use this end-of-meeting debrief indefinitely or at every single meeting. It is a good idea, however, to use it regularly for a month or two, especially as your team is working to habituate these best practices. Then, when you've made visible progress, move to a biweekly or monthly cadence.

GREAT MEETINGS ARE POSSIBLE

Great meetings don't happen by accident; they're the result of intentional design and disciplined execution. When you combine a clear Statement of Achievement, the right people in the room, and structured ways to start and end meetings, you create an environment where real work gets accomplished. But perhaps most importantly, when you leverage the unique talents of your Directors, Stabilizers, Harmonizers, Achievers, and Trailblazers—and use tools like debriefs to ensure those talents are being fully utilized—your meetings become engines of progress rather than drains on productivity. The difference between a meeting that energizes your team and one that depletes them often comes down to these seemingly simple but powerful practices. By implementing them consistently, you'll transform your meetings from necessary evils into catalysts for team success.

CHAPTER REFLECTION GUIDE

- Think about the last meeting you attended. Did it have a clear Statement of Achievement? If not, how might defining one have improved the focus and outcomes of the meeting?
- Have you noticed patterns where certain individuals dominate meetings while others remain quiet? What steps could you take to ensure all voices are heard, especially those less likely to speak up?
- How could tools like AI-generated meeting summaries or accountability tracking improve the productivity and clarity of your meetings? Are there specific meetings where you could experiment with these technologies?
- Have you ever conducted or participated in a meeting debrief? What insights do you think your team could gain by asking questions like, "How well did we harness everyone's talents?" or "What should we do less of in future meetings?"

Visit **www.leadershipiq.com/teamplayers** to find more resources, such as exercises, assessments, and additional tools.

CHAPTER 12

SELECTING NEW PEOPLE TO JOIN YOUR TEAM

T HERE WILL INEVITABLY COME A TIME WHEN YOU'LL NEED TO bring a new member onto your team. In an ideal world, that new member will fit perfectly and give your group exactly what it needs.

When Steve Jobs rejoined Apple, it was his decisiveness as a Director that most immediately snapped the company out of its financial funk and reinvigorated the brand. When the personal computer revolution needed technical perfection, it was Steve Wozniak's laser focus and hands-on brilliance as an Achiever that birthed the Apple I and II. And when Google's founders made the inspired choice of Eric Schmidt for CEO, it was his penchant for providing "adult supervision" as a Stabilizer that enabled their growth from $90 million to $38 billion in annual revenues.

When Dr. James P. Allison faced widespread skepticism about immunotherapy, it was his preternatural doggedness and innovation as a Trailblazer that led to the development of a revolutionary cancer treatment. And when Bristol Myers Squibb needed to bridge the gap between that groundbreaking science and corporate investment, it was Rachel Humphrey's transformative diplomacy and savvy as a Harmonizer that facilitated the development of the drug Ipilimumab.

Jobs, Wozniak, Schmidt, Allison, and Humphrey each fit a vital role perfectly. They were all smart and skilled, of course, but the real magic was how well their personalities, traits, and attitudes fit their particular role.

Those examples illustrate a crucial point: When bringing new people onto your team, role fit and attitude are often more important than technical skills alone.

One of my previous books is called *Hiring for Attitude*. In the research undergirding the book, my team and I tracked more than 20,000 hires across hundreds of organizations. The results were eye-opening: Forty-six percent of newly hired employees fail within eighteen months, while only 19 percent achieve unequivocal success. But here's the kicker—contrary to popular belief, technical skills are not the primary reason for these failures. In fact, a staggering 89 percent of hiring failures are due to attitudinal issues, while only 11 percent stem from a lack of technical skills.[1]

The research underscores why Jobs, Wozniak, Schmidt, Allison, and Humphrey were such perfect fits for their roles. It wasn't just their technical prowess that made them successful; it was their attitudes—their decisiveness, focus, stabilizing influence, persistence, and diplomatic savvy—that truly set them apart. These traits allowed them to not only excel in their individual capacities but also to click and synergize with their teams and organizations.

When you're bringing a new member onto your team, it's tempting to focus solely on their resume and technical qualifications. However, the *Hiring for Attitude* research, coupled with all the real-world examples we've seen throughout this book, demonstrates that attitude should be at the forefront of your selection process. The right attitude—be it the visionary drive of a Director, the meticulous focus of an Achiever, the steadying hand of a Stabilizer, the innovative spirit of a Trailblazer, or the connective sense of a Harmonizer—can make the difference between a hire that merely fills a position and one that transforms your team.

THIS IS ESSENTIALLY HIRING

If you've gone through Chapter 7 on curating your team and you're still missing a role or two, you've entered the realm of hiring. Whether you're looking inside or outside the organization, the task is fundamentally the same: selecting someone to seamlessly fill the missing role.

There's a reason why I'm framing this as a hiring decision: Choosing someone to join your team shouldn't be done capriciously, based on hearsay, or simply because they have a pulse and space on their calendar.

You've undoubtedly experienced the torture of being on a team with someone who's a terrible fit or, worse, a difficult or toxic personality. Not only do they add little or no value to your team, but, if they're problematic enough, their negative attitude will infect the rest of the group. It's called *emotional contagion*, and it's been well-studied. For instance, one experiment found that displays of negative emotions, such as irritation or hostility, led to a group reporting 30 percent less cooperation and experiencing a noticeable increase in conflict.[2]

The risks of harming your team with a new addition are too great to not take this seriously. Even if you've previously met someone, had a few passing conversations, or said hello in the hallways, treat the addition of a new team member like any other hiring decision. In other words, even if you're considering someone from down the hall, interview them.

If you'd like to explore the nuances of hiring, please grab a copy of my previous book. Meanwhile, what I'm going to share here is how to choose someone who fits seamlessly in each of the five roles.

THE SCIENCE OF INTERVIEW QUESTIONS

Because we're going to treat selecting a new team member as a form of hiring, we're going to use questions that you'll recognize as behavioral interview questions. But there's a little twist, because most of the behavioral interview questions you've seen before contain a ruinous flaw.

These typical questions follow a pattern where the interviewer asks about a specific situation, action, and result. They often start with phrases like "Tell me about a time when..." or "Give me an example of..."

But many interview questions are subtly phrased to nudge candidates toward sharing a success story. For instance, a question like "Tell me about a time when you successfully balanced competing priorities" is directing interviewees to speak about a situation where they emerged successfully. The inclusion of words like "successfully," "adapted," or "persuaded" signals that the interviewer is looking for a positive outcome.

Questions that include phrases at the end like "how you did it successfully" or "what you did to make the job more interesting" are signaling a desire for positive outcomes. If the question includes "and how did you solve it?" or "and how did you overcome that?" it's giving away the right answer: The interviewer only wants to hear successful stories about problem-solving.

By adding words to the end of the question, like "and how you overcame it," the interviewer explicitly tells the interviewee not to talk about the mistakes they couldn't overcome. It sends the message that the interviewer doesn't want to hear about gut-wrenching mistakes; rather, they just want the mistakes that were easily overcome.

But which of those mistakes (the gut-wrenching one or the one easily overcome) will reveal more about the person you're considering for your team? You will always learn more when someone talks about their struggles than you will from their recitation of polished success stories.

In short, you won't learn whether someone truly fits the Director, Stabilizer, Harmonizer, Achiever, or Trailblazer roles if you spoon-feed them the correct answers.

A QUICK WORD ON BIAS

My wife and I were out for a nice dinner when our drinks arrived, the waiter smoothly delivering our bourbon and pinot grigio. He set the pinot grigio in front of my wife and the bourbon went to me. There was just one problem: I don't drink bourbon, and my wife doesn't drink pinot grigio.

My wife is a petite, fit, and polished clinical psychologist, so I guess she doesn't give off a bourbon vibe. I've got a dad bod and graying facial hair, so, apparently, I shouldn't be drinking a light white wine. We avoid this situation only when the waiter pays enough attention to remember our specific orders; otherwise, it's a regular occurrence.

Drink order mix-ups are inconsequential in the grand scheme of things, but I'm mentioning it because this sort of stereotyping and bias is a frequent occurrence in hiring. There's an abundance of research on hiring bias, and when it comes to the roles on teams, my colleagues and I regularly run experiments.

When we ask people to choose between realistic-sounding profiles of potential Directors, Stabilizers, Trailblazers, Achievers, and Harmonizers, male-sounding names (e.g., Michael) are more likely to be chosen for the Director role than female-sounding ones (e.g., Michelle). The same is largely true for Trailblazers. But when it comes to Harmonizers, Michelle gets picked more often than Michael. The Stabilizer and Achiever roles have thus far been more immune to bias than the others.

My ask is simple: When you're considering candidates for each role on your team, recognize that Directors and Trailblazers don't have to be men, and Harmonizers don't have to be women. Think hard about any prejudgments that might lurk in the back of your mind about the ideal person for each role. For instance, if you've only ever worked with male Directors and female Harmonizers, is that history creating a prejudgment about who could or couldn't fill your team's Director and Harmonizer roles? All of us have histories that impact how we make present-day decisions. Those histories aren't necessarily bad; we just need to ensure that they're not biasing our current choices in a way that limits our ability to create a diverse and high-functioning team.

SELECTING A DIRECTOR

A quick way to test if someone has classic Director traits is to ask about their experience making difficult decisions in the face of opposition. Do this by asking them: "Could you tell me about a time you were faced with making an unpopular decision?"

This question reveals how the candidate handles the pressure of making decisions that may not be universally liked, their reasoning process, their ability to stand firm on their choices, and how they communicate and implement unpopular decisions. It also gives you some insight into their leadership style, their willingness to take responsibility, and their capacity to balance team dynamics with the need for decisive action.

Now let's look at examples of good and bad answers to this question.

Example Good Answer: "In our last major project, we were facing a tight deadline, and I realized we needed to cut a popular feature to ensure timely delivery. Many team members were emotionally invested in this feature, having worked on it for weeks. I called a meeting to explain the situation, presented data showing we couldn't complete everything in time, and outlined the risks of missing our deadline. I listened to everyone's concerns but ultimately decided to cut the feature. It was tough, but we delivered on time, maintained our reputation with the client, and eventually implemented an even better version of the feature later. This experience taught me the importance of making hard choices for the greater good of the team and project."

Why it's good: This answer demonstrates the candidate's ability to make difficult decisions, effectively balancing team morale, short-term difficulties, and long-term benefits. It shows they can analyze a situation, make a decisive call, and stand by their decision while still being sensitive to team dynamics.

Example Bad Answer: "Well, I try to avoid making unpopular decisions. I believe in always finding a consensus and making sure everyone is happy. In my experience, if a decision is unpopular, it's probably not the right one. So, I usually just keep discussing until we find something everyone agrees on, even if it takes a while. I can't really think of a specific example where I had to make an unpopular decision."

Why it's bad: This answer suggests the candidate is conflict-averse and may struggle with the decisive nature of the Director role. It indicates a tendency toward prolonged discussion and an inability to make tough calls when necessary. The lack of a specific example is also concerning, as it may indicate a lack of leadership experience or an unwillingness to take responsibility for difficult decisions.

SELECTING A TRAILBLAZER

To quickly get a handle on someone's ability to recognize inadequacies in existing systems and their willingness to challenge established norms—key Trailblazer qualities—try this question: "Could you tell me about a time when the status quo or conventional way of doing things wasn't working or wasn't good enough?"

This question invites potential Trailblazers to demonstrate their innovative thinking, problem-solving skills, and courage in proposing unconventional solutions. It also allows the interviewer to assess someone's ability to identify opportunities for improvement, their creative approach to challenges, and their capacity to drive change within a team or organization.

Here are some example answers:

Example Good Answer: "In our last product development cycle, we were struggling with a tight deadline and using our standard waterfall methodology. I noticed that this approach was causing bottlenecks and hampering our ability to adapt to rapid market changes. Despite initial resistance, I proposed we switch to an agile framework. I organized a team workshop to explain the benefits and address concerns. We started with a pilot project, and the results were impressive—we reduced time-to-market by 30 percent and increased customer satisfaction scores. This success led to the adoption of agile methodologies across all our product teams. It wasn't easy challenging our long-standing processes; it took a lot of persistence and convincing across dozens of conversations, and I probably got a bit annoying for a while. But by focusing on the potential benefits and involving the team in the transition, we were able to make a significant positive change."

Why it's good: This answer demonstrates the candidate's ability to identify inefficiencies, propose innovative solutions, and lead change. It shows their willingness to challenge the status quo, resilience in the face of resistance, and their ability to implement new ideas successfully.

Example Bad Answer: "Well, I generally try to follow established procedures because they're there for a reason. I remember once our team was having issues with project delays, but I figured it was just a temporary problem that would sort itself out. I didn't want to rock the boat or upset anyone by suggesting changes. Eventually, management stepped in and made some adjustments, and things got better. I guess sometimes you just have to wait for problems to resolve themselves."

Why it's bad: This answer shows a lack of initiative and an unwillingness to challenge the status quo, which are essential qualities for a Trailblazer. The candidate demonstrates a passive approach to problem-solving and a reluctance to propose innovative solutions. They also show a lack of ownership in improving team processes, waiting for others to make changes instead. This mindset is antithetical to the Trailblazer role, which requires proactive thinking and a willingness to drive change.

SELECTING A HARMONIZER

The question "Could you tell me about a time you worked with a difficult colleague?" is an effective Harmonizer question because it directly probes the candidate's ability to navigate challenging interpersonal situations.

This question allows the interviewer to assess the candidate's emotional intelligence, conflict resolution skills, and capacity to maintain positive relationships even in difficult circumstances. It provides insight into how the candidate approaches interpersonal challenges, their ability to empathize with different perspectives, and their strategies for fostering collaboration in the face of adversity.

Example Good Answer: "In our last project, I worked with a colleague who was known for being confrontational and dismissive of others' ideas. Instead of avoiding him, I made an effort to understand his perspective. I scheduled one-on-one meetings where I actively listened to his concerns and ideas. I discovered he felt undervalued and was passionate about improving our processes. I acknowledged his expertise and suggested ways to present his ideas more collaboratively in team meetings. I also mediated discussions between him and other team members, ensuring everyone's views were heard and respected. Over time, his communication improved, and the team's productivity increased. This experience taught me the importance of empathy and open communication in resolving conflicts and building a cohesive team."

Why it's good: This answer demonstrates the candidate's ability to approach difficult situations with empathy and a problem-solving mindset. It shows their skill in active listening, mediation, and fostering better communication within the team. The candidate didn't just solve a personal conflict but improved overall team dynamics, a key aspect of the Harmonizer role.

Example Bad Answer: "Oh, I try to avoid difficult people as much as possible. There was this one colleague who was always causing problems, so I just stopped inviting them to meetings and worked around them. It's easier to just focus on the people who are easy to work with, you know? In the end, the project got done, and that's what matters, right? I think if someone is being difficult, it's not really my job to fix their attitude."

Why it's bad: This answer shows an avoidance of conflict rather than a willingness to address and resolve it. The respondent demonstrates a lack of empathy and an unwillingness to understand or help improve challenging team dynamics. They prioritize personal comfort over team cohesion and effectiveness, which is a disturbing sign for a Harmonizer.

SELECTING AN ACHIEVER

To select an Achiever, ask about someone's ability to tackle challenging tasks with a detail-oriented and results-driven approach. You can do this with the question: "Could you tell me about a time you were assigned a task or project that seemed overly ambitious or unrealistic?"

This question allows the interviewer to assess the candidate's problem-solving skills, work ethic, and ability to deliver high-quality results under pressure. It also provides insight into how the candidate handles seemingly impossible tasks, their ability to break down complex problems into manageable parts, and their commitment to excellence even in difficult circumstances. You'll also likely hear about the candidate's capacity for deep focus, their drive for perfection, and their ability to immerse themselves in the nitty-gritty details of a project.

Example Good Answer: "In our last product launch, we were tasked with developing a new feature that would typically take three months, but we were given only six weeks due to market pressures. Instead of dismissing it as impossible, I broke down the project into smaller, manageable tasks. I focused on the core functionality first, optimizing our coding process to eliminate redundancies. I worked extra hours to dive deep into the technical challenges, often staying late to solve complex problems. I also collaborated closely with the QA team, integrating testing throughout the development process rather than leaving it to the end. This approach allowed us to identify and fix issues quickly. We managed to deliver the feature on time, and it performed better than expected in beta testing. This experience taught me the importance of efficient prioritization, attention to detail, and persistence in achieving seemingly unrealistic goals."

Why it's good: This answer demonstrates the candidate's ability to tackle challenging tasks head-on, break them down into manageable parts, and focus intensely on the details to deliver high-quality results. It shows their commitment to excellence, willingness to put in extra effort, and ability to optimize processes—all good traits for an Achiever.

Example Bad Answer: "We get unrealistic deadlines all the time. In our last project, the manager wanted us to complete a month's worth of work in just a week. I told them it was impossible and that they were being unreasonable. I suggested we either extend the deadline or reduce the scope of the project. When they insisted on keeping the original timeline, I just did what I could in the given time. The quality wasn't great, and we missed some key features, but that's what happens when you set unrealistic expectations. It's not my fault if the higher-ups can't plan properly."

Why it's bad: This answer shows a lack of problem-solving skills and a tendency to give up when faced with challenges, traits that do not fit the Achiever archetype. The candidate doesn't demonstrate any attempt to find innovative solutions or to dive deep into the task to make it work. They also show a lack of ownership and a tendency to blame others, which goes against the Achiever's typical drive for personal excellence.

SELECTING A STABILIZER

To test if someone is a fit for the Stabilizer role, assess their ability to bring order to chaos and implement structure in disorganized situations. You can accomplish this with the question: "Could you tell me about a time you were assigned to a project or team that wasn't as organized as it could have been?"

You'll quickly see someone's organizational skills, attention to detail, and ability to create and maintain processes. The question also provides insight into how someone approaches challenges related to lack of structure and their capacity to implement systems that enhance productivity. You'll also see whether they have a natural inclination toward creating order, a crucial aspect of the Stabilizer role.

Example Good Answer: "In our last product launch, I was assigned to a team that lacked clear timelines and defined processes. Recognizing the potential for missed deadlines and confusion, I took the initiative to create a detailed project plan. First, I met with each team member to understand their tasks and timelines. Then, I developed a Gantt chart to visualize our timeline and dependencies. I also implemented a daily stand-up meeting to track progress and address issues promptly. To improve communication, I set up a shared digital workspace where we could centralize all project documents and updates. This structured approach helped us identify and mitigate risks early, leading to a successful launch that was both on time and within budget. The team appreciated the clarity and organization, and these processes were adopted for future projects across the department."

Why it's good: This answer demonstrates the candidate's ability to recognize organizational issues and take proactive steps to implement structure and processes. It shows their skills in planning, communication, and creating systems that enhance team efficiency. The candidate also highlights the positive impact of their actions, both on the immediate project and for future team operations.

Example Bad Answer: "Disorganized projects happen all the time. In my last team, things were pretty chaotic. No one really knew what was going on, and deadlines were constantly shifting. I just tried to focus on my own tasks and not get caught up in the mess. I figured it wasn't my job to fix the team's problems, so I just kept my head down and did my work. Eventually, the project got done, even though it was late and over budget. I guess that's just how things go sometimes in a big organization."

Why it's bad: This answer shows a lack of initiative and willingness to address organizational issues, which runs counter to the Stabilizer mindset. The candidate demonstrates a passive approach to challenges and a reluctance to implement structures or processes to improve team efficiency. They also show a lack of concern for the overall success of the project and team, focusing solely on their individual tasks. This would likely perpetuate disorganization rather than bring the stability and structure that a Stabilizer provides.

FITTING THE FINAL PIECES

In the event you need to bring someone new onto your team, remember that it's not just about technical skills; it's about finding individuals whose natural inclinations align with the Director's decisiveness, the Trailblazer's innovative spirit, the Harmonizer's diplomatic skills, the Achiever's attention to detail, or the Stabilizer's organizing prowess. Pay attention to the language people use, their past experiences, and their approach to challenges. When you find the right attributes, you'll get a team where each member complements the others and elevates the group as a whole.

CHAPTER REFLECTION GUIDE

- Think about a recent hiring decision you were involved in. Did you prioritize technical skills or role fit and attitude? How did that decision impact the team dynamic and performance?
- How do you ensure that the strengths of a new hire complement the existing team rather than duplicating or clashing with other team members' roles?
- Are there areas where your team could benefit from greater diversity in thinking styles or approaches? How can you ensure your hiring process encourages this without introducing bias?
- Have you experienced the impact of a poor team fit? Reflect on how a single hire can affect team dynamics, morale, and productivity. How can you prevent this in future decisions?

Visit **www.leadershipiq.com/teamplayers** to find more resources, such as exercises, assessments, and additional tools.

CHAPTER 13

CONCLUSION

Throughout this book, we've explored how to solve the paradox of teams. While conventional wisdom often focuses on merging everyone into a single homogeneous entity, we now know that truly great teams embrace the distinct, diverse roles and talents of their members.

That's why we delved into the critical roles that form the foundation of high-performing teams: Directors, Stabilizers, Achievers, Trailblazers, and Harmonizers. We've seen how each role contributes uniquely to a team's success and how the right balance can lead to extraordinary results.

Now it's time to do a quick recap and put this knowledge into action.

1. ASSESS YOUR CURRENT TEAM

The first step in transforming your team is to gain a clear understanding of its current composition and dynamics.

- Implement the Team Role Map Exercise: Gather your team and have each member identify the role they believe others see them fulfilling most often. Remember, this isn't about pigeonholing people; rather, it's about understanding their natural inclinations and strengths. You can also supplement that exercise with the Team Role Assessment at www.leadershipiq.com/teamplayers.

- Analyze Role Distribution: Once you have your Team Role Map, assess the distribution of roles. Are all five roles represented? Is there an overabundance of one role and a scarcity of another?
- Identify Gaps and Overlaps: Look for areas where your team might be lacking. Perhaps you have multiple Directors but no clear Harmonizer, or several Achievers but no Trailblazer.
- Consider Secondary Roles: Remember to note any secondary roles that team members expressed interest in developing. This information can be valuable for future role balancing and personal development.
- Find Everyone's Comparative Advantage: Everyone has an area that they're relatively best at. That's their comparative advantage, and you want to find that for every member of your team.

2. EMBRACE AND CULTIVATE ROLE DIVERSITY

With a clear picture of your team's composition, your next step is to actively embrace and cultivate role balance and diversity.

- Address Role Gaps: If your assessment revealed missing roles, create a plan to fill these gaps. This might involve developing existing team members, reassigning roles, or bringing in new talent.
- Develop Existing Team Members: Identify team members who show potential in underrepresented roles. Provide them with opportunities to develop these skills, perhaps by assigning them to projects that allow them to exercise these new muscles.
- Consider New Hires: If you're unable to fill crucial gaps internally, consider bringing in new team members. Use the hiring

strategies we discussed in Chapter 12 to identify candidates who can complement your existing team dynamics.

- Implement Adaptive Hierarchies: Remember the concept of adaptive hierarchies we discussed in Chapter 9? Allow leadership to flow to the person best suited for each situation or task, regardless of their formal position.

3. FOSTER A CULTURE OF MUTUAL APPRECIATION

One of the insights we explored is the power of reciprocal expertise affirmation. When team members understand and appreciate each other's unique talents, collaboration improves dramatically.

- Conduct the Role Appreciation Exercise: Go through the exercise in Chapter 7 where each team member describes a time when they worked with someone amazing in each of the five roles.
- Address Role Biases: Be aware of and actively work to counteract any biases against certain roles. For example, ensure that Harmonizers' contributions to team cohesion are valued as highly as Achievers' tangible outputs.

4. ENHANCE TEAM DECISION-MAKING PROCESSES

We've explored various techniques to combat groupthink and enhance team decision-making. Your next action should be to implement these strategies systematically in your team's decision-making processes.

- Implement Pre-Meeting Independent Thinking: Before important decision-making meetings, have team members independently write down their thoughts, including rationales, pros and cons, and potential risks.

- Use Structured Sharing Techniques: In meetings, use techniques like round-robin sharing or anonymous idea submission to ensure all voices are heard.

- Leverage the Herding Effect Positively: Remember how we discussed using the herding effect to elevate underrepresented voices in Chapter 10? Strategically order the sharing of ideas to give weight to perspectives that might otherwise be overlooked.

- Use AI-Assisted Analysis: Leverage AI tools to analyze meeting transcripts and identify patterns in participation and decision-making. Use these insights to continually refine your processes.

5. REVOLUTIONIZE YOUR MEETINGS

Meetings are a crucial part of team functioning, yet they're often ineffective. Your next action should be to overhaul your meeting practices using the strategies we've discussed.

- Implement Statements of Achievement: For every meeting, create and share a clear Statement of Achievement that defines what the meeting needs to accomplish.

- Curate Attendee Lists: Be intentional about who attends each meeting. Only include those who are essential to achieving the meeting's stated objective. That might include trying the two-pizza rule from Chapter 11.

- Conduct Regular Meeting Debriefs: At the end of each meeting, use the four-question assessment we discussed in Chapter 11:

  1. How well did we meet our Statement of Achievement?
  2. What is one thing you'd like to see more of?
  3. What is one thing you'd like to see less of?
  4. How well did we harness your talents?

- Leverage Technology: Use tools like AI-assisted transcription and analysis to gain insights into meeting dynamics and effectiveness.

6. REFINE YOUR TEAM MEMBER SELECTION PROCESS

When bringing new members onto your team, it's crucial to focus not just on technical skills but also on attitude and role fit.

- Develop Role-Specific Interview Questions: Create a set of interview questions designed to assess candidates' natural inclinations toward each of the five key roles (or just use the ones in Chapter 12).
- Be Aware of Bias: Remember our discussion about bias in hiring from Chapter 12? Be conscious of any preconceptions you might have about who is a good fit for certain roles.
- Look for Attitude, Not Just Skills: Remember, our research showed that 89 percent of hiring failures are due to attitudinal issues, not lack of technical skills.

7. CULTIVATE CONTINUOUS LEARNING AND ADAPTATION

Building a great team is an ongoing process that requires continuous learning and adaptation.

- Implement Regular Team Assessments: Schedule quarterly team assessments to review your Team Role Map, discuss team dynamics, and identify areas for improvement.
- Encourage Role Switching: Remember how we discussed the benefits of team members trying on different roles in Chapter 7? Create opportunities for team members to step into different roles on specific projects.

- Use the Greek Theater Mask Analogy: When encouraging team members to try new roles, remind them of the Greek theater mask analogy we discussed. This can help them understand how roles can amplify different aspects of their abilities.

FINAL THOUGHTS

Creating an extraordinary team requires consistent effort, open communication, and a willingness to adapt. By implementing these strategies, you're setting your team on a path to exceptional performance.

Remember, the power of a well-balanced, highly functional team cannot be overstated. When Directors, Stabilizers, Achievers, Trailblazers, and Harmonizers work together and balance each other, there's no limit to what you can accomplish. Each role brings unique strengths and perspectives that, when properly leveraged, create a whole that is truly greater than the sum of its parts.

As you embark on this journey, be patient with yourself and your team. Change takes time, and there may be bumps along the way. Celebrate small victories and learn from setbacks. Keep the lines of communication open, and always be willing to adjust your approach based on what you learn.

Remember also that, as a leader, you set the tone for your team. Model the behaviors you want to see. Be willing to adapt your own role as needed, appreciate the contributions of all team members, and foster an environment where diverse perspectives are not just tolerated but actively sought out and valued.

The strategies and actions outlined in this book are not just theoretical concepts—they are practical, actionable steps that have been proven effective out in the real world. By consistently applying these principles, you can transform your team into a high-performing unit capable of tackling any challenge.

Acknowledgments

Every author says there are too many people to thank, and it's true. However, I do need to highlight a few individuals without whom this particular book simply wouldn't have been possible.

My wife, Andrea Burgio-Murphy, PhD, is not only the love of my life, but she's also an esteemed clinical psychologist whose insights have drastically improved all of my books. My children, Isabella and Andrew, are my everything. Their love, humor, and, now that they're in young adulthood, deep conversations, kept me going throughout the process.

Jill Sutherland is my indefatigable and invaluable aide-de-camp and Leadership IQ's Stabilizer par excellence. Much like the example of Eric Schmidt at Google, she expertly manages the chaos and organizes the company to enable my book-writing process.

On the book itself, two people must be mentioned as the driving forces behind bringing this creation to life; their trailblazing vision and insights into the book's possibilities and necessity ensured its path to the market and its broader reach.

First is Esmond Harmsworth, my agent at Aevitas Creative Management. I am deeply indebted to him for believing in this book, seeing its potential, and making transformative contributions to honing the book's message and refining its positioning. This book idea doesn't become a reality without him.

Of course, Esmond is also responsible for creating the relationship with the other catalyst, my editor, Colleen Lawrie. Colleen's insights, edits, and refinements, along with her passion for this team model, have made this book the high-water mark of my career. I also want to thank her colleague Emily Taber for her great work and support during the editorial process.

I can't say enough good things about the teams at Basic Venture and Aevitas Creative Management.

Notes

INTRODUCTION

1. Ramona Shelburne, "How the Nuggets Cultivated the NBA's Most Dynamic Duo," ESPN.com, June 13, 2023, www.espn.com/nba/story/_/id/37846076/nba-finals-2023-how-nuggets-cultivated-nba-most-dynamic-duo.

2. Wynton Marsalis, "How the Rhythm Section Swings," Harvard University, November 6, 2017, YouTube, 3:14, www.youtube.com/watch?v=Xi27zn7YNFo&ab_channel=HarvardUniversity.

CHAPTER 1: THE FIVE TEAM ROLES

1. Dan Pompei, "The Dream Team That Wasn't: A Cautionary Tale for Free Agency," Bleacher Report, October 3, 2017, https://bleacherreport.com/articles/2621230-the-dream-team-that-wasnt-a-cautionary-tale-for-free-agency.

2. Associated Press, "Michael Vick: Eagles No 'Dream Team,'" ESPN.com, October 5, 2011, www.espn.com/nfl/story/_/id/7063196/michael-vick-philadelphia-eagles-finished-dream-team-label.

3. Boris Groysberg, Jeffrey T. Polzer, and Hillary Anger Elfenbein, "Too Many Cooks Spoil the Broth: How High-Status Individuals Decrease Group Effectiveness," *Organization Science* 22, no. 3 (June 2011): 722–737, https://doi.org/10.1287/orsc.1100.0547.

4. Ilaria Barberis et al., "The History of Tuberculosis: From the First Historical Records to the Isolation of Koch's Bacillus," *Journal of Preventive Medicine and Hygiene* 58, no. 1 (March 2017): 9–12, accessed November 12, 2024, www.jpmh.org/index.php/jpmh/article/view/728.

5. Martin Placek, "Topic: LED Lighting in the U.S.," Statista, accessed January 13, 2025, www.statista.com/topics/1144/led-lighting-in-the-us/.

6. Mark Murphy, "Never Stop Challenging the Conventional Wisdom, and This Nobel Prize Winner Shows Why," *Forbes*, September 9, 2022, www.forbes.com/sites /markmurphy/2022/09/08/never-stop-challenging-the-conventional-wisdom-and-this -nobel-prize-winner-shows-why/.

7. Peter Schmidt, "Grand Jury Blames Richmond Bankruptcy on Board," *Education Week*, September 13, 2021, www.edweek.org/education/grand-jury-blames-richmond -bankruptcy-on-board/1991/06.

8. Henry Pitt, *The House: The Dramatic Story of the Sydney Opera House and the People Who Made It* (Allen & Unwin, 2018).

9. Tim Harford, host, "Cautionary Tales: The Tragedy of the Sydney Opera House," *Cautionary Tales with Tim Harford* (podcast), September 15, 2023, https://timharford .com/2023/09/cautionary-tales-the-tragedy-of-sydney-opera-house/.

10. Joe Taysom and Tom Taylor, "Pink Floyd: The Long and Brutal History of Roger Waters and David Gilmour's Feud," *Far Out Magazine*, February 7, 2023, https:// faroutmagazine.co.uk/pink-floyd-roger-waters-david-gilmour-feud/.

11. "Naked Mole-Rat," Smithsonian's National Zoo and Conservation Biology Institute, April 25, 2016, https://nationalzoo.si.edu/animals/naked-mole-rat.

CHAPTER 2: THE DIRECTOR

1. Jeffrey Powers, "October 6, 1997: Michael Dell: 'I'd Shut Apple Down,'" Day in Tech History, October 6, 2024, https://dayintechhistory.com/dith/october-6-1997-michael -dell-shut-apple-2/.

2. John Leyden, "Printer Ink Seven Times More Expensive than Dom Perignon," The Register, July 4, 2003, www.theregister.com/2003/07/04/printer_ink_seven_times_more/.

3. Walter Isaacson, *Steve Jobs* (Simon & Schuster, 2011, Kindle edition), 338–339.

4. Isaacson, *Steve Jobs*, 338–339.

5. Géraldine Schwarz, *Those Who Forget: My Family's Story in Nazi Europe—A Memoir, a History, a Warning*, trans. Laura Marris (Scribner, 2020).

6. Ruth Bender and Valentina Pop, "Austria to Build Fence on Slovenia Border to Slow Flow of Migrants," *Wall Street Journal*, updated October 28, 2015, accessed November 13, 2024, www.wsj.com/articles/austria-to-build-fence-on-slovenia-border-to-slow -flow-of-migrants-1446024586.

7. Bryan Walsh and TIME Photo, "Alan Kurdi's Story: Behind the Most Heartbreaking Photo of 2015," *TIME*, December 29, 2015, https://time.com/4162306/alan-kurdi -syria-drowned-boy-refugee-crisis/.

8. Carlo Angerer and Alastair Jamieson, "71 Dead Refugees Found in Truck on Austria Highway: Officials," NBCNews.com, August 28, 2015, www.nbcnews.com/storyline /europes-border-crisis/71-dead-refugees-found-truck-austria-highway-officials-n417536.

9. Kati Marton, *The Chancellor: The Remarkable Odyssey of Angela Merkel* (Simon & Schuster Paperbacks, 2022).

10. Raea Rasmussen and Jacob Poushter, "People Around the World Express More Support for Taking in Refugees than Immigrants," Pew Research Center, August 9, 2019,

www.pewresearch.org/short-reads/2019/08/09/people-around-the-world-express-more
-support-for-taking-in-refugees-than-immigrants/.

11. RJ Reinhart, "Germans May Be Ready for Change as Merkel Exits," Gallup, September 24, 2021, https://news.gallup.com/poll/354950/germans-may-ready-change-merkel
-exits.aspx.

12. Mark Murphy, "How CIA Sabotage Tactics Could Be Ruining Your Team Meetings," *Forbes*, March 26, 2023, www.forbes.com/sites/markmurphy/2023/03/26/are-cia
-sabotage-tactics-ruining-your-team-meetings/.

CHAPTER 3: THE STABILIZER

1. Chris Yeh, "CS183C Session 8: Eric Schmidt," Medium, October 15, 2015, https://medium.com/cs183c-blitzscaling-class-collection/cs183c-session-8-eric-schmidt
-56c29b247998.

2. Luke Salkeld, "Is This the Man Who Sank the Titanic by Walking Off with Vital Locker Key?" DailyMail.com, August 29, 2007, www.dailymail.co.uk/news/article-478269
/Is-man-sank-Titanic-walking-vital-locker-key.html.

3. Jared Knott and Winfred Blevins, *Tiny Blunders, Big Disasters: Thirty-Nine Tiny Mistakes That Changed the World Forever!* (Jefferson Central Publishing, 2020).

4. Susan Clary, "Willie King Said: 'Doctor, That's the Wrong Leg,'" *Tampa Bay Times*, updated October 3, 2005, www.tampabay.com/archive/1995/03/10/willie-king
-said-doctor-that-s-the-wrong-leg/.

5. Ahsan Zil-E-Ali et al., "Is Surgery on the Right Track? The Burden of Wrong-Site Surgery," *Baylor University Medical Center Proceedings* 36, no. 5 (July 5, 2023): 657–660, https://doi.org/10.1080/08998280.2023.2231714.

6. Sandra G. Boodman, "The Pain of Wrong Site Surgery," *Washington Post*, June 20, 2011, accessed November 13, 2024, www.washingtonpost.com/national/the-pain-of
-wrong-site-surgery/2011/06/07/AGK3uLdH_story.html.

7. Arvid S. Haugen, Nick Sevdalis, and Eirik Søfteland, "Impact of the World Health Organization Surgical Safety Checklist on Patient Safety," *Anesthesiology* 131, no. 2 (August 1, 2019): 420–425, https://doi.org/10.1097/aln.0000000000002674.

8. Fred I. Greenstein, *The Hidden-Hand Presidency: Eisenhower as Leader* (Basic Books, 1982).

9. Jean Edward Smith, *Eisenhower: In War and Peace* (Random House Trade Paperbacks, 2013).

10. Knott and Blevins, *Tiny Blunders, Big Disasters*.

CHAPTER 4: THE TRAILBLAZER

1. Mark Murphy, "If You've Ever Had a Great Idea Snubbed, This Nobel Laureate Wants You to Know You're Not Alone," *Forbes*, June 2, 2022, www.forbes.com/sites/
markmurphy/2022/06/02/if-youve-ever-had-a-great-idea-snubbed-this-nobel-laureate
-wants-you-to-know-youre-not-alone/.

2. "Managers Don't Love Innovators," Leadership IQ, August 21, 2022, www .leadershipiq.com/blogs/leadershipiq/managers-don-t-love-innovators.

3. Nicholas Wade, "American and Briton Win Nobel for Using Chemists' Test for M.R.I.'s," *New York Times*, October 7, 2003, www.nytimes.com/2003/10/07/us/american -and-briton-win-nobel-for-using-chemists-test-for-mri-s.html.

4. Marc Randolph, *That Will Never Work: The Birth of Netflix and the Amazing Life of an Idea* (Little, Brown and Company, 2022).

5. Hayley C. Cuccinello, "Netflix Cofounder Marc Randolph on Why He Left, Becoming a Mentor and His Love of Chaos," *Forbes*, September 17, 2019, www.forbes.com/sites /hayleycuccinello/2019/09/17/netflix-cofounder-marc-randolph-memoir/.

6. Randolph, *That Will Never Work*.

7. Henry Blodget, "I Asked Jeff Bezos the Tough Questions—No Profits, the Book Controversies, the Phone Flop—and He Showed Why Amazon Is Such a Huge Success," Business Insider, December 16, 2014, accessed November 17, 2024, www.businessinsider .com/amazons-jeff-bezos-the-business-insider-interview-2014-12.

8. Brad Stone, *The Everything Store: Jeff Bezos and the Age of Amazon* (Little, Brown and Company, 2018).

9. Stone, *The Everything Store*.

10. Mark Murphy, "This Nobel Prize Winner Explains Why You Need a Dose of 'Soft Insanity' to Be Successful," *Forbes*, May 24, 2022, www.forbes.com/sites/markmurphy /2022/05/24/this-nobel-prize-winner-explains-why-you-need-a-dose-of-soft-insanity -to-be-successful/.

11. Murphy, "Nobel Prize Winner."

12. Mark J. Perry, "Fortune 500 Firms in 1955 vs. 2014," August 18, 2014, accessed November 18, 2024, www.aei.org/carpe-diem/fortune-500-firms-in-1955-vs-2014-89-are -gone-and-were-all-better-off-because-of-that-dynamic-creative-destruction/.

CHAPTER 5: THE HARMONIZER

1. Tim Cato, "'The Nicest Human I've Ever Met': Boban Marjanovic, the NBA's Best Teammate," *New York Times*, July 13, 2020, accessed November 17, 2024, www.nytimes .com/athletic/1916610/2020/07/13/the-nicest-human-ive-ever-met-boban-marjanovic -the-nbas-best-teammate/.

2. Ursula Burns, *Where You Are Is Not Who You Are: A Memoir* (Amistad, 2022).

3. *Jim Allison: Breakthrough*, directed by Bill Haney, (Uncommon Productions, April 27, 2020), 1:30, www.pbs.org/independentlens/documentaries/jim-allison-breakthrough/.

4. Benoit Denizet-Lewis, "The Man Behind Abercrombie & Fitch," Salon, January 24, 2006, accessed November 13, 2024, www.salon.com/2006/01/24/jeffries/.

5. Total Retail Staff, "Top Women in Retail 2018: Fran Horowitz, Chief Executive Officer, Abercrombie & Fitch Co.," Total Retail, February 6, 2018, www.mytotalretail.com /article/top-women-in-retail-2018-fran-horowitz-abercrombie-fitch-co/.

6. Mark Murphy, "This CEO Shows How You Get Ahead by Not Hogging the Spotlight," *Forbes*, April 11, 2023, www.forbes.com/sites/markmurphy/2023/04/11/this-ceo-shows-how-you-get-ahead-by-not-hogging-the-spotlight/.

CHAPTER 6: THE ACHIEVER

1. "The Machine That Changed the World; Interview with Steve Wozniak," GBH Open Vault, January 1, 1992, accessed November 17, 2024, https://openvault.wgbh.org/catalog/V_7CCEDE8F8CE246889EBAAB8BCB225EB5.

2. Josh Ong, "Apple Co-Founder Offered First Computer Design to HP 5 Times," AppleInsider, December 7, 2010, https://appleinsider.com/articles/10/12/06/apple_co_founder_offered_first_computer_design_to_hp_5_times.

3. Ong, "Apple Co-Founder."

4. John R. Pierce, "ECHO—America's First Communications Satellite," Southwest Museum of Engineering, Communications and Computation, accessed November 17, 2024. www.smecc.org/john_pierce___echoredo.htm.

5. Jon Gertner, *The Idea Factory: Bell Labs and the Great Age of American Innovation* (Penguin Books, 2013).

6. Pierce, "ECHO."

7. Walter Isaacson, *Steve Jobs* (Simon & Schuster, 2011, Kindle edition).

CHAPTER 7: CURATING YOUR TEAM

1. Jeff Fedotin, "Chiefs Star Patrick Mahomes Bought Golf Carts Worth More than $100,000 for Linemen," *Forbes*, December 22, 2023, www.forbes.com/sites/jefffedotin/2023/12/22/chiefs-star-patrick-mahomes-bought--golf-carts-worth-more-than-100000-for-linemen/.

2. Boris Groysberg, Ashish Nanda, and Nitin Nohria, "The Risky Business of Hiring Stars," *Harvard Business Review*, accessed August 1, 2014, https://hbr.org/2004/05/the-risky-business-of-hiring-stars.

3. Satya Nadella, Greg Shaw, and Jill Tracie Nichols, *Hit Refresh: The Quest to Rediscover Microsoft's Soul and Imagine a Better Future for Everyone* (William Collins, 2018).

4. Xiaoxiao Hu et al., "Do Employees Know How Their Supervisors View Them? A Study Examining Metaperceptions of Job Performance," *Human Performance* 27, no. 5 (October 20, 2014): 435–457, https://doi.org/10.1080/08959285.2014.956177.

5. Thomas F. Oltmanns et al., "Meta-Perception for Pathological Personality Traits: Do We Know When Others Think That We Are Difficult?" *Consciousness and Cognition* 14, no. 4 (December 2005): 739–751, https://doi.org/10.1016/j.concog.2005.07.001.

6. Hanneke Grutterink et al., "Reciprocal Expertise Affirmation and Shared Expertise Perceptions in Work Teams: Their Implications for Coordinated Action and Team Performance," *Applied Psychology* 62, no. 3 (February 16, 2012): 359–381, https://doi.org/10.1111/j.1464-0597.2012.00484.x.

7. Tom Brady and Nitin Nohria, "Tom Brady on the Art of Leading Teammates," *Harvard Business Review*, accessed August 15, 2024, https://hbr.org/2024/09/tom-brady-on-the-art-of-leading-teammates.

8. James Herbert, "Steve Kerr on Team USA's Joel Embiid, Jayson Tatum Getting DNPs at Olympics: 'We Have Options for Everything,'" CBSSports.com, August 1, 2024. www.cbssports.com/olympics/news/steve-kerr-on-team-usas-joel-embiid-jayson-tatum-getting-dnps-at-olympics-we-have-options-for-everything/.

9. Marc J. Spears, "Kevin Durant Now the Gold Standard for USA Men's Basketball," Andscape, August 11, 2024, https://andscape.com/features/kevin-durant-now-the-gold-standard-for-usa-mens-basketball/.

10. Ben Stinar, "Charles Barkley's Honest Quote About Jayson Tatum Benching," Fastbreak on SI, August 13, 2024, www.si.com/fannation/nba/fastbreak/charles-barkley-honest-quote-about-jayson-tatum-benching-celtics-team-usa.

11. Brian Windhorst, "Jayson Tatum Says Limited Role in Paris Won't Affect '28 Decision," ESPN.com, August 10, 2024, www.espn.com/nba/story/_/id/40813393/jayson-tatum-says-limited-role-paris-affect-28-decision.

12. Hiroya Fujikake et al., "Directional Bias in the Body While Walking through a Doorway: Its Association with Attentional and Motor Factors," *Experimental Brain Research* 210, no. 2 (March 16, 2011): 195–206, https://doi.org/10.1007/s00221-011-2621-3.

13. Alexandros Tsilfidis et al., "Function and Acoustic Properties of Ancient Greek Theatre Masks," *Acta Acustica united with Acustica* 99, no. 1 (January 1, 2013): 82–90, https://doi.org/10.3813/aaa.918591.

14. Alexander Oettl, "Reconceptualizing Stars: Scientist Helpfulness and Peer Performance," *Management Science* 58, no. 6 (2012): 1122–1140, https://doi.org/10.1287/mnsc.1110.1470.

CHAPTER 8: LEARNING TO THINK LIKE ALL FIVE ROLES

1. Carl Rogers, *A Way of Being* (Houghton Mifflin Company, 1980), 140.

CHAPTER 9: HIERARCHY IS NOT A BAD WORD

1. Jack El-Hai, "The Chicken-Hearted Origins of the 'Pecking Order,'" *Discover Magazine*, November 20, 2019, www.discovermagazine.com/planet-earth/the-chicken-hearted-origins-of-the-pecking-order.

2. Benedict C. Jones et al., "Facial Cues of Dominance Modulate the Short-Term Gaze-Cuing Effect in Human Observers," *Proceedings of the Royal Society B: Biological Sciences* 277, no. 1681 (October 28, 2009): 617–624, https://doi.org/10.1098/rspb.2009.1575.

3. Rawan Charafeddine et al., "How Preschoolers Use Cues of Dominance to Make Sense of Their Social Environment," *Journal of Cognition and Development* 16, no. 4 (July 22, 2014): 587–607, https://doi.org/10.1080/15248372.2014.926269.

4. Meghan Oliver, "Disrupting to Stay the Same: Culture Insights from Zappos," Human Synergistics, January 4, 2024, www.humansynergistics.com/blog/constructive

-culture-blog/details/constructive-culture/2017/03/16/disrupting-to-stay-the-same
-culture-insights-from-zappos.

5. Emily M. Zitek and L. Taylor Phillips, "Ease and Control: The Cognitive Benefits of Hierarchy," *Current Opinion in Psychology* 33 (June 2020): 131–135, https://doi.org/10.1016/j.copsyc.2019.07.015.

6. Jinyu He and Zhi Huang, "Board Informal Hierarchy and Firm Financial Performance: Exploring a Tacit Structure Guiding Boardroom Interactions," *Academy of Management Journal* 54, no. 6 (December 2011): 1119–1139, https://doi.org/10.5465/amj.2009.0824.

7. Nir Halevy et al., "When Hierarchy Wins," *Social Psychological and Personality Science* 3, no. 4 (October 6, 2011): 398–406, https://doi.org/10.1177/1948550611424225.

8. "All Time Leaders: Stats," NBA.com, accessed November 17, 2024, www.nba.com/stats/alltime-leaders?StatCategory=FG3M&SeasonType=Regular%2BSeason&PerMode=Totals.

9. Kirk Goldsberry, *Hoop Atlas: Mapping the Remarkable Transformation of the Modern NBA* (HarperCollins, 2025).

10. "Paul George Says, 'I Gotta Get the Last Shot,' after CJ Miles Fails to Hit Game Winner," ESPN.com, accessed November 17, 2024, www.espn.com/nba/story/_/id/19167326/paul-george-indiana-pacers-upset-take-final-shot-game-1-loss-cleveland-cavaliers.

11. Gregory A. Bigley and Karlene H. Roberts, "The Incident Command System: High-Reliability Organizing for Complex and Volatile Task Environments," *Academy of Management Journal* 44, no. 6 (December 1, 2001): 1281–1299, https://doi.org/10.2307/3069401.

12. Bigley and Roberts, "The Incident Command System."

13. Hank Gilman, "The Most Underrated CEO Ever," *Fortune*, March 21, 2004, www.kuratrading.com/PDF/TheMostUnderatedCEOEver.pdf.

14. Paul Gatling, "David Glass' Leadership Path Did Not Include Shortcuts," *Talk Business & Politics*, February 4, 2020, https://talkbusiness.net/2020/02/david-glass-leadership-path-did-not-include-shortcuts/.

15. Winston Churchill, "Blood, Toil, Tears, and Sweat" (speech, House of Commons, London, England, May 13, 1940), International Churchill Society, https://winstonchurchill.org/resources/speeches/1940-the-finest-hour/blood-toil-tears-sweat/.

16. Francis Sill Wickware, "Psychosomatic Medicine: Upset Emotions Can Cause Illness, Obesity, Even Accidents," *LIFE*, February 19, 1945, 53.

17. "Barry J. Marshall Interview," NobelPrize.org, March 6, 2014, accessed November 17, 2024, www.nobelprize.org/prizes/medicine/2005/marshall/interview/.

18. Pamela Weintraub, "The Doctor Who Drank Infectious Broth, Gave Himself an Ulcer, and Solved a Medical Mystery," *Discover Magazine*, April 17, 2023, www.discovermagazine.com/health/the-doctor-who-drank-infectious-broth-gave-himself-an-ulcer-and-solved-a-medical-mystery.

19. Adam Lashinsky, "Tim Cook: The Genius Behind Steve Jobs," *Fortune*, November 24, 2008, https://fortune.com/2008/11/24/apple-the-genius-behind-steve/.

20. Lashinsky, "Tim Cook."

21. Tim Carmody, "Why Tim Cook Is the Best Choice to Run Apple," *Wired*, August 25, 2011, www.wired.com/2011/08/why-tim-cook/.

22. Harry McCraken, "What Apple Has Lost—and Gained—Since Steve Jobs Died 10 Years Ago," *Fast Company*, October 5, 2021, accessed November 18, 2024, www.fastcompany.com/90682991/what-apple-has-lost-and-gained-since-steve-jobs-died-10-years-ago.

23. McCracken, "What Apple Has Lost."

24. Joanne Chen, "American Dreamers: Zoom Founder Eric Yuan on Making His Mark in Silicon Valley," *Forbes*, July 11, 2022, www.forbes.com/sites/joannechen/2022/07/11/american-dreamers-zoom-founder-eric-yuan-on-making-his-mark-in-silicon-valley/.

25. Ben Thompson, "An Interview with Zoom CEO Eric Yuan about Surviving COVID and Building Moats," Stratechery (blog), March 14, 2024, https://stratechery.com/2024/an-interview-with-zoom-ceo-eric-yuan-about-surviving-covid-and-building-moats/.

26. Thompson, "An Interview with Zoom CEO."

27. Chen, "American Dreamers."

28. Emdad Islam and Jason Zein, "Inventor CEOs," *Journal of Financial Economics* 135, no. 2 (February 2020): 505–527, https://doi.org/10.1016/j.jfineco.2019.06.009.

29. Noelle Baird and Alex J. Benson, "Getting Ahead While Getting Along: Followership as a Key Ingredient for Shared Leadership and Reducing Team Conflict," *Frontiers in Psychology* 13 (June 27, 2022), https://doi.org/10.3389/fpsyg.2022.923150.

30. John W. Aaron, interview by Kevin M. Rusnak, January 26, 2000, accessed November 17, 2024, transcript, NASA Johnson Space Center Oral History Project, https://historycollection.jsc.nasa.gov/JSCHistoryPortal/history/oral_histories/AaronJW/AaronJW_1-26-00.htm.

CHAPTER 10: MAKING BETTER DECISIONS ON YOUR TEAM

1. Solomon E. Asch, "Studies of Independence and Conformity: I. A Minority of One Against a Unanimous Majority," *Psychological Monographs: General and Applied* 70, no. 9 (January 1956): 1–70, https://doi.org/10.1037/h0093718.

2. Quy Huy and Timo Vuori, "Who Killed Nokia? Nokia Did," INSEAD, August 18, 2022, https://knowledge.insead.edu/strategy/who-killed-nokia-nokia-did.

3. Huy and Vuori, "Who Killed Nokia?"

4. Aaron De Smet, Gerald Lackey, and Leigh M. Weiss, "Untangling Your Organization's Decision Making," McKinsey & Company, June 21, 2017, www.mckinsey.com/capabilities/people-and-organizational-performance/our-insights/untangling-your-organizations-decision-making.

5. "Elements of Amazon's Day 1 Culture," AWS (Amazon Web Services), accessed January 13, 2025, https://aws.amazon.com/executive-insights/content/how-amazon-defines-and-operationalizes-a-day-1-culture/.

6. Mark Murphy, "This CEO Has a Better Rule for Making Faster Decisions," *Forbes*, April 18, 2023, www.forbes.com/sites/markmurphy/2023/04/18/this-ceo-has-a -better-rule-for-making-faster-decisions/.

7. Murphy, "This CEO Has a Better Rule."

8. Irving Lester Janis, "Groupthink," *Psychology Today*, November 1971, accessed December 27, 2024, https://agcommtheory.pbworks.com/f/GroupThink.pdf.

9. Irving Lester Janis, *Groupthink: Psychological Studies of Policy Decisions and Fiascoes* (Wadsworth, 2013).

10. Karen Girotra, Christian Terwiesch, and Karl T. Ulrich, "Idea Generation and the Quality of the Best Idea," *Management Science* 56, no. 4 (April 2010): 591–605, https://doi .org/10.1287/mnsc.1090.1144.

11. Elijah Mayfield and Alan W. Black, "Analyzing Wikipedia Deletion Debates with a Group Decision-Making Forecast Model," *Proceedings of the ACM on Human-Computer Interaction* 3, no. CSCW (November 7, 2019): 1–26, https://doi.org/10.1145/3359308.

12. Elisabeth Noelle-Neumann, "The Spiral of Silence a Theory of Public Opinion," *Journal of Communication* 24, no. 2 (June 1, 1974): 43–51, https://doi.org/10.1111/j.1460 -2466.1974.tb00367.x.

13. Danielle Z. Bolling et al., "Dissociable Brain Mechanisms for Processing Social Exclusion and Rule Violation," *NeuroImage* 54, no. 3 (February 2011): 2462–2471, https:// doi.org/10.1016/j.neuroimage.2010.10.049.

14. Joanna Z. Li, Alina Herderich, and Amit Goldenberg, "Skill but Not Effort Drive GPT Overperformance over Humans in Cognitive Reframing of Negative Scenarios," preprint, submitted April 19, 2024, https://doi.org/10.31234/osf.io/fzvd8.

15. Francesco Salvi et al., "On the Conversational Persuasiveness of Large Language Models: A Randomized Controlled Trial," preprint, submitted June 5, 2024, https://doi .org/10.21203/rs.3.rs-4429707/v1.

16. Alex G. Kim, Maximilian Muhn, and Valeri V. Nikolaev, "Financial Statement Analysis with Large Language Models" (working paper, University of Chicago Booth School of Business, Fama-Miller, 2024), https://doi.org/10.2139/ssrn.4835311.

17. Alan Karthikesalingam and Vivek Natarajan, "AMIE: A Research AI System for Diagnostic Medical Reasoning and Conversations," Google Research (blog), January 12, 2024, accessed November 17, 2024, https://research.google/blog/amie-a-research-ai -system-for-diagnostic-medical-reasoning-and-conversations/.

18. Karan Girotra et al., "Ideas Are Dimes a Dozen: Large Language Models for Idea Generation in Innovation," preprint, submitted August 2, 2023, https://doi.org/10.2139 /ssrn.4526071.

CHAPTER 11: THE SCIENCE OF GREAT MEETINGS

1. Nicholas Carlson, "What Happened When Marissa Mayer Tried to Be Steve Jobs," *New York Times*, December 17, 2014. www.nytimes.com/2014/12/21/magazine/what -happened-when-marissa-mayer-tried-to-be-steve-jobs.html.

2. Benjamin Laker et al., "Dear Manager, You're Holding Too Many Meetings," *Harvard Business Review*, March 9, 2022, https://hbr.org/2022/03/dear-manager-youre-holding-too-many-meetings.

3. Leslie A. Perlow, Constance Noonan Hadley, and Eunice Eun, "Stop the Meeting Madness," *Harvard Business Review*, June 26, 2017, https://hbr.org/2017/07/stop-the-meeting-madness.

4. David Smith, "50 Surprising Meeting Statistics for 2024," Flowtrace, May 12, 2024, www.flowtrace.co/collaboration-blog/50-meeting-statistics.

5. Steven G. Rogelberg, Cliff Scott, and John Kello, "The Science and Fiction of Meetings," *MIT Sloan Management Review*, January 1, 2007, https://sloanreview.mit.edu/article/the-science-and-fiction-of-meetings/.

6. Sabrina Skorski and Chris R. Abbiss, "The Manipulation of Pace within Endurance Sport," *Frontiers in Physiology* 8 (February 27, 2017), https://doi.org/10.3389/fphys.2017.00102.

7. Chris R. Abbiss et al., "Difference in Pacing between Time- and Distance-Based Time Trials in Trained Cyclists," *International Journal of Sports Physiology and Performance* 11, no. 8 (November 2016): 1018–1023, https://doi.org/10.1123/ijspp.2015-0613.

8. Andrew Mao et al., "An Experimental Study of Team Size and Performance on a Complex Task," *PLOS One* 11, no. 4 (April 15, 2016), https://doi.org/10.1371/journal.pone.0153048.

9. Joseph A. Allen, Nale Lehmann-Willenbrock, and Steven G. Rogelberg, "Let's Get This Meeting Started: Meeting Lateness and Actual Meeting Outcomes," *Journal of Organizational Behavior* 39, no. 8 (March 24, 2018): 1008–1021, https://doi.org/10.1002/job.2276.

10. Scott I. Tannenbaum and Christopher P. Cerasoli, "Do Team and Individual Debriefs Enhance Performance? A Meta-Analysis," *Human Factors* 55, no. 1 (June 4, 2012): 231–245, https://doi.org/10.1177/0018720812448394.

CHAPTER 12: SELECTING NEW PEOPLE TO JOIN YOUR TEAM

1. Mark A. Murphy, *Hiring for Attitude: A Revolutionary Approach to Recruiting and Selecting People with Both Tremendous Skills and Superb Attitude* (McGraw-Hill Education, 2017).

2. Sigal G. Barsade, "The Ripple Effect: Emotional Contagion and Its Influence on Group Behavior," *Administrative Science Quarterly* 47, no. 4 (December 2002): 644–675, https://doi.org/10.2307/3094912.

Index

MARK MURPHY is the author of the *New York Times* bestseller *Hundred Percenters*, senior contributor to *Forbes*, and founder of Leadership IQ, a research and training firm. His research has appeared in *The New York Times*, *Harvard Business Review*, *Time*, and *The Wall Street Journal*, among others. He is also the author of *Hiring for Attitude*. Mark lives in Roswell, Georgia.

RAISING READERS
Books Build Bright Futures

nk you for reading this book and for being a reader of books in general. As an
hor, I am so grateful to share being part of a community of readers with you,
I hope you will join me in passing our love of books on to the next generation
aders.

**you know that reading for enjoyment is the single biggest predictor of a
d's future happiness and success?**

e than family circumstances, parents' educational background, or income,
ding impacts a child's future academic performance, emotional well-being,
mmunication skills, economic security, ambition, and happiness.

dies show that kids reading for enjoyment in the US is in rapid decline:

In 2012, 53% of 9-year-olds read almost every day. Just 10 years later,
in 2022, the number had fallen to 39%.

In 2012, 27% of 13-year-olds read for fun daily. By 2023, that number
was just 14%.

Together, we
can commit to
aising Readers
and change
this trend.
How?

- Read to children in your life daily.
- Model reading as a fun activity.
- Reduce screen time.
- Start a family, school, or community book club.
- Visit bookstores and libraries regularly.
- Listen to audiobooks.
- Read the book before you see the movie.
- Encourage your child to read aloud to a pet or
  stuffed animal.
- Give books as gifts.
- Donate books to families and communities in need.

BOB1217

Books build bright futures, and **Raising Readers** is our shared responsibility.

For more information, visit **JoinRaisingReaders.com**

Sources: National Endowment for the Arts, National Assessment of Educational Progress,
WorldBookDay.org, Nielsen BookData's 2023 "Understanding the Children's Book Consumer"